2/2/

Best Prayers

a.C. Hill, #

IN SEARCH OF THE TRUTH

A Real Life Story About What an Attorney Should "NOT" Do!

by Anderson C. Hill, II, J.D., M.B.A.
Edited by The American Conscious (TAC), Inc.
Poetry by Gina's Inkwell
Illustrations by Michael G. Cothran

First Edition

PRIME TIME PUBLISHERS, Inc.

IN SEARCH OF THE TRUTH
A Real Life Story About What an Attorney Should "NOT" Do!

Published by:
PRIME TIME PUBLISHERS, Inc.

750 S. Orange Blossom Trail
Suite 120
Orlando, FL 32805
SAN 299-3651
407.426.8597

Clearinghouse for Book Orders:
4205 E. Busch Boulevard
Tampa, Florida 33617-5937
813.988.8148
800.635.2639(Toll Free)
813.988.8422(Fax)

Publisher's Cataloging-In-Publication
(Provided by Quality Books, Inc.)
Hill, Anderson C.
In search of the truth: a real life story about what an attorney
should "not" do! / by Anderson C. Hill ; edited by The American
Conscious (TAC), Inc. ; poetry by Gina's Inkwell. — 1st ed.
  p. cm.
Includes bibliographical references and index.
Preassigned LCCN: 97-92189
ISBN: 0-9658628-7-9: $14.95 Softcover
1. Hill Anderson C.—Ethics.
2. Legal Ethics.
3. Lawyers—United States—Biography.
4. Afro-American lawyers—Biography.
5. Lawyers—Disbarment, disqualification, etc.
6. Bank fraud. I. Title

KF306.Z9H55 1977   340.092[B]
                           QBI97-40774

TABLE OF CONTENTS

About the author, editor, poet, illustrator

Book order form

DEDICATION

THIS BOOK is for my wife, **SANDRA ALENE**. It is given to you with all my love and courage. There are some words and phrases inside, you asked me not to use, but there was not much choice in telling this story. I trust that you can forgive me. I could not have made it this far, without your strong love and support, for me and our family;

and

for my dear sweet mother, Rosie Lee Hill, and my loving sister, Erma Peterson. The two of you have always been there for me and I love you. It is also written for my father, Archester Hill (1900-1986);

and

for my children, Greg, Andy and Lauren. If anybody reads this, I pray that each of you will. Please do not do the bad things that I have done, but remember the good things that I tried to do. I fell short of my goal, but each of you can make it to the mountain top! I want to look up on that mountain, one day, and see you there;

and

for the people who have personally come into my life, as well as the readers of this book, some of whom I may not know. I acknowledge each of you, and especially Ken and Marlene Guthery, Dr. and Mrs. R.J. Gainous, Jr., Dr. and Mrs. J.C. Bentley, Lee Lambert, Dr. and Mrs. Oswald P. Bronson, Sr., and The Myers Family.

PREFACE

SOMETIMES I can feel just a sprinkle of God's presence, and I become so afraid. Heavenly Power vibrates through my mind and heart. The Bible says that no man could stand to actually look upon God in His raw form. My feelings tell me that this is true. He does exist! I want to muster enough fortitude in my weak soul to see Him, one day. The upcoming text is analogous to Adam hiding in the Garden of Eden, when God called unto Adam, "Where art thou?" I decided to come on out...*Will you join me?*

NUMB POWER

Elevate me and I want it now.
Levitate me and I will tower above
the dust.

I think rich, and I am.
I think intelligent high falooting thoughts.
They must be the truth because I cannot see a lie.

Grains of clouds fill my nose.
Numbing my throat and filling my belly.
I am empowered to dive into forbidden territory.

My sex is ready to explode and cover miles of terrain.
My wild streak is ignited.
I race to get the feeling of no feeling.

1 CRUISING

"When one loses contact with God, it is impossible to discern what the truth really is."
Theologian Dr. Howard Thurman (1900-1981)

THE sleek silver Mercedes Benz sedan slowed to a whisper as it turned into the parking lot of the Friendly Mercedes dealer in Daytona Beach.

Even at such a slow speed, I could feel the power and precision of the fine automobile, the cool air-conditioning blowing on a hot Florida day, the engine purring like a satisfied woman. The car was a loaner. I was here for my new baby. It was the same style as this car, a 560 SEL, and the same, brand new model year. But mine was the coveted color of black. The dealer had to fly an employee to Atlanta to get the limited edition black Benzo and make the ten-hour drive back.

As I pulled into the lot, I saw a short, stocky white salesman standing on the stoop outside the showroom. He drew leisurely on a cigarette, leaning against the wall in a sliver of shade cast by an awning over the door. As he looked my way, I could see his eyes squint as the bright sunshine glistened off the long silver hood. By now, he and the other sales staff knew me well. This would be my fourth new Mercedes from the lot in less than 18 months. Mercedes Benz was my "weapon of choice".

As the salesman threw me a wave, I smiled and waved back.

I thought back to when I had been here just three days earlier, soaring on adrenaline from several big deals that I successfully negotiated. I walked into the dealer showroom and found the nearest salesman - a young white guy, maybe 30 years old with a baby face and an ill-fitting blue polyester-blend suit.

"What's the most expensive Mercedes you sell?"

The sales manager and another salesman quickly made their way over to me. The young guy could tell I must be someone important. I'm 6-foot-2 and weighed 250 pounds then. I towered over the young guy.

"The 560 SEL," he said.

"That's what I want. In black."

"Attorney Hill, we only have the car in silver," the sales manager interjected, addressing me with the courtesy title, "Attorney Hill", which was all the sales staff now used when dealing with me. "Let me show it to you. And you can drive it away today. That car's been waiting for you."

"No, it's got to be black," I replied firmly.

"Well, let's see then. I'll have to make a few calls. Please, have a seat, Attorney Hill. Can we get you something cold to drink, a soft drink maybe?"

When I declined, he turned and walked down a hallway, the young salesman in tow, and into an office. I retreated to the seating area and picked up the local paper, *The News-Journal*. An attorney like myself had to keep abreast of local events. I flipped through it, glancing at stories about crime, politics, Chamber of Commerce happenings and local business dealings.

"Attorney Hill, I found one."

I looked up from the paper and saw the manager stride toward me, a big grin on his face. I sensed that he and the young salesman had run the math and calculated their commission on this sale. Daytona Beach is a small town. These guys weren't selling luxury cars every day. I could tell by the glow of their faces that I had made their day. The young one had probably called his wife already and told her the good news.

"Black, just like you want. It's in Atlanta," the sales manager said. "I'll fly one of the guys up tomorrow and he'll bring it back. Give us a day to clean it up and check it out for you. Should be ready by the end of the week."

"Great," I said and stood, reaching out to shake his hand. "Sounds like you've got yourself a deal."

We walked together back into the manager's office, filling out paperwork and securing a deposit for the car. Sticker price: $60,575. He gave me the keys to the silver 560 SEL. Told me to drive it until mine came in.

Maybe he thought I'd change my mind and keep the silver one. But I learned long ago that black cars make a statement. I had thought about that on the way over to pick up the car. The dealership is a 5-

minute ride from Bethune-Cookman College, a small, historically black college in town where I worked as college attorney and assistant to the president.

The black sedan would put the finishing touch on my image. A black man. A black Benz. Today, I was wearing a black tailor-made suit, which cost $850. I normally ordered three suits at a time. On my wrist was a black and silver faced Submariner Rolex watch. Gold Rolexes were too gaudy for my taste. On my lapel was a pin I wore daily, bearing the corporate logo of my beloved Bethune-Cookman College. The pin was shaped like a triangle with the words, Head, Heart and Hand, on each side, and a diamond in the middle.

One of the proven techniques for success at the college was to dress sharply. College President Dr. Oswald Bronson Sr., a former church pastor and charismatic leader, set the standard on campus with his impeccable taste. I was close behind, trying hard to topple him from his dressing kingship.

The dress-for-success philosophy was instilled in me by my Momma. I can still hear her telling me, "People want you to look like the role you are playing. It makes them feel better about you, besides what is necessarily in your head."

When I was an undergraduate at Clark College in Atlanta, just starting out as an intern at a big accounting firm, Momma took me shopping and bought me 10 suits - one to wear every day for two weeks without having to wear the same one twice. The legal profession was just like my first career in accounting. It was best to dress conservatively. Gray, blue and black suits only. I now had rows of them in my closet.

"Oh shit man, look at that pretty bitch." The words snapped me out of my daydream. Leon Day, the office manager at my law firm and a close friend, was sitting in the front passenger seat beside me. He was looking at my new black Benzo across the lot. "That car looks like it is a mile long. I wonder if the seats in the back automatically move like the seats in this one?"

"Man, this car is too damn comfortable," Craig Watson, the college architect, said from the backseat. "These foot-rests are straight out of a limo."

The four of us looked like we had stepped from some slick

advertisement in Gentleman's Quarterly.

Leon considered himself a real ladies man. His hair was coarse and wavy, his skin dark and smooth, and he had a thick mustache. He had been prowling for women lately, ever since he moved out from his wife, Opal. The two were planning a divorce, a decision their young daughter and I hoped they reconsider.

Married with two kids myself, I maintained high ideals about family and marriage. But I knew I could not unreasonably interfere with Leon's personal affairs. It was his life. I just wanted him to stay with Opal.

All four of us were friends. But Leon and I were close. I often felt we could be twins. I talked him into trading his Volvo for a new black 300E Benz, which is smaller than the four-door sedan I was getting. Leon kept saying he couldn't afford it. I told him I'd make the monthly payments of $648 whenever he couldn't. "Just get the car. We'll pay for it," I told him.

Our matching cars would look great in the parking lot of my law office. The perfect marketing ploy. People like to patronize successful attorneys, even if they pay through the nose for it. I could visualize our cars parked side by side at the law office, by day, and at my riverfront nightclub, The Mirage, after hours. Business was good at both places. The law office employed five full-time and two part-time workers. The Mirage had 15 employees. But I was always looking for ways to boost profits.

Craig Watson, the school architect, was seated behind me in the backseat of the gray sedan. He was a bit portly at 6-feet and 240 pounds, although his gray pinstripe suit hid his weight well. His skin was a shade lighter than Leon's and mine. He was also a family man with two kids. Beside him sat Tommy Huger, director of college construction and renovation. He was the shortest of us four and looked sharp in a button-down, white collared shirt with a snazzy burgundy and small white dotted tie. Tommy was married with three kids. We sometimes teased him about his demanding, but nevertheless sweet wife, Linda. During the day, she would call my law office, where Tommy had an office so we could work together on college construction projects, at least 10 times a day to find out where he was. She kept tight reins on Tom.

I hadn't planned on bringing these guys with me to get the new car, although I always enjoyed showing off my assets. Craig, Tommy and I were wrapping up a meeting about a new multi-million-dollar construction project on campus when the phone rang on my large, solid oak desk.

My secretary screened my calls with the discipline of a military commander. I was far too busy for her not to. If the phone rang in my office without her announcing it on the intercom, it could be only one of a few people - my wife, my children, sister, mother or Dr. Bronson, the college president.

I picked up the phone expecting my wife. The voice didn't belong to anyone on my priority list, however my secretary obviously knew I'd want this call right away. A woman in a high-pitched voice said:

"Attorney Hill, your car has arrived at Friendly Mercedes and is being prepped for delivery. Would you like for us to deliver it to you this afternoon or will you pick it up? Everyone here has been talking about how special this car is. It fits your personality to a tee. You were lucky to get it. Many times when this color rolls off the production line in Germany, the dealers already have the sales lined up."

I was reaching for my suit jacket. "Do I want you to deliver it to me? Are you kidding? I will be over shortly to pick it up, can you pleasseee have it ready?" I asked.

"Certainly, Attorney Hill."

I hung up the phone and bellowed in a tone that carried throughout the two-story, historic wooden house that I had converted into my law office.

"It's here!"

I PULLED the silver sedan alongside my new car. Four salesmen were hanging around the cars on the lot, talking among themselves. I saw one of them glance at us, then turn back to the others and make what appeared to be a wise-ass comment. The men smirked. My instincts told me what the man had said, something to the effect of, "Would you look at those niggers?"

The salesmen were happy to take my money. But underneath

their artificially sweet demeanor, I sensed raw anger and bitterness at seeing four well-dressed black men arrive to pick up a car that they and most other whites could never afford.

Blacks make up a hefty segment of Daytona Beach's population - about 35 percent, three times the number in most of the surrounding cities. But the majority lived below the poverty line. I was a minority within my own minority. Educated to the hilt. A cush job in the upper echelons of a respected college. And enough money for the best Benzo around.

Whether they liked it or not, the salesmen snapped to attention when I arrived these days. The first time I came to this dealership, well, that was a different story. You would have thought I was some wacked-out homeless guy, talking to himself and asking passersby for spare change. No one even looked my way.

I arrived in my plain white Chevrolet Blazer. I walked around the lot for thirty minutes, sweating in the hot sun, pressing my face against the windows of the locked cars, trying to get a sniff of the custom leather inside, I could see several salesmen in the showroom. They were watching me. But not one of them got up.

Finally I tired of that and walked inside. A couple of middle-aged men sat sprawled with their feet on desks in a nicely wooden paneled showroom, dealer achievement plaques lining the walls and air-conditioning blowing briskly. When none of them looked my way, I said loudly, "I need to speak with the owner or manager!"

Hearing my educated-sounding voice, a salesman got up and asked if I needed some help.

I asked for the owner or manager again. "I came in to test drive a new Benz for my wife, but since it appears none of you had the courtesy to assist me, now I am only going to deal with the owner or manager. Unless, of course, one of you is that person. And if that's so, I will take my business elsewhere."

The salesman went into a back office for a few moments. Out emerged a gangly white man, at least 6-foot-4, with bright red hair. He extended a broad hand with a gold class ring on one finger.

"Which car are you interested in?" he asked.

I grasped his hand, squeezed tightly, and replied, "the blue 260E."

The car listed for $35,000. I gave him the name of my personal banker. After one call, he told the sales staff to send a buyer's order for the car. The bank delivered them a check that day. I only paid $32,000 for that car. The sales staff suffered for their rude behavior because the manager cut out their commission. Never again did I mention how I was treated that day. I was born and raised in Little Rock, Arkansas, grew up on the heels of integration. That's how white people treated blacks in a place like this. It always has been that way.

After the abuse at the lot, I was disheartened by my wife Sandra's reaction to the car. I loved surprising her with expensive gifts. But she wanted her old reliable, blue Volvo back. To her, this piece of sheet metal was a waste of money.

Sandra has such light-colored skin that people often assume she's Hispanic or Filipino. Someone once called her a "Florida Cracker;" I kid you not. I'd sometimes catch people glaring at us like we're an interracial couple. And with my dark brown skin, we do look like one. We started dating when she was 15 and I was 16.

"Anderson, why did you trade the Volvo in on that? It was almost paid for."

"Baby, don't worry," I told her. "We have the money. And besides, my lady deserves a real Benz, not an imitation one."

Two months later, I traded in my Chevy white Blazer for a black 300E. That's the car I later gave Leon. Then I got a bronze colored stationwagon, a 300 TE, for Sandra and the kids. Traded in the blue Benz for it. The stationwagon set me back $52,000. Sandra about died when I told her the price. I could tell she was worrying about my erratic behavior.

After purchasing more than $200,000 worth of automobiles, the sales staff acted like Secret Service agents around the President's car when I drove into the lot these days. Seeing us four men in the silver sedan, the four salesmen each hurried to one of the doors, opening them almost simultaneously.

I heard Leon whisper under his breath, "Would you look at these mothers, Andy? What have you done to these guys besides buy all of their cars?"

I said nothing as I extended my leg out of the door and boldly stood up. If someone had been lying on the ground, they would have seen all of our pants legs fall right into place, slightly crumpled above the shoes.

I could have flashed an attitude. This was my show and I knew that. But I had learned from business dealings and from courtroom etiquette that one should always make immediate and friendly eye contact. A little graciousness goes a long way. I wanted my companions to see that.

"Thanks for letting me borrow this nice car. Is the black sedan ready?"

"Yes, sir," the salesmen said in unison.

"Here are your keys. Enjoy the new car," one salesman said. "You know the routine of bringing it back in for the service."

We piled into the car.

"It's on now," Leon said.

I was too busy thinking about the $1,200 monthly car note that was due in thirty days. I needed more money. As I fiddled with all the switches and knobs on the dashboard, I tallied in my head the big deals I had in the works. They should help my cash flow in the short-term. Heck, last year, I grossed $300,000. At least that's what I said on my 1040 tax form.

I was partnering in a new business venture and expected my income to soon soar. The relationship could gross me as much as $600,000 in the coming year.

At that time I thought, money was imbued with medicinal qualities. Whenever I found myself down, money was the thing to lighten my psychological load. It had to be cash or cashier's check. People who did business with me knew my rule. I had lived by it, since a couple of big checks bounced.

Money was like a stimulant. It was terrific when I was high and loaded with cash in my pockets. As it disappeared, I felt desperate and hungry for more. There was only a fleeting sense of relief. Not that many years before I earned $30,000 a year as an accountant. I thought that was plenty to raise a family. Now, that sum would barely last one month. The old adage is true, "I was much happier with a little, than with a lot." A famous rapper, the Notorious B.I.G. or Biggie Smalls, said in a posthumous chartbuster rap song; *Mo Money, Mo Problems!*

But, oh, what a ride I'd take before that lesson sunk in.

BY THE time we were cruising back toward town in my new Benzo, it was almost 5 p.m. Normally, by this time on a Friday, we'd be all heading in our separate cars to the Mirage. The happy hour on Fridays was the best. By 6 p.m., the place was packed.

Today, we would all arrive in my new car, which would help me to show it off. First, I needed to stop by the bank and deposit a cashier's check for $25,000, which I had in my breast pocket. Yet another successful deal sealed by the "Midas Touch", as I jokingly referred to my business acumen.

I couldn't wait to drive my new ride on campus. Everyone would wonder what was going on. Black colleges aren't like MIT or Stanford - a bunch of rich kids and wealthy scientists driving around in BMWs and Acuras. Half of the student body at Bethune-Cookman managed to attend by the Grace of God. Financial aid was the norm. The college president constantly raised funds to keep the college afloat. Surrounding the small scenic campus, with its majestic live oak trees draped in Spanish moss and its weathered red brick buildings, sat the poorest neighborhoods in Daytona Beach. A constant reminder of what life held for most black people.

Housing projects. drug dealers. unemployed men of all ages sitting on wooden boxes in front of dilapidated stores, windows covered with steel grates.

Even in a tourist town like Daytona Beach, the 560 SEL would be a mobile billboard. Heads would turn and people would wonder who was behind the wheel. I learned in college, and from Momma, there was more than enough pie to go around in America. If I worked hard, I'd get my share. But a lot of people didn't see it that way. Becoming successful brought unwanted jealously and mean-spirited gossip. There's a tendency among many black people - maybe people of all races, for that matter - to respond to good news about someone's accomplishments by thinking, Well, How come that's not happening to me? I must admit, I've thought that way, too.

"Where's he getting all that money?" would be the question around campus. "Yesterday a gray Benz, now back in black. What's up?" The students and staff had stopped to stare at the gray sedan. Wait till they saw this one.

"Andy, how are you going to ride around here on a daily basis in these large cars? All of the niggers and the crackers are going to be jealous," Craig said from the backseat. The guys laughed and chimed in with their wise cracks. I knew I had to handle it with tact. Otherwise, the car could cause serious problems.

The Bethune-Cookman College family, as the staff liked to call themselves, was a tight-knit group. My work environment felt comfortable because of it. But it also meant people got up in your business all the time. There already were rumblings on campus about my earning power. Some of the college's Cabinet members, essentially the top-level administrators, surveyed other colleges not long ago to see what they paid their attorneys.

The Cabinet members were making only $40,000 to $60,000 a year. I, on the other hand, had purchased a $350,000 home in a gated subdivision, called Pelican Bay, the nicest address in town. I had a two-story law office just a four-minute drive from campus. It was a historic landmark, a large Colonial-style home with white siding and black shutters. I also owned a $1 million nightclub. The smaller Mercedes had been tolerable to those envious people around me. But the 560 may be the straw that would break my back.

I call it "the crab syndrome." When one crab reaches the top, the other crabs grab it and pull it back in. I knew I needed to take action to offset the obvious jealousy and stop further prying into my financial status.

Too many people were saying I was next in line to ascend to the college presidency. I was flattered by their confidence in my abilities, but the comments also made me shudder. "Brother Hill, when is Dr. Bronson going to retire and let you take over?" they'd say at college functions and social events.

My response was well-rehearsed. "I am not interested in the presidency until Dr. Bronson sees fit, and not a day sooner. I have plenty of time."

But I knew that wouldn't satisfy the rabble-rousers. By the time my words got back to Dr. Bronson, I reportedly had said, "I'll be glad when he retires, so I can run things the way they should be to make the college prosper."

When you're riding high like I was, you better grow eyes in the back of your head. Sneak attacks come from all directions, often by the people you trust the most.

A friend had just told me the Volusia County Narcotics Task Force was targeting my nightclub for an undercover investigation. Word on the street was I used the club as a base to sell drugs. Not long ago, I spent months minimizing the damage of a rampant rumor, which said three friends and I were arrested for trafficking drugs in Orlando, an hour drive from Daytona Beach. According to the rumor, we were caught with a big shipment. No one seemed to question how, if the rumor were true, I could be driving around Daytona and not be locked up in federal prison.

I was accustomed to such stereotypes. If a black man has money and is not a professional athlete, then surely he's selling drugs. I wasn't trafficking in drugs, nor were any of my friends. The undercover agents could snoop around all they wanted. That wasn't a problem. But the car could be.

"Hey, I can handle it," I told myself. "Who is going to mess with me."

Craig Watson started in, "What can I do to get me one of these? I am tired of driving my 300. But my wife will kill my ass, if I buy another Benz. We really cannot afford this one with our new house note. I should have been a lawyer because you're making all of the paper."

Tommy joined in. "At least you guys have Mercedes, so quit crying or give it up, and I will show you all how to parlay."

My mind jumped to the night of drinking ahead at the club. Given my training and instinctual cunningness, which served me well as a lawyer, I should have paid better attention to their comments that evening. Events were beginning to take shape around me. But not until years later would I look back and understand how the pieces fit together.

Part of it was naiveté. And some of it stemmed from letting down my guard in a black environment. Growing up in Little Rock and attending two predominantly white state universities, I learned to stay alert when interacting with the majority culture. I intentionally sought out employment in a black environment and thought of Bethune-Cookman as my sanctuary from a racist world, which had never appreciated my

talents. I don't mean to sound like I hated whites. I buried myself in a
black haven to stay out of trouble, I thought. Paranoia grew in me, like
it did for many blacks, while living in South in the 1950s, 60s and early
70s.

I TURNED the Benz off International Speedway Boulevard and
headed south on U.S. Highway 1 toward my nightclub. The Mirage
overlooked the Halifax River, which separates the mainland from the
barrier island and the beaches. The club was in the city of South
Daytona, right next to Daytona Beach.

I punched the accelerator and felt the hood of the car lift up as
the car surged ahead, reaching 80 mph in the seconds before I let up on
the pedal. I was itching to test the limits of the car. But this stretch of
road was posted at 45 mph. I didn't want to push my luck, although
Leon, Craig and Tommy were expecting me to top 100 mph as we blew
past South Daytona's City Hall and adjoining police station.

My friends were used to hair-raising rides when I test drove my
latest Benz on the public testing grounds, known as Interstate 4 between Daytona Beach and Orlando, a rather straight 40-mile stretch of
four-lane highway.

My record speed to date: 135 mph.

I liked seeing how much speed the car could withstand without
the steering wheel or car shaking. Even at top speeds, I never felt the
tiniest vibration. A Benz felt solid and dug deeper into the road the
faster it went.

My most infamous speed tests occurred on the way home from
Orlando Magic basketball games. Unless my family was on board.
Because Sandra would not have tolerated such reckless and dangerous
behavior.

The first year Orlando got an NBA team, I bought four season
tickets and renewed them every year. The tickets were in hot demand
and I used them to entertain clients and friends. We had a blast, drinking
liquor and sometimes doing lines of coke before, during and after the
games. After games, we'd slide on downtown, a few blocks from the
Orlando Arena, and hung out at the Blue Note Jazz Club, drinking and

partying until the early morning.

On the way back to Daytona Beach, once we reached the quieter stretch of I-4 on the outskirts of Orlando, I'd say, "WATCH THIS!"

Off we'd go. The passengers quickly snapped into their seat belts and started praying. At 120 mph, objects pass by super-quick. I'd be weaving in and out of traffic. A few foolish young drivers would try unsuccessfully to keep up with me in their Cameros and Mustangs.

My biggest fear was spooking some slow-poke driver from Ohio, who, seeing me fly up in the rear-view mirror, might start frantically changing lanes to get out of my way. Dangerous. I'd have no time to react to their sudden moves. That or a tire blow-out would mean instantaneous death.

"Slow down, fool," a passenger would yell.

"I'm going to kill you if you don't slow this car down."

I remain fixated on the road ahead, concentrating so hard that I didn't respond to them, much yet soothe their fears. One miscalculation and we'd be dead. No matter how responsive the car feels, it cannot drive itself.

As my passengers' protests grew louder, I'd come to my senses and slow down to a reasonable speed. Surprisingly, I was never pulled over by the Florida Highway Patrol troopers who constantly run radar on I-4 to catch all the tourists speeding to get back home.

I just wanted to fly. When I was a boy, I told Momma I wanted to be a jet pilot. I didn't pursue that dream. Roaring down the highway at 135 mph in a Mercedes Benz, was the closest I'd get. The experience - although unfair to my passengers and fellow drivers - provided a feeling of power and success. It sated my desire to live dangerously.

THE Mirage parking lot was filling up as we pulled up to the front. As the owner, I parked right along the front walkway.

Seeing the Mirage always gave me a thrill. The entire building was curved, so that as your eye scanned the front, it never hit a sharp corner. Even the roof sloped across the top of the building, giving the place a sleek and classy look that carried through to the inside.

Patrons started waving at us as soon as we stepped from the car.

Once inside, the staff greeted us like we were royalty. I had barely reached the dancing area when a waitress handed my usual, tequila and water, just a little ice. She took the other guys' order and disappeared in the crowd.

About 20 couples were gyrating on the dance floor. The six sets of speakers produced enough bass to rumble your chest. A disco ball splashed a rainbow of colors around the room; dry ice provided intermittent layers of smoke.

Along the back wall were solid windows. Automated shades on the windows turned back and forth, providing a view of the Halifax River. At night, they offered a picturesque scene of lighted homes on the distant riverbank and an occasional lighted boat making its way down the Intracoastal Waterway.

The Mirage was 7,000 square feet. I called the decorations a "French motif." The tables were covered in deep burgundy table cloths, which matched the fabric on the bistro chairs and the carpeting and wallpaper. The place looked like a fine supper club. It offered a full menu and could be converted into several banquet rooms where, among others, Bethune-Cookman College had held formal presidential dinners and receptions.

The place looked expensive and it was.

Craig was with me the first time I walked in the place. We had stopped by for a drink. I fell in love with the place and felt intuitively that it would be mine someday. Owning a restaurant/lounge seemed like the perfect sideline. My friends and I were always hanging around places like this, just like you see on T.V. Whether you were a gangster, a player, or just one of the guys, you had to hang out in restaurants.

"I'm going to buy this place," I told Craig that night.

"You can't be serious, Andy."

Of course, I was.

Two days later, I learned the Mirage would be auctioned off. The timing seemed like an omen. I called the real estate agent handling the sale and asked what it would take to stop the auction. The agent, an Egyptian named Sherif Guindi, who wore a star on his forehead, called me back the next day and said I had to pay a $30,000 deposit.

My banker had already called and said Guindi was checking out my financial status. The deal was coming together. I should have looked for investors to go in with me, which was Sandra's suggestion. But I waved if off. I wanted the club to myself.

Sandra and I spent several nights at the dining room table, working up the numbers for the new business. Sandra had been a fund-raiser in the development department at Bethune-Cookman College and was as adept at business as I. She had resigned from her job to raise our two young children.

We figured how many patrons we'd need each night to meet our fixed costs. We calculated the Overhead, Payroll, Taxes, Mortgage and Escrow payments. We were working on the financial analysis when Guindi came by for the $30,000 non-refundable deposit and the $200,000 down payment.

"Mr. Hill, I must tell you not to buy this club," Sherif said. I had greeted him and led him back to the pool deck behind my home to enjoy the bright orange sunset. "I feel I must inform you that I and my partners are about to open a new nightclub in Daytona Beach. Ours will have a much better location than yours in South Daytona. I don't think you will be able to survive."

My face must have shown my indifference to his words. Before I could reply, Sherif added, "So it is. You are going to be engaged in severe competition with me and my associates. I want you to know this, Mr. Hill."

I began asking him questions about the closing date on the Mirage and what documents I must prepare. As he rose to leave, I said Sandra and I wanted the sale to remain confidential. We made the decision for several reasons. For starters, I didn't need to be flashing anymore money around town. And secondly, the club needed to attract black and white patrons to survive. By announcing a black owner, we could lose support.

Blacks alone could not provide enough customers for the club. And anyway, blacks do not usually go out of their way to support black establishments. That's a well known fact. I can't tell you how many times I saw middle-class blacks in the courthouse with white attorneys, especially in civil cases where a huge settlement was on the line.

Sherif looked surprised at my explanation. He folded my checks and put them in his jacket. As he walked out, he looked back at me and said, "I will keep it quiet. Don't worry."

Two days after the real-estate closing, I picked up *The News-Journal* and saw the headline at the top of the business section. "Attorney Anderson C. Hill II purchases the Mirage Nightclub for $1 million."

The article quoted Sherif at-length. Obviously, the reporter hadn't picked up the sale from public records. Sherif sent out a press release. He played street ball, making a underhanded, but sly, move to bolster his soon-to-open entertainment complex. And I, well, I erred by not putting a confidentiality clause in the sales contract.

FRIDAYS were my late nights at the club. I was far too busy during the week to stay out late. And on Saturday nights, I had to get home at a decent hour so I looked presentable at the 10:50 a.m. Sunday church service. As a deacon at Greater Friendship Baptist Church, I couldn't look hung over or smell like alcohol and cigarettes on Sunday mornings.

Sandra never expected me home before 3 a.m. on Saturday mornings. I'd circulate from table to table all night, talking to friends and acquaintances. The club was my home turf. I owned the place figuratively and literally. All nightclubs develop their own personality over time. The same people tend to visit regularly, which helps build a feeling of camaraderie and friendliness within the establishment. It helps if newcomers can sense this immediately and that way are drawn to return again and again.

The Mirage had such a click. A nice mix of black and white patrons, most of them in their late 20s to early 40s, and with professional careers. People dressed up, danced till they sweat, drank wholeheartedly and cruised for the opposite sex.

For me, it was like going to a jammin' party every Friday night. Everyone knew me and wanted my attention. As college attorney, assistant to the college president and a restaurant/lounge owner, I was becoming a local celeb in town. I was active in the Chamber of Commerce, spoke regularly on Dr. Bronson's behalf at civic and social events, and handled a few noteworthy court cases in my private law practice. The list of duties frequently landed my name and picture in the local newspaper.

I could tell that some club patrons thought of me as a good luck charm. If they could get close to me, then some of my magic touch would rub off on them. Their faces would look like they thought I was the luckiest man alive. And I couldn't deny that luck helped me many times. But I've noticed that people minimize the amount of sheer determination, discipline and hard work that account for wealthy people's successes in life.

I worked long days during the week, and it wasn't uncommon for me to return to my law office on Saturday and Sunday afternoons to meet all my commitments. My biggest responsibility was serving as college attorney. I handled real-estate purchases, oversaw multi-million-dollar building projects, and handled all lawsuits for and against the college, including taking steps to resolve any possible problems before they wound up in court.

My presence was required at all meetings of the college Board of Trustees, all Cabinet meetings and sometimes several meetings a day with Dr. Bronson. He asked me personally to oversee several special projects and college committees, and I diligently accommodated such requests.

Meetings of the Cabinet, which set college policy and handled internal issues, would start as early as 7 a.m. and conclude at 2 p.m. It was important to stay alert and think quick at these meetings because there was constant jockeying among the administrators to impress Dr. Bronson.

Many days, I didn't stop for lunch unless it was a special luncheon with Dr. Bronson or visiting dignitaries on campus. Sandwiched between my college responsibilities, I tried to build my private law practice. I'd dash off to court hearings between college meetings, prepare legal documents, research case law and supervise the employees in my law office.

At nights and on weekends, I'd keep an eye on business at the Mirage.

Since childhood, I had always enjoyed rigorous physical exercise. At this point in my life, there was time only for mental calisthenics. I knew the life was taking a toll on me and my family. My family, which I loved dearly, was being substantially ignored.

This was a marked shift from my past. I once had spent every evening with Sandra and the kids, Andy, born in 1982, and Lauren, born in 1984. I could tell it was bothering them, although no one had yet to complain to me.

Sandra and I rarely argued, but I guess I should have seen the blow-up coming. We were driving home from one of her sorority functions, Delta Sigma Theta. Our only nights out as a couple these days were always for some formal event. I now owned three different tuxes, with the banquets and parties for my fraternity, her sorority, the college, the church, civic organizations and business affairs.

I was bragging about my new black Benz.

"Anderson, you are going overboard with these cars. What is your problem?"

"Everything is all right. I'm only trying to live a dream that I've had for many years."

"What dream is that?" she asked and turned down the radio, which was playing "Don't Push Me 'Cause I'm Close to the Edge," a rap tune about societal problems encountered by black males. It was one of my favorite songs.

"To own a big Benzo," I said and turned the volume back up.

"A big Benzo?" Sandra said, her voice rising. "What is wrong with the ones we already have? You need to wake up and realize that you're not thinking clearly. Your problem is with alcohol and cocaine. Please stop what you're doing, for the sake of me and the kids. Everyone can see what's wrong. You may think people don't know, but they know. This town is too small, Deacon Hill."

I pulled the car into our driveway and waited for the automatic garage door to finish opening.

"I'm just trying to help you, me, and the kids," Sandra continued. "Don't you care or have the drugs taken over?"

"You don't need to worry, San," I replied in my most charming voice. "I'm not going to let the drugs and alcohol take command of our lives. I know better than that."

She seemed distant from me and remained aloof as we walked in the house. I paid the baby-sitter and took her three blocks away to her home. When I returned, Sandra was already in bed. I undressed and crawled in beside her. I wanted to reach out and hold her. But I knew she was mad at me and probably already asleep. I laid there for awhile and couldn't get to sleep.

Instead, I got up and went into my closet to where I had just hung up my tux jacket. I slid my hand in the breast pocket and felt the little brown bottle of cocaine.

I crept downstairs into the family room and flipped on the T.V. It didn't matter what show was on. The sound and picture kept me company. I poured myself a drink and sat down on the gray leather sectional couch. I dipped out a tiny spoonful of white powder and stuck it up my left nostril. By clamping down on my right nostril with my thumb and snorting quickly, the powder shot deeply into my left nostril. That first burst of tingling euphoria was what I lived for. I dipped the spoon again and inhaled it into my right nostril.

Lift off.

I dropped my head on the back of the couch, closed my eyes and enjoyed the sensation. This latest batch made me a feel a bit more on edge than my usual supply. A few cocktails would smooth that out. I settled back with my drink and flipped through the stations until I came to an old Clint Eastwood movie.

Coke is such a seductive and troublesome drug. It's illegal, yes. And very expensive. But even worse, it wears off too quickly. You spend the rest of the night packing your nose with more powder in a vain attempt to recapture the initial rush. And guess what? It never happens. Coke users know this. They've been through it time after time. But for some sick reason, they just don't get it. Like some monkey in some sick experiment who keeps pushing the lever over and over even though each time the lever delivers an electrical zap to its brain.

"First contact." That's what coke users chase after so frantically and pathetically. The intense pleasure that comes when the fine white grains first make contact with the mucous membranes high in each nasal cavity. The membranes are teeming with nerves that are wired direct to the brain, which is jolted awake and overwhelmed by feelings of well-being, invincibility, physical strength and intense energy.

By the tenth spoonful, your brain is overloaded and shuts down. Now all you feel is wired and hollow. Delusions and paranoia take hold. When the cocaine runs out, you spend hours searching through every pocket in your clothes, hoping to find some forgotten stash. Of course, you never do. What started as fun turns into a long, sleepless night.

Which is exactly the hell-hole I fell in about 4:30 a.m.

I projected a solid self-assurance to the world, but several things had been worrying me lately. Despite my "Midas Touch", I had suffered two big setbacks in recent months. By day, I tried to shake off the defeats. At night, lying wide awake just before dawn, I sensed these events did not portend well for the future.

I HAD trained for several years to become the college's executive vice president, second in command after the president. Dr. R.J. Gainous Jr., who also owned the black funeral home in Daytona Beach, held the position for many years. My title was College Attorney and Assistant Executive Vice President. It was assumed that I would move into his position when Dr. Gainous retired.

His retirement announcement had come six months earlier. However, instead of promoting me into the job, the college set up a committee to study whether the position should remain. A month later, the committee reported that the position should be eliminated. I learned about the decision through the college rumor mill. That afternoon, I had a previously scheduled meeting with Dr. Bronson and I asked him about it.

"Brother Hill," he said. "This was not my decision. It was the decision of the committee. I know you had hoped to move into that position. I was thinking of making you Assistant to the President instead."

My gut told me something was amiss. I had been around long enough to know that college committees were created by Dr. Bronson's urging and therefore they normally recommended whatever he wanted. By having a committee study an issue and determine a course of action, Dr. Bronson could distance himself from controversial decisions.

I didn't know all the details about what was behind this decision. But years later, after I left the college, I learned my instincts were right. For again, the college now has an executive vice president.

I had watched many years earlier, shortly after I started working at Bethune-Cookman, another top administrator fall from grace. He was the college Provost, Dr. Israel Tribble Jr. Rumors had flown around the campus that Tribble was next in line for the college presidency. Dr.

Bronson had been president since the mid 1970s. People expected him to retire any year. Within a few months, the college decided to eliminate the position of provost and Dr. Tribble disappeared. He later surfaced in Tampa, Florida, in a grand style. Dr. Tribble became president of the powerful Florida Education Fund and the first African-American President of the Tampa Greater Chamber of Commerce. Dr. Bronson found himself having to ask Dr. Tribble for student scholarship consideration at the college.

I, too, had become the golden boy. I rose quickly through the ranks of the college administration. I had started as an accountant and applied to law school after Dr. Bronson said the college would help pay for my law degree. I returned to the college three years later as a lawyer in training, working under the guidance of a law firm in town that was under contract with the school.

I continued to rise quickly. I knew Dr. Bronson and others could view me as a threat. I kept reminding myself of Dr. Tribble and became much more subservient to Dr. Bronson. Because I wanted him to know, that in my mind, he was always in charge. I would constantly say to him, "It was you, Dr. Bronson, who made me who I am. I'll never forget that." It was more than just playing up to him. I knew it was a necessity for my survival. I didn't want him or others to feel that I thought that I was better than they, and I was truly grateful for the opportunity.

I knew Dr. Bronson was uncomfortable about the home I had purchased. I heard him remark off-handedly many times to people in a joking tone, "I live in a middle-class subdivision. But Brother Hill lives in Pelican Bay, an upper-class subdivision."

Our house was 3,800 square feet with a swimming pool and three-car garage. Out back was an exquisite view of the only island hole on the golf course, the 13th hole. Several canals flowed around that area of the golf course. A quaint little bridge crossed over one canal right behind our house.

Word spread fast that we had purchased a large home. Many people from Bethune-Cookman tried to drive into the subdivision to look at it, but they'd be stopped by the security gates. The guard would call us and say some people wanted to drive by our house. The people usually stopped in for a full tour of the house. For awhile we had so much company it was unbelievable.

I knew stories about our house were racing around campus, which caused a slight alienation of affection from Dr. Bronson. He was, after all, supposed to be king of the campus. And now his prodigy was receiving all the attention.

Dr. Bronson and his wife were among the first people we invited over for dinner. They seemed to be truly happy for us. Dr. Bronson commented, "This house would be great to entertain in. We can have college functions here."

I quickly agreed. "Sandra and I would be more than happy to entertain whoever you want in our home. That's no problem."

THE Mirage was the other source of my worries. The name should have been my first warning that the business might not do well. The dictionary says a mirage is *something that falsely appears to be real. (See delusion.)*

The club was losing money from the moment I opened the doors. But I thought I had another way to make money off it. The club sat at the front of a deep piece of property stretching from U.S. Highway 1 to the river. The land behind the club, abutting the river, had more than enough room for condominiums. Sandra and I had figured we could put up a high rise, add some boat slips and make more than enough money to pay off the property.

I hired architects and surveyors to complete the necessary development plans. The planners at the South Daytona city hall encouraged the project and thought it would receive a definite go-ahead. Once the city staff signed off on the plans, we needed only to go before the Planning and Zoning Board to request a change in zoning from commercial to multi-family on the back tract of land.

The P&Z board voted unanimously to recommend the rezoning to the city commission. Tommy Huger and I had a big celebration that night, giving each other high 5's, dreaming about big profits. Tommy and I figured we'd be in and out of the meeting in an hour. When we pulled up to city hall, on our next scheduled appearance, the parking lot was filled with cars. A large number of people were milling around the front entrance. I knew I was in trouble. Usually only a couple people attend city commission meetings. These people were here about my project.

When the Mirage development came up on the agenda, the city manager said he recommended it, and P&Z had approved it. The commission chairman opened the meeting to public comments. A line of people, all white, moved toward the podium. For almost an hour, they all seemed to say the same thing.

"We don't want a low-income housing development in this community. Those people will be driving by all night, stealing and raping." They were scared to death that black folks would take over their bedroom community.

Finally, it was my turn to respond. "There is no basis for these comments except for racism. The sales price for an individual unit would be at a minimum of $100,000. There is no way this facility is going to become designated as a low-income or a housing project."

The commissioners, playing to their electorate, had already made up their minds. The vote was unanimous against the project.

I went over to the Mirage and sat there until after closing, nursing one drink after another. Without the condominiums, I'd never be able to pay off the debt on this place. I sat there wondering, Should I keep the place or let it go? I knew the answer. But my pride wouldn't let me put up a "For Sale" sign.

GET BILL OFF OF
THAT MOON WILL YOU

Goon done gone to the moon
and become a fool.

Don't want to be beat up by the
moon no more.

The moon can kick some booty.

Shed that old skin and become akin
to the likeness of Bill.

Bill is slick like Rick.
He knows all the latest tricks.

The skin fits old Willie who is now Bill(y) very well.

We think that we see you, but nobody will ever tell that it
is ol' Willie hiding under that skin.

Cause your name is now Bill and you are destined
to give all who want to ride, cheap yet expensive thrills.

2 WILLIE GOON

"We live in a world which respects power above all things. Power, intelligently directed, can lead to more freedom. Unwisely directed, it can be a dreadful, destructive force." Dr. Mary McLeod Bethune (1875-1955)

I WAS sitting in the family room, kicked back, watching the tube, when the six o'clock news reported that Bethune-Cookman College's head baseball coach had just been arrested by the Daytona Beach police.

"San, come here quick," I yelled. She scurried in from the kitchen, where she was making dinner, and caught the end of the newscast. A police mug-shot of Johnny Randolph flashed onto the screen. He was charged with two counts of attempted first-degree murder. He had allegedly shot two men at the home of his estranged wife. The motive was unknown, according to the prissy blonde TV reporter, who was broadcasting live in front of the brown-brick city police station. Randolph was being held in the local jail.

Sandra and I were sitting speechless when the phone rang.

"Brother Hill, did you hear the news report?"

It was Dr. Bronson. There was worry and alarm in his voice.

"Yeah, we just heard it on the TV," I said.

"Well, what can we do?" Bronson stammered. "What could have happened to cause such a reaction from Johnny? We've got to help him, Brother Hill."

As the college's attorney, I was the go-to man whenever an employee may have needed personal legal representation, especially at times like this when an incident could reflect badly on the college. I had handled relatively few criminal cases. Although I had little experience in criminal law, The University of Florida Law School had pounded the basics into me, enabling me to be somewhat proficient for the court-appointed and walk-in cases that I took into my private law practice. My professional career had been devoted to real-estate law, contracts and other documentary type legal work.

A few times, when I had to attend hearings in the new three-story courthouse, designed in a modern style with dark bricks and large tinted glass windows, I would pop into another courtroom if a big criminal trial was going on. The back three or four rows would be crowded with young assistant public defenders and assistant state attorneys, reporters and private attorneys like me, all eager spectators to watch the town's best criminal defense attorneys take on the state prosecutors.

Only a handful of the defense attorneys in town would draw a big crowd. Word spread through the courthouse when these big names were handling a trial. Watching them rivaled the performance of a Broadway show. They would argue passionately before the jury, having planned a sophisticated strategy that we less experienced attorneys could only admire. High profile criminal cases were a different ball game. If I had dedicated myself to the craft, I could have developed those skills. But by choice, I took another course in my professional practice.

"I'll make sure he's got a bail bondsman," I said to Dr. Bronson. "He should be able to get out of jail tomorrow, if the bond isn't set too high. I'll go down there and speed things along."

"Good," Dr. Bronson replied. "Johnny needs you now, Brother Hill. Call me tomorrow. I'll need an update."

Dr. Bronson had more on his mind than Johnny's fate. As college president, he knew the local media would call his office first thing in the morning, wanting to know the college's position. Would Johnny be suspended? Fired? Was the college shocked by the news?

Dumb questions. At a white college, incidents like this warranted no more than a three-paragraph brief, buried on the bottom of page three. A scandal at a black college seemed to send the white media into a feeding frenzy. TV reporters might be waiting outside the stately White Hall, the college's main administration building, when he drove up in the morning. Just the thought of it made Dr. Bronson sigh and seem to suddenly feel very tired.

"Thanks, Brother Hill," he said and hung up before I could reply.

Attempted first-degree murder is a serious crime. If convicted, Johnny faced life in prison. In Florida, a conviction could put Johnny in prison for a minimum of 25 years, before he would become eligible for parole.

I knew I had my work cut out for me. It would not be right to assign the case to one of my associates. This case I would definitely have to handle myself. I'd give it my best effort and would call in a good criminal trial attorney if I needed help. First my task would be to dig out my old law-school textbooks at home and freshen up on criminal procedures. An endless series of motions and countermotions must be filed before the prosecutor and defense attorney even contemplate a trial date. Discovery. Depositions. Motions to compel. Motions to quash.

The research and drafting of legal documents would take me twice as long as an experienced criminal attorney. I had to be thorough, especially because Johnny was a longtime close friend. We were fraternity brothers in Kappa Alpha Psi. And Sandra and I were godparents to his daughter, Jasmine. My handling of the case would be under the watchful eye of Dr. Bronson, who would possibly judge me by whatever happened. I sagged under the thought of another stressful project right now. But I had no choice.

Just months before, Johnny was the idol of the campus. He had been selected to become an agent for the Federal Bureau of Investigation after completing a rigorous selection process that few people got through successfully. Johnny had resigned his job as head baseball coach and left for FBI headquarters in Quantico, Va., to begin training.

Sadly, Johnny didn't last long there. I don't know if he failed the training or couldn't withstand the separation from his wife, Jeanette. Within a few weeks, he was back at Bethune-Cookman, asking for his old job back. After all the fanfare, Dr. Bronson was disappointed to see him back. But Johnny was a Bethune-Cookman alumni and a loyal employee. He was part of the Bethune-Cookman family - a distinction that allowed him to return anytime.

College employees who were B-CC alumni enjoyed a special status among the college staff. My wife and I had worked for the college since 1976 and 1977, respectively. We were considered honorary members of the local alumni chapter. But several administrators and other staffers had told me point-blank over the years that we were still considered outsiders.

I repeatedly suggested that Johnny retain a more experienced criminal attorney. But he wouldn't hear it.. His faith in my ability stroked my ego and also made me work even harder for him, which may have been his intent all along. The case would be tough to win because it had been assigned to a circuit court judge - a woman - renowned for her stiff sentences and no-nonsense attitude in court. I regret that later in her career, the first woman judge of Volusia County, Gayle Graziano, was removed from the judicial bench for misuse of her power, by the Supreme Court of Florida.

As the trial date approached, I became engulfed in the case, working 10 to 12 hours a day on the case in addition to my other responsibilities. At night I would unwind at the Mirage, drinking the usual tequila until late into the night. Then I would dip heavily into the cocaine. A line here, a line there. By the end of the week, it added up to an eight ball, or more than $500 for the drugman.

I told myself the cocaine kept me going. Clear the mind, and the butt will follow. Just like caffeine, but with a lot more octane. Foolish thoughts created by a foolish drug, but when you are on it, those ideas seem to be fresh and creative. It made me feel like I could conquer the world, until the last snort when I felt more powerless than ever. Once I started a coke session, it was always "time for another hit," no matter where I was. If I was in public, I'd head to the nearest restroom.

The drugs, alcohol, late nights, and pressure had begun to distort my personality into a gross deformity, which only those closest to me could see. I once had been a well-grounded, determined, even cautious, young man. "Conservatism" was my motto. I was a long time member of the Republican Party and, to the disgust of many of my black friends, truly adhered to many of its political philosophies. The local party officials had asked me to run for public office. "You could win and beat the best at the state level," they told me. "The office would be yours with our assistance."

I had always declined their offer. "I am not interested in running for any political office. True money and power rest in the private sector," I told them. But now increasingly, the cocaine was filling me with irrational feelings of grandeur and invincibility. The drugs and liquor would whisper, ever so sweetly, "You can do anything you want, Big Daddy. Go ahead and give it a try."

I thought I'd easily win Johnny's case. The two male victims had initially attacked Johnny when he arrived at his estranged wife's home, forcing Johnny to defend himself. His wife was dating one of the guys - a big guy, 6-foot-1 and in his late 20s, several years younger than she. The guy with him was his brother, an even bigger guy, maybe 6-foot-3. Johnny, by comparison, was 5-foot-10. My strategy was to emphasize the size difference, that it was two guys against one, and get Johnny off on justifiable use of deadly force.

But the facts of the case muddied our defense. Johnny shot the two men, one time each during the fight. When the boyfriend's brother tried to run away, he tried to shoot him in the back, but his gun jammed. Then he turned to the boyfriend, lying on the pavement, blood covering his clothes. Johnny stood over him screaming obscenities. He pointed the pistol right in the guy's face. Said he was going to blow his fuckin' head off.

Jeanette tried to calm down her husband but Johnny didn't drop the weapon until two police cruisers squealed into the driveway and the officers, squatting behind their car doors with pistols drawn, ordered him to drop it and get down on the ground.

At the trial, under my questioning, Johnny couldn't avoid the self-incriminating details. Asked why he shot the man a second time, Johnny said, "I lost it, and feared the young buck would retaliate against me one day." Only Johnny and I knew the pistol had jammed as he stood over the guy and squeezed the trigger. Johnny's story was the best we could do. It was best for him to say it under my questioning than under the harsh cross examination by the prosecutor. I knew the jurors weren't buying it. I could see the looks of disbelief on their faces.

The jury deliberated for more than six hours. They rejected Johnny's excuse of justifiable force but they did not convict him of attempted first-degree murder. Despite pleas from the prosecutor for the jury to throw the book at Johnny, the jury found him guilty of the lesser included offenses of aggravated assault.

When we heard the court clerk read the verdict, I knew Johnny and I had made a serious mistake. Just a week before, the prosecutor had offered a plea bargain. Johnny could plead no contest and receive three years in prison. That was the best the prosecutor could do because, under Florida law, anyone who used a firearm during the commission of a crime had to serve a minimum of three years in state prison.

Johnny had said he didn't want to deal. I thought we might do better at trial, too. Now, I wasn't so sure. My thoughts ran to little Jasmine and I could imagine how she'd feel when she heard the news. Her daddy was going to prison, maybe for a long time.

I knew the impact of that on a child. At 8 years old, my father went to prison in Arkansas. Because he had shot and wounded my mother's sister. Then Archester Hill burned down our home, because Momma was threatening to divorce him. My father could be a very mean drunk and he was drinking excessively and more frequently. Rosie Hill wanted out of the marriage of twenty years.

Visiting my father in prison, was distressful, to say the least. It always saddened me to see that enormous, towering man locked up, ordered around like a dog by mean, white prison guards. Little Jasmine could grow up with those images, too.

I filed several motions and a stack of supportive letters, asking the judge to disregard the stiff sentence recommended by state guidelines and give Johnny probation. We hoped and prayed for the best. As the sentencing day came, Johnny tried to convince himself that it might just work out.

THE morning of sentencing, before leaving the law office to drive the few blocks to the three-story courthouse in midtown Daytona Beach, I happened to glance at my day's calendar and saw an appointment that was surprising. It only took a second to buzz my personal secretary, Teresa.

"Why is Robert Billingslea coming over here today," I sternly asked. It was my immediate hope that there wasn't anything wrong with the "endowed chair" contract. Billingslea worked for Walt Disney World in Orlando and had been selected by Disney to serve on the college's Board of Trustees. Bob now served as chairman of the powerful trustee's development committee. Disney had agreed to donate quite a substantial sum to Bethune-Cookman College and wanted a position on the board in exchange. Disney officials reasoned that it would help them oversee their donations to the hospitality management program at the college.

Billingslea and I had gotten to know each other very well. We had faxed drafts of the agreement back and forth, before the final signing. The college was expecting a check for $50,000 from Disney any day, out of the total $250,000 grant. I nevertheless had to get to Johnny's sentencing hearing. There simply was no time to worry about the contract right now.

"Mr. Billingslea called last week and said it was extremely important for you to meet with him and a Mr. Bill Williams," Theresa explained.

I shrugged and figured to concern myself with it later. I had better not be late for the sentencing hearing. Circuit Judge Gayle Graziano might hold me in contempt of court, the way she had done one other time. My punishment was to give a cash donation to the college of

$25.00. She made me bring her the college's receipt, before ordering my formal release. At first I thought that she was just kidding about the donation, but her words were, "Don't try me Attorney Hill, because I will put you in jail." No more was needed to be said. After seeing my father in jail, I knew I never wanted to be there, except when I had to visit clients in jail. Even knowing that I could walk out when I felt like it, I found jails a bit nerve-wracking.

I can remember after my father was released from prison and I'd go visit him. He'd tell me all his prison stories and warn me, "It is not a place that you want to be, son. Stay out of trouble, so you will not end up there. Too many black men go to prison for foolish things that can be avoided." I tried to heed these words, remembering vividly from my childhood visits when the bell would ring and visiting time would end, he had such a sad, trapped look on his face.

Johnny was waiting for me outside the second-floor courtroom, looking nervous and dressed in a new gray suit. My dress was my usual tailor-made dark suit. In the courtroom, I argued the best I could, telling the judge that the jury had not evaluated all the facts and evidence and should have returned not-guilty verdicts on both counts. "The jury's findings were indeed contradictory to the evidence, your Honor. If it was not attempted murder, then how is it aggravated battery?"

"Johnny is a role model in the community, your Honor. He's successful, educated, reliable and hard-working. He poses no threat to the community and has learned his lesson. Both victims in this case have fully recovered and admitted the error of their ways by initiating the confrontation."

The judge was unmoved. "This may not have been premeditated, but it certainly was an act of confused passion," she said and promptly sentenced Johnny to 10 years in state prison. "Court adjourned," she added and walked out a side door.

My heart sank. I turned to Johnny, who looked calm and stoic. "I'm sorry, Johnny."

My head and body felt like a wreck. Suddenly, I could feel the severe hangover from the tequila and cocaine the night before. Johnny must have read my expression, because he began to reassure me about my performance on the case.

He said it could have been worse. The jury could have convicted him of attempted first degree murder and the judge could have sentenced him to the max - life in prison. That's what usually happened to black men, especially ones that came to court with black attorneys. Many people in the black community openly said after Johnny's conviction, "He should have hired a white attorney. It would have increased his chances of getting off."

Maybe they were right, I thought. A black defendant faces an uphill battle to sway a jury. Then when the jurors see me, regardless of how well I perform, they can't see past my black skin. What more could I have done, other than not taking the case? What will the community and Dr. Bronson think of me and my skills as a trial attorney?" These were some of the thoughts running through my mind.

As Johnny was led away in handcuffs, I headed back to the office. On the short drive, I wondered what lay ahead for Johnny. Tears came to my eyes as I felt the depth of my despair about his future. I'd seen many people sentenced to prison during my years of practice. But this time was different. I knew Johnny personally and was worried about his ability to hold up in a demoralizing and dangerous prison system.

I pulled into my law office parking lot and parked my new Benz beside one just like it, except gray. I knew it was my next appointment. I loved the looks of these expensive German cars. Pure class, I thought.

Bob Billingslea and Bill Williams, Jr. were seated in the waiting room. As soon as I walked through the door, Bill jumped from his seat and extended a hearty "soul-brother" handshake.

I scanned his physique and wondered if I could take him in a game of one-on-one basketball. At six-foot-two, I didn't normally have to look up to many people. But Bill stood three inches taller than I and seemed to look down on me as he stroked his neatly trimmed, salt-n-pepper colored beard.

As successful black men, the three of us knew how to speak in perfect white diction. But we reverted to the ebonics from our childhood at certain times during our conversation on that day. It built feelings of camaraderie.

"You two are bigger niggers," Bob said, laughing, as he introduced Bill. "I'm the little fish in this ol' pond," he said sarcastically, a play on his status as a college trustee and Disney executive.

I continue studying this new man's appearance. He commanded attention. He was well-groomed and projecting an air that said he knew how to live graciously. He reminded me of an accounting professor I admired at Clark College, named Mr. Drake. Mr. Drake wore tailor-made suits and drove a new Benz . The first time I saw him, I thought he had attained a level of success that most black men could only dream of. Looking at myself now, I could see I had shaped myself into a carbon copy of Mr. Drake, especially my love of a Mercedes Benz or a "Merk" as we called them back in my undergraduate college days.

I looked over Bill again. I could probably take him to the hole, a vernacular used in basketball, but not with an inside post game. It would be my outside shots that would kill him. I could feel my competitive streak kick in. The two of us drove the same cars and dressed alike. Success and self-confidence exuded from both of us. The three of us standing there in the waiting area probably wore $7,500 or more in clothes, jewelry and watches.

I loved seeing successful black brothers. That's why I had chosen to go to Atlanta to attend Clark College. After growing up in Little Rock, it expanded my horizons to see such large numbers of black police, doctors, lawyers and other types of professionals. In Atlanta, even the mayor was black.

"We're here to make things click," Bob continued. "Together, you two will be awesome."

"Nice to meet you, Bill," I said. "Why don't you and Bob come upstairs to my office?"

As we walked out of the waiting area and up the stairs to my office, I remembered that Bill Williams Jr. had called me several times and left messages. He owned a large construction company in Orlando and wanted information about bidding on several construction projects at Bethune-Cookman. I hadn't returned any of the calls, although I mentioned them to Tommy, the college's construction manager. He didn't seem interested in contacting the man either. Calls from black-owned construction companies were nothing new to us. Often they showed up unannounced at our office with big promises and a hundred variations of the same sales pitch, which usually started with Surely-you-want-to-help-a-black-brother-out. I would have liked to help them all, but we were unable to find one that could meet the stringent requirements imposed by the federal government when it handed out money for construction projects.

Tommy and the architect had scoured the United States looking for a qualified minority to participate. We were frustrated by the lack of a qualified pool of minorities to choose from. We were on the verge of giving up and advising the board of trustees that minorities for our size of construction projects just were not available.

I closed my office door behind the two men and took a seat at my polished oak desk. I noticed Bill checking out my maroon color scheme. He seemed to be wondering who had done my interiors. I would have gladly told him my wife Sandra, but naturally he did not want to ask and appear overly impressed by his surroundings. As we were getting settled, there was a bustling of activity outside my door. I figured it was Tommy trying to figure out who I was seeing and wondering why he hadn't been invited to the meeting.

The men sat down in the two antique chairs that faced my desk. The richly-colored soft-bottom cushions on the chairs matched my deep burgundy leather executive chair. I made eye contact and leaned back. They knew I was in charge of this fiefdom.

"Now, Anderson, Bill here, is the kind of person who has the financial and professional capabilities to make many things happen," Bob said. "I don't know what the problem is around here. I told Bill to call Tommy and talk to him about some of the college's construction projects, but Tommy gave him the cold shoulder."

I glanced at Bill, who sat quietly, nodding his head occasionally, as Bob spoke. His eyes didn't blink behind the dark rimmed spectacles. It was as though he was staring at me, not in a hostile way, just with a sense of keen intellect.

As Bob kept talking, a tone of desperation creeping into his voice. Bill's company, Renselear Development Corporation, had done substantial work at Walt Disney World. Bob could vouch for Bill's professional qualifications. As a college trustee, Bob knew the board was pressuring Tommy and me to hire minority contractors for two big construction projects that were about to start on campus. One project would be a dorm and classroom building; the other a fine arts center.

At the last board meeting, the trustees' executive committee had rejected Tommy's and my construction plans. The committee said our projections for minority participation were far too low. The recorded minutes of the meeting summed up their complaints: "If a black college does not have certain levels of participation, then how can we advocate such with other organizations. We must increase our efforts. This plan is unacceptable. Bring us something with higher minority percentages. The (recently) completed science-hall annex project was disgusting in terms of minority involvement."

As I recalled the committee's instructions, Bob pushed ahead with his marketing pitch for Bill Williams. "This is your man. As you are aware, Disney has a vested interest in the future long-range construction plans for the fine arts center, which will house the hospitality management program. The contract states Disney can provide consulting from time to time. My professional advice is to hire this man's company, pronto. He can do what we need and you won't have to look any further. Disney wants Renselear's substantial involvement. Need I say anything further to you, Brother Hill? Hire Bill's company on the dormitory project."

I felt like I had no choice but to hire him.

"We wanted to talk to you about this matter before I take Bill to meet Dr. Bronson," Bob continued. "We'd like your unqualified support on this, Anderson. The college will benefit, Disney will benefit, and I think you personally could benefit, too," Bob said.

The plan would be to hire Renselear Development Corp. as a major subcontractor on the dormitory project, called the Living Learning Center, which would be used to house those students with the highest grade-point averages. We couldn't award the whole project to Renselear, because the college had already hired a local company, Allen Green Construction Co., to handle the $2.6 million project.

However, as a major subcontractor on the Living Learning Center, Bill would be in an advantageous position to get the full contract for the next project - construction of a $2.8 million fine arts center, paid for by the U.S. Congress in honor of the college's founder, Dr. Mary McLeod Bethune (1875-1955).

Bob continued his speech. "You know, the board has ordered you to get more minority participation. Just think what will happen, if you do not do it. The Board will probably look for someone who can do what we think is feasible," Bob said. "Now you have your method to be successful as Bill's firm can do all of the construction work for the college."

I wasn't sure if this was a threat or if Bob was being overly dramatic. He leaned forward in the chair and lowered his voice to an almost conspiratorial tone. "Just to let you know, Anderson, Bill also has several large projects ongoing in Orlando." With that, he turned to Bill, who began speaking as if on cue.

"Yes," Bill began, speaking for the first time. "I'm in the process of purchasing the Grand National office complex off International Drive for $13 million. I've been looking for an attorney to handle some of the paperwork. Bob said you may be available. There is also a project called Splendid China, a new theme park that will be built in Orlando and valued at $34.5 million dollars. Your expertise could be used there, as well."

I had dollar signs in my eyes. The Mirage was draining me of cash. My bills were mounting and several payments were past due. Also, I needed to repay $35,000 to an escrow account for Bethune-Cookman College that I had taken without permission. If the Florida Bar Association found out I misused escrow account funds, I'd face disciplinary action.

At the time, I rationalized that the college owed me the money. I was waiting for the final installment of a $113,004.56 bill for legal work submitted at the end of the previous year. The college was also behind in the rent due to me for Tommy's office in my firm. Dr. Bronson had not yet realized that I had "borrowed" the money, as I told myself. I knew every day was borrowed time until he asked for it back.

I needed money, badly. How did Bob know that? Was it that obvious? Were they trying to bribe me for my recommendations to Dr. Bronson and to the construction manager on the dormitory project? The cocaine, I reasoned, was probably making me paranoid. They couldn't know anything about my financial dilemmas. The man needs an attorney. So what. Of course, he'd come to me. How many successful black attorneys are there in Central Florida?

Bob seemed to sense my hesitation.

"Now, frat brother, you and I have known each other for a long time. I wouldn't do anything to hurt you or your career. This is your lucky day. I'm telling you, this nigger is big. He has it all. He lives over in Bay Hill. He's got limousines and Rolls Royce's. I'm telling you that this man is IT! Everything he does, is successful. So, you'd better do yourself a favor and get to know him. Brother Hill, he can help you. I will recommend to Dr. Bronson that the college allow you to work on Bill's projects. What more can you ask for?"

I KNEW the whole thing was too good to be true.

Something wasn't right, but I ignored the uneasy feelings in my gut. As college attorney, it was my duty to conduct thorough background investigations on companies doing business with the college. I would not do one in this case. I was aware that it was a risk. I figured Bob, as a college trustee, also would bear some of the fiduciary responsibility. If anything went wrong, I could blame him.

Bill Williams looked so successful. How could anything go wrong? His whole demeanor spelled money. And Bob associated only with upper-class black professionals in Orlando. If he knew this guy, then he must be legit. Bob wouldn't risk his career for some fly-by-night operator. Maybe Bob had accepted a bribe, my conscious questioned. Naw, not Bob.

I turned away from my sense of caution. It was easy to believe that everything would work. Since my days at Clark College in Atlanta, I had met many black men and women who took a personal interest in me and helped me along. Somehow, I was blessed with a Midas Touch. Surely this was one of those times.

"Are you sure he can handle this project," I asked Bob.

"Absolutely," Bob said and recounted a list of Renselear's projects - skyscrapers, prisons, federal buildings, city projects, etceteras. Renselear qualified for the highest level of bonding capacity, which was a sign of financial strength and one of the toughest requirements to overcome before qualifying for a federally-funded construction projects, which was the major obstacle for most minority companies. They lacked the financial resources to obtain bonding, a kind of insurance policy that ensures a project will be completed.

"Hey, I'm not here just to take the college's money," Bill said, sounding a bit defensive about my questioning. "If I work for you, I will make significant financial contributions to the college. I believe in giving back to the community, especially to a great institution like this. How many white contractors have ever given something back to the college?"

"I bet Bill does so much for the college that Dr. Bronson will want to put him on the board of trustees," Bob said.

"Based on what you've told me, I have to agree," I said. "An invitation might be extended."

Bill smiled his charming smile. "So, it sounds like we've got a deal. Let's get busy!" That, I would learn, was Bill's favorite saying:

Let's get busy.

With the business talk concluded, Bob suggested I show Bill around Daytona Beach. Bob had already told Bill about my gorgeous club. We all agreed a few drinks were warranted to celebrate our new business arrangement.

We climbed into my black Mercedes as Tommy said his good-byes to us. He knew that something major was up, after the long muffled discussion coming from his boss' office. On the way to the Mirage, I decided to show off a bit and drive past my house on the western edge of town, a short trip out of the way from the club. As the security guard waved my car through the gated entryway, Bill said, "Mmmmmm. I'm telling you boy. You're doing all right for yourself."

I glowed in his admiration, especially because he was so much wealthier than I. "Well, you know, I'm doing okay for an old country boy," I said with a chuckle. "There's not too much to me. But I've managed to be successful in my years with Bethune-Cookman, thanks to the help of people like Dr. Bronson and even Bob."

We approached my house, one of the largest in the development, an immense two-story, light brown cypress wooden house with a sharp-angled roof and wooden shingles. Thick St. Augustine grass surrounded the house. Two large pine trees grew beside the three-car garage, which was attached to the right side of the house. The hedges and crepe myrtle trees grew lush from the daily waterings of the automatic sprinkler system and the attentive constant care of our lawn service.

"OOOOhh,ooooh! Look at this black nigger," Bill laughed.

We didn't stop. I wanted to get to the club, have some drinks and relax. I no longer felt hesitant about this relationship. I now wanted to impress this man and convince him that I could keep up with him. My financial worries appeared to be over.

I did the math in my head as Bob and Bill chatted on the 10-minute ride to the club. If Bill spends $13 million on the office project, I could reap $100,000 to $150,000 in legal fees. Hey, hey. It's party time. Wait till Bill sees my club. It'll blow his mind.

Bill repeated his praise as we pulled up to the Mirage. "OOOOh,ooh!" he said. "Boy, I've been to nightspots on the East Coast to the West Coast and I've never. Are you sure you own this? Come on, you're playing with me. Take us to your spot. I don't want to go to some white man's nightclub."

"Oh, my neutron brother," I crooned, enjoying the attention. "Just hold on. You ain't seen nothing yet."

We parked in front of the doorway. As we walked into the foyer, the beat of the music was awesome and overtook us. Bob and Bill exchanged high five's.

"You see, everything I told you about this nigger is true," Bob said to Bill. "This nig is rough. He's Dr. Bronson's main man. Whatever Brother Hill says, goes, I tell you."

The staff swirled around us as we took a seat, bringing a steady stream of drinks. They could tell their boss was entertaining some important clients. We talked about Bethune-Cookman College and the millions of dollars that would be spent on the upcoming construction projects. There was money to be made, we said. Time for black folks to start skimming off the cream.

Hours later, when I finally made it home, Sandra and the kids were in bed asleep. These wee hours of the night were my favorite time of the day. I poured myself another tequila and settled into the family room. Out of my suit jacket pocket, I pulled the little brown vial of cocaine. I spoke to the bottle and said, "Baby, tell me what I am doing is right! This is the major leagues, but with one error, I will get thrown out before I can make it around the bases." I continued to snort the cocaine, drinking and watching music videos.

My mind raced non-stop. I played out scenario after scenario - the conversations, the demands, this new relationship with Bill. The alcohol had loosened up all our tongues at the club. Bill talked freely about his business ventures. He had so many projects in the works, I could devote a whole law practice to this man.

At the same time, Bill and Bob were speeding down Interstate 4 in Bill's Benz. Bob had passed out in the passenger seat and Bill was thankful to have the time alone to replay the events of the day. At this time of night, the interstate was clear and offered a mindless and relaxing hour-long drive back to Orlando. It was almost 3 a.m. but Bill picked up the cellular phone and called his closest friend, Arthur Finley, in Cleveland, Ohio.

"Hey Art, will you guess what?" Bill said with the excitement of a young child.

Art had been sound asleep. "Man, what have you done now? You are always into something. When you call me this late, I know you've found someone new to hook onto your leash. You better be careful, Bill", he said slightly angered to be waked at that time of morning.

"Fin man, let me freak you my brother. Today I met this nigger named Anderson Hill and he is too bad. This boy has his hands on millions of dollars and we can get rich. He has the coldest spot that I have ever been in. The place is in Daytona, but it should be in Vegas, Fin. I am going to work this. He is going to be my attorney."

Art responded in disbelief, "You're going to hire a black attorney? I've never known you to hire a black lawyer, besides George Forbes. Is this boy on that level? You're the one always saying that the only thing a black attorney can do for you is give you the name of a white lawyer, am I right or wrong, Billy?"

"Fin, this boy is strong," Bill said. "As a matter of fact, I don't believe he appreciates where he is or who he knows. He hasn't played on our level, but I'm going to give him a nose bleed because we're about to move high and at lightning speed. Hey Fin, that's all I can say now. You never know who's listening on these damn phones. I will check you later, my brother."

Bill thought about all he already knew about Anderson Hill. Yeah, he's a country boy, all right. A country boy in way over his head. In his line of business, Bill had learned to quickly discern someone's weaknesses and use them to his advantage. With Hill, there was a whole list to cultivate. Bill noticed right away that Hill had a drinking problem. Bob had told him on the ride over about Hill's rumored cocaine abuse and that nightclub was sucking him bone dry. Bill knew no one made money off nightclubs.

A vulnerable man, this Anderson Hill. Bill would have him right where he wanted him in no time. Hill would be easy to manipulate because no other black in town could offer him what Bill would.

If there was one thing Bill knew, it was that money can make people do things they wouldn't normally do.

This might just be easier than Bill thought.

VERY FEW PEOPLE knew, where Bill had actually come from, before showing up in Orlando, Florida. In Bill's earlier days, it has been said that a southern baptist minister preached to the congregation on a sweltering hot day in a small, white, wooden church in the backwoods of Arkansas. It was in the days before air-conditioning, back when people in the South literally sweated out the summers. They fanned themselves non-stop from May to September with whatever magazine or folded piece of paper they could find.

"The wages of sin surely is death," the minister bellowed. "We must obey the words of the Lord, because only the Lord will guide, strengthen and protect us. Oh, I'm telling you brothers and sisters, we must follow the teachings of our Lord and Savior, Jesus Christ. The devil is all around us. If we're not careful, the devil will live in us."

On that cue, a little boy, tall for his age, started to play the guitar and sing in the sweetest of voices. "Yes, Jesus loves me. Yes, Jesus loves me. Yes, Jesus loves me 'cause the Bible tells me so."

The congregation rang out, "Amen". Their faces softened as they watched the boy. The preacher said surely his son, little Willie Williams Jr., was destined to be a preacher.

Willie was born on Nov. 6, 1946, in Waheeken, Arkansas. Early in his childhood, his family moved to Cleveland, Ohio. The transition was tough for Willie, moving from a small wholesome town to harsh urban life.

Willie was a big kid, shy, awkward and timid. Neighborhood kids hounded him like hunting dogs following a trail of blood from a wounded animal. The kids slapped Willie and shoved him to the ground. Willie had a brother, Donald, but he was younger and too small to come to his rescue. Willie's best friend, Arthur Finley, constantly told him to stand up for himself. "If you don't fight back and stand your ground, the kids will beat you down unmercifully and call you a punk", Art told him over and over.

On the basketball court one day when Willie was 12, a kid named Steve Antwine - a real wiseass and bully - walked up to Willie and tried to rip Willie's nice leather basketball out of his hands. To everyone's surprise, Willie swung quickly and punched Steve before the bully knew what was happening. Steve, in his embarrassment, knowing all the kids were watching him, yelled back at Willie: "You ain't nothing but a Goon."

All the kids laughed. They knew they had witnessed a major event - scrawny little Willie Williams fighting back for the first time. "Willie Goon. Willie Goon. Willie Goon," the kids chanted. The name stuck.

As one of the tallest kids in his class, Willie Goon excelled at basketball, starting in junior high and then becoming a high school star. Whenever he entered games or walked into the school cafeteria, he was always greeted by the same words, "Willie Goon." He grew to hate the nickname more than anyone imagined.

Some kids used the nickname to needle Willie. They were jealous of such a lucky kid. Willie was a track star, basketball star and decent student. As the minister of church, Willie's father was considered among the city's solid black middle-class. At 15, Willie was driving his father's new Buick and wearing new suits to school.

Willie stood 6-foot-3 by the time he enrolled in a local community college in Cleveland and started playing ball for the college team. His abilities caught the eye of coaches throughout the region, and Willie went on to join the basketball teams at Cleveland State University and Missouri Southern State College.

Later, Willie would tell people that he graduated from college. But in actuality, he never did earn a degree. He left school, thinking he would try out for the NBA and make big money. He was never drafted by a team.

That was okay with him, though, because his true love had always been money. As a teenager, he worked on a garbage truck and then as a parking lot attendant in the summers. He told his friend, Art, "Someday I am going to own this parking lot." And years later, he did purchase it. The deal was done by proxy. Willie was sure the racist owner would never have sold it to a "nigger".

While at Missouri Southern College, a white, bank vice president took Willie under his wing. The man became Willie's mentor and helped him get a job as a teller at a Cleveland bank. Willie worked long hours and soon was promoted to bank manager. He learned the business of money, loans, financing strategies and investment portfolios.

It was great experience, but Willie knew he'd never become a millionaire working at a bank. So, although only in his early-20s, he had saved a tidy sum of money from his paychecks, and he went into business for himself by opening a window-installation company.

He didn't know a thing about window installations, and didn't really care to. He saw potential and acted on it. The federal government spent billions of dollars each year, building, refurbishing and maintaining low-income housing. As a minority, his company would be given preference in the bidding process. While working at the bank, he saw people make quite a bit of money off the federal government.

He had watched others excel at the game and knew he could do it better, utilizing the machinations of politics. He changed his name to Bill Williams, Jr., and ran for city councilman at the young age of 22. He told Art, "Finley, I know I can't win, even with all the support I have from my father's church. I just want people to know me as Bill Williams. I have got to shake that "Willie Goon" label. That has never been me."

Bill later switched to the Republican Party, an unheard of move for a black in those days. He worked the Party system, donating to the campaigns of Republican candidates, hosting fund-raisers and sticking campaign signs in front of his business. He worked his way through the ranks and came to be known as one of those behind-the-scenes supporters that can make or break a local campaign.

Whenever a big fund-raiser was planned in Cleveland, the organizers would call Bill, who could always be counted on to write a check for thousands of dollars to whatever Republican candidate was in need. He also generously supported his church, which won him a seat on the national board that oversaw the church. His status was rising greatly in Cleveland, especially within the black community.

Of course, the political candidates reciprocated in the most generous of ways. They made sure Bill got all the government contracts he could handle. It created a symbiotic relationship: Money gets power gets more money gets more power gets more money gets more power.

To Bill's way of thinking, campaign contributions were the cost of doing business. Bill would tell his associates, after getting off the phone with some powerful Republican, who had been looking for more money, "This donation is going to make me millions." He'd happily make out the check. Bill knew he had to pay to play.

Business boomed. Bill sold the window-installation company at a huge profit. He opened a construction company in Shaker Heights, a suburb of Cleveland. He preferred to do business outside his hometown. His reputation could be sullied if his business dealings turned dirty.

"Can't have a company within the city of Cleveland," he'd say. "It's not the right image for me."

Soon, he opened a larger construction company, called Bill Doc, named for himself and his partner, Larry Doctor, a banker who could help with financing big projects. The company took off overnight, winning all sorts of government contracts from the federal and Ohio state governments. Bill Doc specialized in building prisons, a growing market. Governments always were building prisons. The country's rising crime rate would ensure a lifetime of profitable work for Bill.

With his newfound wealth, Bill gravitated toward a flamboyant and indulgent lifestyle. He lived for a short time in Washington, D.C., and learned how rich and influential people really live. He rarely socialized with his old gang in Cleveland, anymore. Everything was about business - the people he knew, the political events he attended, the parties he attended. There wasn't time for people and events that could not benefit him, financially. He bought a Rolls Royce and a limousine, hired a private driver and leased a private jet. He moved his family into one of the most expensive homes in Pepper Pike, a prominent suburb of Cleveland, where homes start at $500,000.

To succeed in business, he developed a shrewd personality. Events in his life also contributed to his cold streak. His younger brother died of kidney failure, and his first wife, of natural causes.

His business expanded beyond Ohio, and soon his company constructed public facilities in numerous states east of the Mississippi River. He earned more and more, and correspondingly, he spent more and more. It seemed incomprehensible but at times this man, who earned hundreds of thousands of dollars a year, faced intense financial pressure. He came to a crossroad and took a path that would shape the rest of his life.

Bill was so committed to wealth, he decided if he couldn't be rich honestly, he'd do it dishonestly. This decision occurred gradually as his business and financial pressure mounted. *The Cleveland Plain Dealer* had recently labeled him a slum lord during their series about dilapidated apartment complexes. Bill, and his business partner, Larry Doctor, owned a big one. The heat was on. That kind of publicity always scared off bankers, whom Bill needed to continue financing his construction projects. There were also rumors that he had run off with the proceeds from a black charity fund-raiser.

Bill was juggling his finances, acquiring loans based on trumped-up loan information. To conduct business this way, he had to give away a percentage of whatever money he received. Everyone down the line needed a small payoff to make them cooperate and keep them quiet.

Greed motivates people, and it allowed Bill to keep up the

payments on his expensive lifestyle while he worked to get more government contracts. When those contracts weren't forthcoming, his scam unraveled.

Politicians, bureaucrats and bankers - the people who had helped Bill for so long - were now running for cover. They had stuck their necks out to get Bill government contracts. Now, state inspectors were complaining about his shoddy work. Contracts weren't being completed on time and within budget. Subcontractors were yelling about not getting paid on time. Wholesale suppliers were filing liens against the government because they hadn't been paid in months. A couple of reporters were beginning to sniff around, sensing a scandal that could reach high into Ohio's state government.

The politicians said Bill would not receive any more government work. Bill, thinking about all the chips he could call in with influential people, still thought he could turn everything around. He had attended fund-raisers in the White House. On his office walls hung his two most prized possession, autographed pictures of him standing beside two U.S. Presidents - George Bush and even hugging Ronald Reagan. A big black man hugging Ronald Reagan! The effect that picture had on people was priceless.

Williams contacted his powerful law firm in Washington, D.C., and asked for the firm to work the halls of Congress on his behalf. He thought, if a few Congressmen called the mayor of Cleveland on his behalf, the water would again turn to wine.

But the first rule of politics is survival. No matter how much a person contributed yesterday, if they become a liability today, they're gone. The general consensus was Bill would have to face this trouble alone. The lawsuits began arriving. He received a notice from his bank that his signature red Rolls Royce was about to be repossessed. Bill knew it was time to high-tail it out of town. And quick.

Bill had already borrowed money from Norm Nixon, the former LA Lakers basketball star. Unable to repay the original money to Norm, he couldn't ask for more. All his sources were tapped out.

Bill liquidated all his assets at rock-bottom prices. His interest in a chain of 10 Kentucky Fried Chicken restaurants netted $1 million. He could have used the money to pay off his debts. But he needed money to start another business. So he left town with his debts unpaid. All of them.

To save his beloved Rolls Royce, Bill hid it in a secret garage, so the repo man couldn't find it. He wasn't going to lose that car.

BILL Williams decided to move South. His personal flair and professional shrewdness would make him successful in the slow and unsophisticated South.

First he tried Atlanta.

He spent months working the town, taking all the right people out for expensive dinners, joining the Chamber of Commerce, getting his Washington pals to make a few calls on his behalf. His efforts reaped a few, small, government-funded construction projects, but not nearly what he had hoped for.

Atlanta is a black town, so there were plenty of minority contractors, therefore the competition was stiff. The other black contractors grew suspicious of Bill. They weren't as naive as he thought. They started checking on him and spread the word. Bill was trouble. He had had severe financial trouble in Cleveland, and was running from many hundreds of thousands of dollars in debts and civil judgments.

Bill moved on, scouting for a new location. He chose Miami, then Tampa and finally settled on Orlando, because a Washington politician had told him about a large federally funded project in Orlando.

Bill got the contract and began building a huge affordable housing project in Orlando. He set up the business headquarters of Renselear Development Corp. in a palatial suite on the south side of town, not far from Universal Studios Florida, which was then under construction.

He leased an expensive 4,500-square-foot home in gated community of Bay Hill, where the Professional Golfers Association holds an annual Arnold Palmer Golf Tournament. His friends called the mayor's office on his behalf, even the governor, passing along that useful tidbit that a major political contributor had moved into the neighborhood. He started a Black Businessmen's Club and recruited prominent black leaders in the town to join.

Through these relationships, he met Robert Billingslea, head of the equal employment office for Walt Disney World and its other developments in Orlando. One night at the Blue Note Jazz Club, in downtown Orlando, Bob Billingslea ran into Art Finley, who was visiting Bill. Bob, in previous conversations with Art, knew Art was from Cleveland.

"I understand there's a nigger from Cleveland in town named

Bill Williams. I got a call from my boys in Ohio and they said whatever I do, I better meet Bill Williams."

Art smiled and pointed at a table full of people across the room. "There he is right over there," Art said. "Come on, I'll introduce you."

Bill knew immediately that he needed to cultivate Bob as a friend. Here was a man who could help him, for two important reasons: (one) because of Bob's ties to Disney, which for 20 years had run Orlando like a company town, and (two) Bob's recent appointment to the Board of Trustees at Bethune-Cookman College. Bill had heard through the grapevine that Bethune-Cookman had been awarded millions of dollars in grants and low-interest loans from the federal government to build several new buildings on campus.

Bill needed to get his foot in the door over at the college and start pursuing those contracts. He broached the topic with Bob Billingslea over dinner a few days after their first meeting. Bob told him to call the college's internal construction manager, Tommy Huger, because the college desperately was looking for a minority contractor. Bill left countless messages for Huger and, when he received no reply, went back to Bob for help.

This time, Bob suggested he call the college's internal attorney, Anderson Chester Hill II, who also oversaw construction on campus. Anderson was the college president's right-hand man, Bob said.

Bill started calling Anderson. But the calls went unreturned. Bob finally promised to set up a personal meeting with Anderson. As the meeting approached, Bill pumped Bob for all the information he could get on Anderson.

Bob said concerns had been expressed at a recent trustees' executive committee meeting about the constant rumors of Anderson's alcohol and cocaine abuse. A couple of trustees were uncomfortable with Anderson's sideline venture in the nightclub business. It was common knowledge that he was losing his shirt on the place. For years, Anderson had been the golden boy on campus. He rose through the ranks quickly and was expected to be appointed college president when Dr. Bronson retired.

But recently, he suffered his first major setback and it seemed Dr. Bronson and the trustees were losing confidence in him. In a controversial move, a trustees' committee had voted not to select Anderson as the new Executive Vice President, second in command at the college. Instead, the position would go unfilled.

It was said Anderson had taken the news hard.

All of this Bill knew before he even met Anderson. Bill was doing his homework. His success in Central Florida hinged on this man. He needed to ensure things went smoothly. Bill didn't want to scout for another city. He had to make this work.

As the days neared to their meeting, Bill convinced Bob to say his Renselear Development Corp. was working for Walt Disney World because Bill knew it would carry weight with Anderson. In exchange, Bill paid Bob $5,000.

Of course, it worked wonders. The meeting went superbly. Bill hadn't felt better in years _ not since his prosperous days in Cleveland. Bill felt he had turned a corner; he was on his way back up. He thought of Anderson and knew he could work this man to his advantage. From what he'd seen so far, Anderson loved money and tequila.

Bill would make sure he had plenty of both.

BUTT FOR THE WHITE FOLKS

*Can a woman raise a man to be
a law abiding citizen, successful,
God fearing and loving to all mankind.*

*I reject the devil's evidence that says it
cannot be.*

*For a man is borne of a woman.
Out of her womb he submerges.
God knows what course his life must take.*

*But for the white folks she don't want him
to make a butt out of himself.*

God knows what course his life must take.

*Sometimes Mother, the son becomes the butt
of the joke. He has to bear the brunt of humility.*

God hates a proud look and a froward heart.

*But as for the white folks who will see.
The devil's evidence was rejected and the son
who is now a man soars forever more.*

3 BAIT FOR THE WHITE FOLKS

"We come to the question presented: Does segregation of children in public schools solely on the basis of race, even though the physical facilities and other 'tangible' factors may be equal, deprive the children of the minority group of equal educational opportunities? We believe that it does."

U.S. Supreme Court Chief Justice Earl Warren in the unanimous decision,
Brown v. The Board of Education of Topeka, May 17, 1954

ON a cold Thursday night in February 1959, at the tender age of 4 1/2, I was sprawled in front of a black and white console TV, flat on my belly on the living room floor, my face a foot from the bright screen, watching adventures of a boy named Theodore Cleaver. *Amos and Andy* was my favorite show because it was one of the few TV shows with Negro actors. My second favorite was the "Beave."

A pillow was pushed underneath my small chest, which, along with the long-john pajamas, provided a barrier against the cold and hard wooden floor. It was dark in the room except for the glow of the TV set and the flames from a gas heater, cranked on high in a vain attempt to push back the damp and chilly Arkansas winter air, which seeped into our second-story apartment from every direction - through the floor, around the window frames and in a crack under the front door.

My knees were bent and my lower legs stuck up in the air. I alternated between slapping my feet together and racing my fat stumpy legs back and forth, letting one foot hit my butt and the other one kick the floor. I loved *Leave it to Beaver*, but my little body had too much energy to sit still for very long.

Tonight, the Beave lost the money that his mother gave him for a haircut. Afraid to tell her what happened, he gives himself a trim, with help from brother, Wally. The botched haircut only worsens Beave's trouble. "Boy, Beave, are you gonna get it," Wally says.

Mother June is moving around the kitchen, the quintessential 1950s mom, looking nurturing and wholesome in a starched white apron, a delicate string of pearls around her neck, and her makeup and lipstick softly applied. Beave is outside, working up the nerve to go in and show her.

Rrrrr-boooooooommmmmMMMMM.

The floor vibrated under my belly and snapped my attention back into the room. I hadn't noticed before, but now I could hear it. My parents were yelling in the back bedroom, loudly. Daddy must have thrown something.

"I'm telling you, Rosie Lee," as father's voice bellowed through the house. "You're not going to see them anymore. You understand me?"

"Chester, honey." Momma's voice was calm but hollow. Sometimes, she had to talk for hours to settle down her husband. After awhile her voice sounded tired, empty, like she was reciting a speech by memory, saying it over and over until she got the words right.

"Quit making this stuff up in your mind," she continued. "You've got no reason to dislike my sister and family. You say they don't like you, but it ain't true. They've been nothing but good to us, Chester."

"I told you to stay away from 'em. I'm tired of it. I know your sister wants you to leave me. She don't like me, ...fine. But I won't let her poison your mind."

"You need to stop drinking, Chester. It's your mind that's gettin' poisoned."

My mother's footsteps echoed across the bedroom floor. I could picture her in her bleached-white maid's uniform and white shoes. She put on that uniform six days a week, left the house early and rode the bus to work, cleaning house for Mrs. Grayson, the white lady up in Pulaski Heights, the wealthy white section of Little Rock. Momma got $25 a week.

She had to work. Our family needed the money. Daddy did all right, especially for an uneducated black man in the Deep South. He drove his rusty dark-blue pickup truck around all day, collecting discarded appliances and other junked items. He refurbished and resold them. He worked hard and was known to be good with his hands.

There were two houses on the property he owned on West 23rd Street. He built them both with his own hands. From the ground up. Put in the electricity and the plumbing. Knew how to plaster walls and shingle the roofs. The property was deep and slanted steeply from east to west with our home in the back and a second house nearer the road. The front house was divided into three apartments, two upstairs and one down. Our house had two apartments - a small one downstairs and a larger one for us upstairs. It had six rooms: three bedrooms, a bath, living room and kitchen in the rear.

My daddy, Archester Hill, was an entrepreneur for his time, a businessman, clever at earning money. Between what he and Momma earned, plus the rents from the apartments, our family did all right. We lived simply but never went without food, toys and a good pair of clothes for Sunday church.

Just west of our house sat the Little Rock Natural Spring Water Company. A handful of blacks worked in the concrete building, bottling water from a spring that started under daddy's property and flowed toward the bottling plant, where it was pumped out.

The company's livelihood depended on Daddy's generosity with the water-supply. We got all the bottled water we could drink, plus the owner of the company always paid for our plumbing repairs, both parts and labor. The owner, a white guy who wore brown khaki suits - a lightweight cotton fabric that was popular in the days before air-conditioning - wanted to show his gratitude. And he also wanted to make sure no rust or unnatural substance polluted his precious spring water.

From the front windows of our living room, I could look down on the front house and the tree-lined street. Neither our lot nor the surrounding neighbors had plush green lawns. There were some trees on our property but the ground was scrubby, a mix of mowed down weeds and patches of rocks with dirt.

I would sit at the front windows for hours, secretly wishing for the day when our family would move into the front house. It looked pretty much the same as our house, but with one big difference: It had a shingled roof. Ours had a tin roof. Oh, how I hated tin roofs. Hated...Hated...Hated them.

"The boy from the tin roof ... The house with the ugly tin roof." It seemed like that's all I heard from the neighborhood kids. Ours was the only house in the neighborhood with a tin roof, shining bright in the hot Arkansas sun, its glare fueling the relentless teasing.

Cccrrrraacccck. My parents' argument continued in the bedroom. It sounded like something hit the bedroom wall, shattered and crackled as it hit the floor, probably shards of broken glass.

"Get back in here, damn it. I'm not done with you, woman."

I sadly glanced back at the TV set. The Beave, Wally and his parents were seated in their crisp, immaculate living room. The Beave's father was lecturing the boys in a calm and concerned tone.

My mind tried to make sense of the two different worlds I was watching, and stumbled on a solution. I pushed myself off the floor and scampered into my bedroom, the first room down a narrow hallway on one side of the house. My parents' room was down another hallway off the kitchen at the opposite side of the house. Their door was ajar, and the light spilled into the hallway, along with my daddy's angry words.

I dug feverishly through the clutter in the bedroom closet, moved to the bed and searched underneath, clawing and dragging out an assortment of dusty and forgotten objects. Next I moved to a pile of toys in the corner, and found what I was looking for under a ragged stuffed bear. The object was shinny and silver, and felt cold as I clutched it in the palm of my right hand.

I made my way back into the hallway and could see my sister's bedroom door closed just beyond my room. A ray of light shone under her door. I knew she was curled up in bed with a book. At seven years old, she was already a bookworm.

I crept up to the door of my parents' room and edged through the doorway. I saw my mother backed into a corner beside the bed. Daddy stood in front of her, blocking any attempt by her to escape his verbal abuse. "It's your sister whose giving you these ideas about leaving.. Can't you see she wants to ruin what we got."

I lifted the gun to waist-level, aiming at my father's back. My beautiful mother was looking past her drunk husband and right at me, with those teary large brown eyes.

"Daddy. Stop it!" my little voice squeaked. "I am not scared of you. Leave my Momma alone, or I'll shoot you."

He spun on the heels of his work boots and struggled for a moment to keep his balance with a pint of whiskey pumping through his veins. To me, he seemed like a giant of a man. He reached down and snatched the toy pistol out of my shaking hand.

"Boy, you don't ever pull a gun on me again, you hear?" My father voice quivered at the thought that his young son would threaten him, even with a cap gun.

It's funny, I would think to myself later, when I became a grown man, at 6-foot-2, a full three inches taller than my father, how that was the only serious run-in I ever had with the man, even after all the pain he caused our family. That was the only time Daddy spoke harshly to me.

Now, Momma was a different story. She was dead-set determined to make sure I didn't end up like my father. End up as "bait for the white folks," as she was taken to say. When she lost her temper, standing over me, a tall, thick woman with caramel skin and muscular arms that could crack a wooden switch across me and my sister so quickly and so painfully that it was useless to try to high-tail it out of the way.

"You had better not run," she'd say after she caught us by surprise with an unsuspecting lick on the back or butt. I'd stay still and take the whipping. No sense making Momma even madder. I knew from experience, if she had to chase me down, I'd get twice as many licks.

If men are the doers in the world, then women are the keepers of its morals. My Momma, like the women in many black families, was the pillar of strength. She set the rules and made sure we complied. Thank goodness, she didn't settle for me growing up as some street rogue.

THERE was a grain of truth to my father's drunken ranting. My mother's family did hate him. Didn't like him from the first look. Not only was he a drunk, they'd complain, he was a mean drunk.

Rosie Lee could've done better, they said. She was 20 years younger than Archester. Her smooth skin and deep brown eyes so alluring that any man would have thanked the Lord to crawl into her lovely arms.

She fell for Archester and her family never understood why. But if my father was anything like me, which, of course, he was, he knew how to finesse a lady when he wanted. Despite my father's flaws, Momma always loved him deeply, I could tell.

My mother was his second wife. His first wife supposedly threw him out of the house. "Ill-natured" is what she called him. She decided it would be easier to raise two kids, William "W.M." and Dolores "Baby Sister," on her own. My sister and I had little contact with them as we were growing up. I'm not sure why, probably their mother and my mother felt some jealousy about my father.

Archester was determined to keep pretty young Rosie Lee by his side. Unfortunately, he was also determined to keep a pint of whisky, wrapped in a little brown paper bag, next to him on the front seat of his pickup. He didn't drink everyday. Usually two or three days a week. He'd crack open a bottle mid-afternoon and, by the time he hit the door in the evening, his mood could turn explosive.

Eventually, Rosie Lee got fed up and did leave him. One day she packed up me and my sister, Erma, and took us on a Greyhound bus for three days travel, to Los Angeles. Her younger brother, Eugene, lived there. We stayed with him until Momma found a job and found her own little apartment in a poor black section of the city, called Watts.

I just remember being struck by the palm trees and the white kids.

In Little Rock, schools were segregated until the early 1960s. The U.S. Supreme Court had ordered public school integration in 1954, which was the year I was born at the black hospital, United Friends, in Little Rock. After a near riot in the fall of 1957, blacks were allowed to attend the white high school in Little Rock. But they were not allowed to attend any other white public school. My sister and I had never gone to school with white kids.

I had seen white people on TV - in those days, that was about all you saw - and was curious about them. I knew they lived in a vastly different world from mine. That was obvious, even to a young child.

White people on TV lived in nice houses and drove the biggest and newest cars. They never seemed to argue, throw things or drink liquor straight from a bottle. I'd noticed white people lived in much nicer neighborhoods. For a long time, I thought all white people were immensely wealthy, with their new cars in the driveway and the black and Hispanic hired-hands cutting their lawns and scrubbing their houses.

On the walks home from school, as I approached our apartment complex in Watts, I noticed the neighborhoods turned drab with weedy yards and old cars lining the street.

School ended for me an hour earlier than for Erma. That meant I got to walk home by myself. Without her to boss me around, I wandered through alleyways and explored different shortcuts. Each day at the same intersection, a busy one with a Safeway grocery store on the corner, I'd encounter the same group of white boys hanging out on the street. They were a couple years older than me, taller and slightly bulkier. They would circle around me like buzzards inspecting road kill, hovering and waiting to move in.

Suddenly, one of them would lunge toward me. He and I would lock arms, tumbling to the ground like sumo wrestlers. No punches were ever thrown. We were six or eight years old, not experienced yet in street fighting. We pushed, shoved, squirmed and panted for breath. But to me, it was a fight for my life.

Somehow, almost on cue, the fight would end and the white boys would walk away, making threats over their shoulders. "Nigger we will see you tomorrow. You better quit coming this way."

I'd stay on the ground until they were out of sight, fighting off another asthma attack and trying to calm my racing heart. I'd collect my scattered books and papers, dust off my clothes and head home. It never occurred to me to take a different route. I wasn't going to go out of my way to avoid a good fight. It's part of my nature to be attracted to controversy.

But I did wonder if the boys would leave me alone if my skin were white.

As I sat alone in our apartment after school, the solution flashed through my ever-calculating mind. I jumped up and turned off the cartoons on TV. I ran through the house collecting what I'd need.

I needed to act fast. Erma would be home shortly. There was just enough time to experiment. I'd clean up and practice again on another day, trying again and again until I got it right. I stripped naked in the bathroom, popped open a jar of Vaseline and started smearing it all over my round body. I looked in the full-length mirror on the back of the door. My chocolate-black skin shined like a newly waxed car.

I grabbed the plastic bottle of baby powder and held it above my head like a shower nozzle. Eyes closed, I shook it and shook it. White dust filled the air and covered my skin like a gentle snow on a winter's morning.

I looked in the mirror, eyes open wide as I scanned my reflection. Patches of dark skin showed through. And my nappy hair gave me away. "This will be harder than I thought," I said aloud to no one. "I gotta do something with my hair."

The front door to the apartment opened and slammed shut. I scrambled for my clothes, yanking on underwear and pants in one frightened jerk. Erma was as nosy as nosy gets. If she saw this, I'd never hear the end of it.

Fiddling with my pants zipper, I heard laughter from the bath-room doorway. It was Momma, standing there with bright eyes, hands on her hips, head thrown back, cackling in delight.

"Momma, I'm sorry." I kept looking at her face, unsure if I was in trouble. Most of the time, Momma had an easy-going nature. But she could turn as hard as nails in a split second. I was in awe of how quickly she could materialize with a leather strap in her hands. Fflfflllllizzzzzp. I'd hear the leather ripping through the air before I felt the sting on my skin.

"Brother, what have you done?" she said. "Brother" was my nickname, coined by my sister. It stuck with me over the years and was used only by people in my immediate family. I didn't answer my mother as she stood there in amazement, after another day of cleaning toilets. I blushed with embarrassment as she continued to laugh.

"Brother," she said again. "It's not going to do any good, child. Your skin is dark. Ain't no hiding it. Now, get in the tub and clean yourself up."

I shed my sticky clothes. "Please don't tell Erma," I said. But Momma told the story to everyone in the family. They laughed and said what a funny boy I was. I learned a lesson from the episode: I'd have to make peace with this God given dark skin.

FROM time to time, Daddy called from Little Rock. I missed him badly. When he wasn't calling, he was writing, begging his Rosie to return. I knew he was making all sorts of promises. Momma was working long hours to support us and was lonely in a big and unfriendly new city. Slowly, she weakened to Daddy's charm.

"We're taking a Greyhound bus back to Little Rock," she announced one day out of the blue. We packed up, said our good-byes and headed to the station. As we climbed aboard, we were all thinking the same thing: "We'll be a family again. This time everything will work out."

It felt great for me to return to my southern routine. Erma and I returned to the black school with all our friends. My parents seemed to be happy again. But within months, Daddy was drinking again, his moods turning more and more volatile. He became obsessed with thoughts that his Rosie would leave him again.

To his generation, the man of the house was entitled to decide who his wife could, and could not, visit. Momma played passive when he was drunk and then stopped by and saw her family on her way home from work. She loved her family and could not let them go.

It turned into a power struggle: Daddy, dead-set on breaking her independent streak and Momma, vowing not to give in. Her younger sister, Otha Lee, gave her constant moral support. Otha Lee was married and lived across town; she and Momma spoke almost every day.

Soon, Momma was threatening to leave again. My father had constructed a new house for his family on Maple Street, a little further west. It was a three-bedroom house, surrounded by woods on three sides and close to the street in the front. For the first time, we enjoyed some privacy. The house was totally ours. We didn't share it with renters.

My mother had devised a plan to move with us back into the upstairs apartment where we once lived. I was then 8; Erma was 10. My father would stay in the new house and would only be a few blocks away to come visit us.

While my mother worked on her plan, my father devised his own. His drinking increased, and, with the help of the whiskey, he plotted a diabolical plan.

Around evening time, as sunshine turned to shadows, he poured gasoline around the base of the house where Momma intended to live. He had built the house with his bare hands. Now, its destruction soothed an angry force inside him.

It was his property, he reasoned in his drunken rage. If he wanted to burn it down, whose business was it? He lit a match and watched the flames skim along the ground. The wooden house ignited quickly. As the flames shot up the sides and reached the second-story roof, he heard sirens in the distance. He left the gas can where it sat and jumped into his truck. A rifle lay on the seat beside him.

A fifteen-minute drive away, he pulled into Aunt Otha's driveway and banged on the door. The rifle hung at his side, hidden behind his leg. Aunt Otha peeked out through the small window in the door. Archester never came alone to visit. She threw open the door, expecting to hear that something awful had happened to Rosie or the kids. She was searching his face - trying to read the wildness in his eyes - and didn't see him raise the rifle to stomach height and pull the trigger.

"My God. No!," she mumbled, too shocked to realize what was happening.

After the second blast, she collapsed in the small foyer of the house. Uncle Coleman came running from the living room. He saw Otha, blood oozing through the fingers she had pressed against her abdomen. He ran to the phone and called the police. Through the window, he could see Archester's truck screeching out of the driveway.

Momma was watching the evening news. I was sitting with her in the living room of our Maple Street home, reading a Superman comic book. Erma was in her room, doing school work, as usual. There was a knock on the front wooden door, and Momma got up to answer it. I wasn't paying any attention until I heard strange men's voices. I got up and craned my neck around the living room wall to see who it was.

A burly black man was holding up a badge and looking past my mother to see who else was in the house. He was a detective with the Little Rock Police Department, dressed in civilian clothes. Beside him stood another detective, a white guy, slender and clean shaven. The black man was talking, "Your sister, a Mrs. Otha Lee Coleman, has just been shot and is in critical condition. We believe your husband tried to kill her. She's in surgery now. The last I heard, they expect her to pull through okay."

The detectives then explained about the fire at the house. It was destroyed by the time the fire trucks arrived. Police officers were searching for Archester Hill throughout the area. When she explained what may have set off her husband - her plans to leave him, the detectives grew very concerned. "It sounds like he's on a rampage. He may be coming here next. I would advise you to stay indoors, keep the doors locked and all the windows drawn."

"Oh, Lord, why would he do these horrible things?," my mother sobbed. Erma came in from her room and, seeing Momma in tears, she started crying, too. I sat on a plaid throw rug on the wooden slatted floor and kept wondering how my father could do anything to hurt us. What have I done wrong to make him not love us anymore? Like a child, I blamed the whole incident on myself. I wasn't mad at him, only at myself. This was all my fault. Maybe it's because I had pointed that toy gun at him, I thought.

Unknown to us, Daddy was watching the detectives and Momma talking at the front door. He was squatting behind a woodpile on the side of the house. He crept around to the back of the house, fearing his cover would be blown. He figured he'd wait until the detectives drove off. Then he'd make his move.

Luckily, the detectives searched the perimeter of the house before leaving. They spotted him moving around the woods and arrested him without a fight. Daddy went to jail. Aunt Otha recovered and was eager to testify against him at his trial. Instead, he pleaded guilty and was sentenced to the state penitentiary.

Erma and I were told only the barest details about what happened. The adults wanted to shield us from such an ugly and senseless ordeal. But in the tightly knit black community, the details were common knowledge. Anything I didn't know was soon learned from the neighborhood kids, who overheard the story in their homes.

"Why do you think Daddy did it? Do you think it's 'cause of me?" I asked Erma on our way home from school one day. "Everyone says he went crazy." We had climbed the last hill before our house, the spot where the few remaining kids turned off. We crested the top of the hill and started down the sidewalk, just the two of us, for the last block home.

The top of that hill was always a special place for my sister and me. When she started elementary school, I'd climb up there and wait for her to walk the eight blocks from school. From such a vantage point, I could see her coming from blocks away and patiently waited for her. It was my self-appointed duty to meet my big sister every day and carry her books home.

Erma always took her role as the eldest, seriously. She was always coming to my rescue. I remember walking home from school when I was maybe seven years old and when an older neighborhood kid, Arthur Crane, started picking on me.

"You live in a house with a tin roof. Your house is ugly and so is your Momma," the bully yelled in my face. He was bigger than me and I had to look up to see his face. A group of kids gathered around and started yelling, "Fight! Fight! Fight!"

I knew I couldn't win. But talking about someone's Momma,

especially mine, well those were fighting words. Arthur raised his hand to slap me. I turned my face to avoid the blow and saw Erma pushing her way through the crowd.

"HEY. ARTHUR! You had better not hit him," Erma stood face to face with Arthur and looked mean enough to freeze him on the spot. Arthur looked at me and back to Erma. He knew he couldn't beat us both. We had kicked his butt before and stood ready to do it again. He gave me a little shove and walked off.

Erma was a comfort to me. As we reached the top of the hill that day, I turned to her and knew she was the only person I could confide in about my pain about Daddy. We rarely spoke about what had happened.

"Do you think Daddy went crazy?" I asked.

"He thought he could make mom stay with him. I think all the liquor messed up his mind," she replied. "I heard mom tell Aunt Otha that she's never going to lay eyes on him again. She's getting a divorce. I don't think daddy will ever live with us again."

I sighed, feeling depressed because I would never have a true family again. Kids were always talking about their fathers, but I couldn't say anything.

"I don't want to be like daddy when I grow up," I said. "The kids at school said we have bad blood. I told 'em to shut up 'cause I'm gonna have the best family in the world. You wait and see."

FROM time to time, Archester's kin would pick me up and take me for visits at the Arkansas State Penitentiary, a massive, scary place that was plunked down in rural farmland about 70 miles south of Little Rock. As a child, it seemed to take forever to get there. I'd daydream as I looked out the windows at fields of cotton on both sides of the highway.

I could tell when we were getting close. Off in the distance stood what looked like a water tower. As we got closer, I could see it was a guard tower. Razor barb wire surrounded the facility, looking like a tangled heap of fishing line rising 10 feet around the perimeter.

Rows of prisoners in white prison uniforms - most of them black men - were working in the fields, raking and hoeing and picking the vegetables used in the prison kitchen. Scattered among the men were a few white prison guards, hefty guys with big round bellies hanging over their belts, wide-brimmed hats and a rifle in their hands. They shouted orders at the prisoners, who leapt at every command.

I sat on the tall steel chair in the visitor's waiting area, feet swinging because they couldn't reach the floor. The waiting room was dingy and crowded but the people seemed so happy. I wondered how people could be happy about a place like this. It made me sad. I hated to see my father here.

I'd hear the steel doors click open, look up and see Daddy standing on the other side of a glass partition, dressed in a white uniform like the men in the fields. Our eyes would meet and we would smile. He knew my visits were special. Erma never came to see him. My sister was deeply hurt by our father's actions. I figured he was my Daddy. I had to see him. I couldn't help but feel love for him.

My mother encouraged my visits and never once attempted to stop me from seeing him in prison nor after his release. Many mothers would not have let their impressionable, young sons go. But my mother was a wise woman, and realized that a boy needs his father, even if the father had made some big mistakes. I certainly needed mine.

Many years later, Daddy was released and bought a small corner market in another part of Little Rock. He'd hand me a cold pop when I visited and tell me horror stories about prison. The guards whipped men with long thick leather straps for the smallest infractions, and sometimes for no reason at all.

My father was proud that he had never been beaten down in such a way. He said it was because he knew how to handle himself in the pen. I figured it was because of his age, too. By then, Daddy was close to 60. He agreed and once told me, "Old black men don't threaten whites like young black boys do. White men try to break the spirit of a black man when he's young and strong. They want to keep them down in the dirt, thinkin' they're worth no more than a dog. Take away a man's dreams and he has no dignity. That way, white folks never have to worry about them standing up for themselves. Be careful. White men love to beat on a young black buck. Gives them bragging rights." His fatherly talks, encouraged me to be cautious as a black man, even if I would not admit it to him or anybody else, back in those days.

"That's crazy, Daddy. No white guy better ever beat me. I ain't scare of no one, white or black."

Daddy would be nipping on his pint of whiskey the whole time we talked. He'd wax philosophical as he neared the bottom of the bottle. He was usually hung over when I arrived and toasted when I left. Only in the last few years of his life did he finally swear off alcohol for good.

During every visit, he'd warn me: "You don't ever want to end up in trouble, boy. Stay on the right side of the law, so the white man won't come and lock you up. Too many niggers in jail, that's all that ever get into trouble, is us. And Brother, believe me, a lot of times we do it to ourselves."

I wondered what he meant by that. Had he done it to himself, too? Sounded like he knew better. Does something just sneak up on black people and pull them into bad times? I guess I should have asked him to explain.

ON a sticky-hot day in mid-July, I sat on the front steps at home, feeling the summer doldrums. Mother dear was working; Erma was in her room. I needed something to do. I was just entering my teens, that difficult age when boys are too old for childish things but too young to drive a car and get out in the world. I figured I'd walk up to the store and get something to snack on.

As luck would have it, I found 45 cents in my dresser drawer and 60 cents in the bowl on the kitchen counter, under the nubby pencils, a pair of scissors, rubber bands and some S&H green stamps.

The Safeway grocery was five blocks from our house, less than a 10 minute walk. Bologna was on my tastebuds. There was peanut butter and jelly in the cupboard at home. But for me, today, I just had to have some of that delicious pre-sliced bologna.

As I walked into the store, a woman passed by with a shopping carts filled with food. My stomach rumbled and I felt hungrier by the moment. I made a bee line to the back of the store, past the aisle with breads and cookies, and went to the deli case. I stood looking at the packs of luncheon meats, trying to find which one was cheapest and weighed the most. I picked up a small pack of bologna. It cost 99 cents, but I also wanted cheese to go with it to make it taste just right. I didn't have enough money for both.

Steal it.

With all the meat in the case, who would miss it? Then I could use my $1.05 for the cheese. I stood there arguing with myself. I'd never shoplifted before. It was exciting and scary at the same time. I knew I could steal both the bologna and cheese. The store would be suspicious if I left without buying anything. Buy one item; steal one item. That became my motis operandi.

I sidestepped down to the next case, loaded with milk, butter and cheeses. I saw a small block of sliced American cheese. The cheese packaging was more compact. It would be easier to steal. The perfect size to hide in my blue-jeans. No one would even see it. I stood in front of the case, heart racing, and felt the refrigerated cold air drying a thin film of sweat that appeared on my skin.

I glanced to the left, then to the right. Two women - one behind the other - were pushing their carts away from me. Their backs faced me, so I knew they wouldn't see anything.

Quick! Do it! Hurry!

I sucked in my stomach, making room in the jeans, and pushed the cheese into my underwear. The cold plastic shocked my skin alive. I shivered and squirmed slightly to settle the package in my groin. I pulled out my shirt tail and pulled it down past my zipper. I scanned the store again. My chest was rising and falling quickly under the cotton shirt.

Oh, Lord. Please don't let me suffer an asthma attack right here. If I start coughing and wheezing, everyone will look at me. I tried to calm myself and knew it was too late to turn back now. I thought about what would happen if my parents found out. Momma would thrash me. Daddy would shake his head. He told me over and over again to stay out of trouble. "A hard head makes a soft butt," he'd say.

I picked up the bologna and headed for the front cashiers. I walked quickly, acting like I was in a big hurry, just rushing inside to buy one thing and my mother was waiting in the car. A check-out line in the middle looked like the quickest escape route. An older woman was ahead of me in line. She could act as a shield for me. The bag boy was standing beside her cart. He had already loaded her groceries into bags and waited to push them outside for her.

I put the bologna on the white Formica counter. The cashier, a middle-aged woman with skin as dark as mine, glanced at me as she fished around in the drawer to give the lady her change. She turned to me next.

"That'll be $1.02," she said while reaching for a small bag. I felt around in the front jeans pocket, rounding up the coins. A tall, husky white man casually walked into the line behind me and emptied an armload of groceries onto the counter. Hamburger meat, ketchup, a few cans of soup, a bag of vanilla wafers.

The cashier had her hand out, my three pennies in change in her fingers. "Thanks," she said as she pushed the brown sack toward me .

I started walking, the glass doors were propped open, 20 feet away. My eyes narrowed as they approached the harsh sunlight.

Ha! Too easy.

A big white hand clamped down on the top of my right arm.

"Hey, kid. Ya'll come on with me."

I was too shocked to respond. Under his firm grasp, I had no choice but to be pulled along down an aisle, through a set of swinging doors, past the EMPLOYEES ONLY sign, around crates of boxes stacked to the ceiling, down a dingy hallway and into an office.

The room was cramped - a gray steel desk, two matching gray steel chairs in front of it, folders stacked on top bulging with inventories, a bulletin board with yellowing papers tacked up. FRIENDLY SERVICE IS OUR MOTTO, one said, and showed a cartoon-like man in a Safeway uniform, his head almost as big as his body with an exaggerated smile and big happy eyes.

The big white man reached down and patted the front of my pants.

"Give it to me or should I get it?"

I reached in and pulled out the cheese. He took it from my hand.

"Now sit down," he said and left.

I was practically hyperventilating when he returned a few minutes later with another white man. He looked like the store manager in his red vest, black tie and black pants. The two of them stood outside the door, speaking in hushed tones.

The taller white man - the one who'd grabbed me - came into the office alone and sat the cheese on the desk in front of me. He wore black cotton pants and a short-sleeved white cotton shirt. Both looked crumpled and I noticed faint yellow sweat stains under his arms.

I expected him to sit down. But he kept standing, reached into his back pocket, pulled out a black wallet and flipped it open. A silver badge was inches from my face. Little Rock Police Department.

"This store prosecutes shoplifters, boy. You're under arrest."

"I'm sorry, sir," I stammered. "I didn't mean. I've...I've...I've never stole nothing, ever, Sir." A few tears dropped down my checks. I licked them with my tongue and tasted the salty drops. I used my shirt sleeve to wipe my nose.

The police department in Little Rock had a bad reputation. Fear was deeply instilled in me as a young boy. I grew up hearing stories about white police officers severely beating black people. Black men were routinely released from jail with bruises and marks on their bodies. I didn't know if they beat kids at the juvenile detention home, but figured, yeah, probably.

"I've never stolen anything before, Mister, I swear to God.."

I looked at the officer's face, then cast my gaze to the floor, submissive and remorseful. I knew better than to have too much direct eye contact. My tears were on the edge of turning into sobs.

"Well, I'll tell you what. I'm going to give you a choice, boy. You can either go home and tell your parents what you've done or you can be arrested. Which do you want?"

I stayed quiet and stared at the dirt and dust on the concrete floor. I couldn't decide which would be worse.

"I want you to give me your parents' names and your telephone number. I'm going to call them tonight. If you haven't told them, I'm coming to arrest you. You understand me, boy?"

"Yes, sir," I mumbled to the floor.

"Now, go on outta here. You should be ashamed of yourself!"

I fled, leaving the sack of bologna on the desk. I ran all the way home, lungs burning from an oncoming asthma attack. I flew into the house, kept running into my bedroom and flopped on the bed. Three hours until Momma gets home. It was like waiting for your own execution.

I heard the door open and knew she was home. She came into my room, looking tired in her white maid's uniform. Her black hair was thick and curly, and softened the lines around her eyes. She looked down at me and said hello. I tried to give her one of my most charming smiles.

Her expression turned hard and I recognized that keen all-knowing look that came into her brown, long eye-lashed, eyes whenever she could tell I'd done wrong..

"Boy, what have you done?" She sounded impatient.

I moped as I sat up on my bed. I hung my head and started mumbling my story. Put cheese in my pants. Policeman. Gonna be arrested. Oh, Momma, I'm sorry,.

"He's going to call you tonight. He let me go but he wants to talk to you to make sure I told you. Momma, I don't want to go to prison."

"I'm...going...to...beat...your...butt," Momma said so deliberately it made me shudder. "There's food in this house. You weren't hungry. You were greedy. I know I've have taught you better than that."

She stormed from the doorway.

"Momma I'm sorry. I won't do it again."

It was no use. I knew what was coming. The strap. A 2-foot long belt-sized piece of brown, aged leather. Momma could make it crack in the air like a seasoned stagecoach driver.

I knew better than to run. Compliantly, I sat on the edge of my bed, braced for pain. She always whipped me across the front of my thighs and calves. I clenched a wad of my bedsheets in both fists By the second hit, I was howling and crying, "Momma, please, I won't do it ever again." I was in pain, but also I knew I had embarrassed her. She shopped at that store and would have to face the store manager.

"Boy, if you don't wise up, you're going to end up in prison just like your daddy. You ... hear ...what .....I'm ..... telling...... you." With each word, she cracked me with the leather, trying to drill the painful message into my defiant teenage head. Erma stood in the doorway watching with a sisterly smile on her face. I could read her thoughts: Get him, Momma. Get him.

"Ain't no child of mine going to end up as bait for the white folks," Momma said as she took one more whack.

WE sat on the porch on an April evening at the home of Lanier Floyd, a good friend of mine who lived on the same block. Erma was with us. She rarely hung out with us, but we were all in a talkative mood that evening because Dr. Martin Luther King Jr. had been shot that day in Memphis.

Dr. King was our idol, a man who had brought about the unimaginable, civil rights for black folks. It was nice to eat in the restaurants downtown and attend a white school, if we so chose. I know some white folks didn't like our newfound power, but to me, this showed the greatness of Dr. King and the movement. Now the future looked uncertain. We had all prayed for hours that day for King to survive. Not only for him and his family, but for black people in general. We needed Dr. King and his wisdom, because his was a voice that both black and white people could hear.

Lanier's parents had stuck their heads out of the front door earlier and announced Dr. King was dead. It was like an evil settled over us. The leader was gunned down 125 miles away. My feelings were so strong that it could have happened here on my block, right before my eyes.

The sound of breaking glass snapped me out of my grief. It came from a few hundred yards away at a neighborhood corner store, owned by a white family. A carload of young men had thrown a firebomb inside. We rushed over and saw the store - where we frequently bought cookies, sodas and my favorite, cinnamon rolls - going up in flames.

Fire trucks arrived and started dousing the blaze. It looked like Schwartz's Grocery would be a total loss. We turned and walked back to the steps of Lanier's front porch. We had barely sat down when Lanier's father stuck his head out the front door and yelled for Lanier to get in the house. All three of us headed for the door.

Lanier walked in first. Before Erma and I could go any further, he stepped in our path. "Get on home. Before you kids end up in trouble."

Sensing there was trouble in the air, Erma and I took off running. I quickly outpaced her, although she managed to stay close behind. Our house was only a half block away, down a big hill, and we picked up speed as we ran down the incline. We just made it into our front yard when a Little Rock police cruiser pulled up behind us with its lights flashing. The tires screeched to a halt and two white officers started screaming for us to stop. I spun around and saw the officers had drawn their guns and were pointing them directly at us.

"Get over here," one of the officers yelled.

"We know what you kids did," the other cop yelled. "Damn kids, firebombing a store."

Erma broke into tears. "We haven't done anything," she sobbed.

I stood quiet, frozen with fear. I couldn't take my eyes off the guns. I figured we'd be shot dead, any second, right there in the street. A white man's store was destroyed. White people killed black people for far less.

Momma had told us about a black man around here who was hanged and burned for allegedly raping a white woman in the 1940s. White men strung him up a tree. After he was dead, they cut him down, tarred, feathered and burned him. They dragged his charred corpse down Broadway, one of the main streets in Little Rock. A strong warning to every black person in town. Keep in your place or else.

If the officers didn't shoot me, they'd certainly haul me off to jail for a good ass-whipping. This was the first incidence of racial violence in Little Rock. I knew the white community would retaliate quickly.

Momma heard the commotion and came out of the front door.

"What's going on?" she demanded of the white officers, walking right up to them, anger overriding any fear she may have felt. "Why do you have my children?"

The heavier of the two officers - he seemed to be the one in charge - said we had just firebombed a store. His tone pronounced us guilty on the spot.

"We're taking them to juvenile detention," he told her.

I turned to my mother and spoke in rapid bursts: "We were up at Lanier's house. We heard a big bang, but we didn't do nothing, Momma, I swear. We heard glass breaking and ran to the corner. The store was on fire when we got over there."

Erma was steadily nodding her head, in agreement with my story. Momma turned to argue with the senior officer as the other slapped handcuffs on my sister and me, and pushed us into the back seat of the black and white squad car. Sweat poured out of my body, both from fear and the short run. I could feel an asthma attack coming on. Erma and I didn't move or talk. We looked out of the window at our Momma bravely standing her own with the two mean looking officers.

The police radio crackled with an alert. Another store had been firebombed. Youths were looting stores. All officers were needed ASAP.

Obviously, the real culprits remained on the loose, causing more damage.

The cops threw open the car doors and unhandcuffed us.

"Stay in the house. I don't want to see you kids out again tonight," the senior officer said as he jumped behind the patrol car's wheel and the men sped away.

As the sirens faded in the distance, Momma began firing questions at me and Erma. "What happened? What were you kids doing up there? Haven't I told you to make sure you stay out of the way of the police?"

Erma explained that Lanier's father had sent us home. We were running home to keep out of trouble. My mother's body stiffened with anger. She told us to get in the house and she stormed off down the street.

She marched up to the Floyd's home and banged on the door. When Momma got mad, she was unstoppable. She gave it to Mr. Floyd real good, as soon as he opened the door.

"What is wrong with you? Don't you ever send my children away in an emergency," she said. "You should have called me to come get them. Our sons play together. You put them in danger! The police were about ready to take them to jail! For no reason! No reason at all! Let me tell you, if they had, you would be dealing with me! You should be ashamed of yourself!"

With that, she spun on her heels and left. Mr. Floyd had violated an unwritten rule in the black community. Black folks were supposed to look out for one another. Momma returned home with a scowl on her face. I was beginning to realize how much trouble black skin could cause.

I thought about my father's years in prison. The incidence with the cheese at Safeway. I promised myself that I wouldn't get in trouble with the law. I understood what Momma meant with her continuous saying, "Don't become bait for the white folks." If I placed myself in the wrong set of circumstances, guilty or not, I could end up in prison. I looked up the word, bait, in the dictionary. *To persecute or exasperate with unjust, malicious, or persistent attacks; to harass.*

For a lady with an eighth-grade education, Momma was darn smart!

I TURNED 14 and was ready for my first real job. I needed something to occupy my time and wanted my own money. With a job, I could help Momma by buying my school clothes. If I was real smooth, I might be able to talk her into letting me have a motorcycle. I was itching for more independence.

A motorcycle was a luxury beyond the reach of most boys in the neighborhood. I knew three, maybe four, guys who rode them. Eddie Paul and Willie Daniels had been fortunate enough to get motorcycles and all the neighborhood guys looked up to them because of it. I had my eye on a Honda 50cc. I'd seen it at the Honda dealership in western Little Rock. Shiny black and chrome with a matching black helmet for $200. My buddies and I would ride our bicycles to the dealer every Saturday morning to look at the motorcycles.

First, I needed a job. I took the bus across town to a stretch of Roosevelt Road that was known as Restaurant Row. A half dozen restaurants sat side by side, the nicest ones in town, the ones where the white people ate. Blacks were allowed inside only to perform the menial jobs - cooks, bus boys, dishwashers. Even the waitresses were white ladies.

I walked to the back of Hank's Dog House. I had passed Hank's Dog House all my life, and noticing the line of white people out front on most evenings, had always wanted to eat in there. But in 1968, blacks knew better than to walk in the front door, even if the "Whites Only" sign had been removed a few years earlier.

I slowly opened the screened door to the kitchen and stepped inside to a steamy and chaotic scene. Waitresses scurrying about with silver trays overhead. Young black men, in white jackets and white round paper caps, rushing around with dirty dishes.

A young friendly black man pointed me toward the restaurant manager, an older white lady, maybe 5-foot-6, heavyset, with glasses and a blonde bouffant hair. They called her Ms. Binky. She told me to report to work the next day. "Go straight to the linen closet and get a jacket and paper cap. One of the boys will show you what to do."

I liked working at the restaurant. The cooks - two middle-aged skinny black men - would ration the leftover portions to us bus boys during the course of our shifts. If I helped close up on a Friday or Saturday night, I got to scarf down whatever was left in the pots and pans. That was the fun time of the evening, all of us eating and dropping lugs.

Dropping lugs was our favorite pastime. Two boys would point out all the other's negative traits. A group would gather round, laughing and watching to see who was wittier, who could dominate the other with verbal finesse.

John, a guy from Westside Junior High, the predominantly white school that I had decided to attend in the fall of 1967, and I started dropping major lugs in the kitchen one night.

"You're so fat, you can't get the ugliest girl at our school, 'cause you a fat pig," I said.

"At least my head will fit into these paper caps we wear, bubble-brains," he replied. We continued our verbal duel all night, in between helping the waitresses carry trays of food to the table. We held the trays as the waitresses served the customers. Then we'd race back to the kitchen to trade insults.

On one break, the words turned from funny to biting. John called my mother a cow. I continued to call him a big fat slob who couldn't get a girlfriend. That was my favorite jab because it was true and I knew it hurt him more than anything else I could say. The exchanges flew back and forth. Each one meaner than the last. I was consistent because nothing hurt a young man's pride more in those days than being without a female's attention. John was bigger than me, a football player at school. He moved in close to me and took a swing. I knew it was coming. I ducked and dodged the sucker punch.

I swung back and landed a hard punch on his jaw. He could beat my butt, so I had to get in a few good punches quick. He barely flinched from the blow. With the speed of a cat, he grabbed me by my waist, lifted me high in the air and tried to slam me hard to the concrete floor. We both tumbled, knocking over a rack of dishes. Shards of glass littered the floor. All work stopped in the kitchen as the employees gasped in disbelief. The boy raised his fist to punch me in the face. Someone grabbed his arm and, Thank God, pulled him off of me.

Orange Edwards was tall, stocky and 35 years old. John was screaming about interference, but knew better than to fight with an adult. I was grateful to Orange. He probably felt obligated to save me. He was the nephew of Mr. Willie, my Momma's boyfriend.

Momma wasn't interested in remarrying. But she and Mr. Willie saw each other steadily for years. Willie Morris was six-foot-tall and very bowlegged. He always drove the newest model pick-up trucks and also owned a 1960 blue Ford Galaxy with white shades in the rear window. Those shades were the coolest thing I had ever seen.

Mr. Willie was a quiet man. He didn't speak much to me. He'd take me fishing out on the lake in his boat and hunting with his hound dogs, an assortment of mixed breeds that he trained to chase rabbits and coons.

His nephew, Orange, had to help me. The manager, Ms. Binky, heard the commotion in the kitchen and came running. The fight disrupted the flow of the busy kitchen on a Saturday night. I tried to apologize, but she wouldn't hear it.

"Ya'll fired. Now, get out of here before I call the police."

Fired from my first job for fighting! I wondered if I'd be in trouble with Momma. She always told Erma and me to protect ourselves. Don't start a fight, but fight back if provoked. I told her John called her a fat cow. I lied a little and said, "Momma when he said that, it was on."

We sat in the small kitchen - barely big enough for a sink, stove, refrigerator and small table in the middle. She laughed as I told and retold the story. We didn't have air-conditioning then. A 3-foot-by-3-foot window fan filled the kitchen with a humming noise and helped keep us cool.

I set out to find another job. I worked briefly at McDonald's and then at Burger King, where some of my school friends had been hired. To my delight, Momma agreed to buy me a brand, spanking new 1968 Honda 50 motorcycle. I was so excited I could barely contain myself. Momma purchased it on credit and I made the payments. I fussed over that bike every minute of the day, polishing the black gas tank until the glare of the sun reflected so brightly I had to look away. I carried a small terry-cloth towel in my back pocket. Shined that gas tank so often it's a wonder the paint didn't wear off.

Momma told me to ride it just around our yard until I got a license and registration tags for the bike. Don't ride it in the street, she repeatedly told me.

Eddie Paul Daniel came over one afternoon to see the beauty and convinced me to take him for a quick spin. I pulled on my black helmet and Eddie Paul went home to get a football helmet to wear. Momma was at work. I knew better than to defy her instructions, but my ego loved showing off. Eddie Paul and I took off and ended up in downtown Little Rock, heading toward the state capital complex. So many people stopped to look at us, I couldn't help but be proud of my new motorcycle.

We stopped and switched drivers. I showed Eddie Paul how to shift gears. We started off again. After only a few blocks, we heard a police siren behind us. The cruiser pulled alongside, its blue lights flashing, and the white officer motioned us to the side of the street.

"Don't you boys know it's against the law to operate a motorcycle without tags," the officer said. He directed the question to Eddie Paul, who was driving. Eddie Paul sat mute.

"We're sorry, sir," I said. " My mother just bought this for me. We're testing it out. We're on our way home right now."

The officer pulled out a binder of traffic tickets and started writing. He asked my name, address, age and other questions, and then handed me a ticket for operating a motorcycle without license tags. I climbed on the bike to drive it back home. A traffic ticket. I was sure to get a whipping.

I dropped Eddie Paul off at his house and headed home. I sat on the front steps and waited, figuring I'd tell Momma right away and get it over with. She just shook her head when I told her and walked right past me. I could hear her in the kitchen, rattling around pans and starting dinner. Her reaction unnerved me. I was relieved that she didn't slap me. But after a few minutes, I felt worse. I got up and went into the kitchen.

She was standing by the window, turning on the fan before she cranked up the cook stove. She didn't look at me as I pulled out a chair and sat down at the table. This was the time of day when I would tell her about my day and she would tell me about hers. Now, there was only silence. As I watched her move about the kitchen, I thought I saw tears in her eyes.

She finally looked at me with her big brown eyes. I knew I'd hurt her.

"Brother, please don't end up like so many of these other boys, spending your time in jail or with the policemen always chasing you. No good will come of your life unless you obey the law and obey your parents. You may think you can get away with something. But sure enough, Brother, it will catch up with you. You'll end up like your father... More bait for the white folks."

Her words stung. "Don't worry, Momma. I'm going to make something out of my life. You'll be proud of me. Just wait and see." I faithfully promised her.

I RETURNED to the white school that fall. I had attended a black elementary school, named Rightsell. But then we had a choice: Enroll at the black Dunbar Junior High School or at the white Westside Junior High, 15 blocks across town.

Erma attended Dunbar, a short walk from our house. I was more adventuresome. I wanted to venture out into the world. See what the white kids had. The year before, I had convinced Erma to come along with me.

It had been an adjustment. I had high hopes of seeing what white people were like. But after a year, I didn't have much more interaction with them than before. Two worlds existed within that small building. I hung out with the same black kids I'd always known. It was a prettier school, but I sensed the teachers and administrators weren't too happy about our presence there.

Erma was a straight-A student. A teachers' pet who basked in their praise. At Westside, she felt only apathy from the teachers, like her participation in class was tolerated but not appreciated. That's why she finished high school at the all black Horace Mann High School.

"I'm going to hang where I am," I told her. "Stick it out. The white folks aren't going to run me off, even if they don't like me. What have we done to them? Nothing at all."

One of my favorite classes was choir. My voice was flat and lacked the depth and resonance that I heard from singers in church. I hoped if I tried hard, I'd sound good, too. Mrs. Summers was the choral director, a white woman in her 60s, five-feet-tall, skinny and a frumpy dresser. She was talented at voice instruction and probably should have taught college-level students. She didn't have the patience for teaching hormone-crazed teenagers. We would get to horsing-around, talking louder and louder, cracking on one another for singing off-tune.

"You, niggers," Mrs. Summers would shout over our voices,

"don't know how to behave yourself."

Among ourselves, we always called each other niggers. But the word always shocked me when a white person said it. It sounded so demeaning, so harsh and ugly. Like a final punch thrown after a guy already went down. Unnecessary. A final jab meant to convey dominance.

At first, the word shocked us into silence. Over the school year, its impact weakened. Mrs. Summers resorted to storming from the room when we got out of hand and returning with Mr. Green, the assistant principal. That shut everyone up quickly.

Mrs. Summers would point out the troublemakers and the students would trail behind Mr. Green back to his office, where they'd get a few good whacks with his famous wooden paddle - holes in the middle of it to increase its force. Then the students would return to class, subdued, their butts stinging.

Once a black boy asked Mrs. Summers why she didn't use the preferred word in those days, Negroes, like everyone else.

"That's how we learned to say Negro in Alabama." No one thought to challenge her logic any further.

I HAD payments to keep up with on the motorcycle. After a series of meaningless jobs, I decided to try for a job with a little prestige. I knew where I wanted to work. I just didn't know if I could pull it off.

In high school, there were only a few ways for kids to improve their status, that is, if they weren't great looking or happened to be born into a family with some money. For the rest of us, it came down to wearing the right clothes, hanging with the right kids, driving the right car and working at a job that didn't involve getting dirty. Jobs in restaurants were easy to come by for black boys. Clean labor was a challenge.

I wanted to work at Safeway. I'd tag along with Momma when she went grocery shopping. I'd watch the employees in their bright red uniforms. Could I ever get such a job and leave behind steamy kitchens, scrubbing dishes and serving food?

I pictured myself in the Safeway uniform: black pants, white shirt and red vest, sweeping floors, stocking shelves and, maybe one day, working as a cashier. Young executive. That's what I'd be. Problem was I'd been caught shoplifting in this same store. How could I ever expect the store to trust me handling its money?

My friends said don't bother. The store manager would laugh in my face. I couldn't walk away so fast. I was more determined, driven, than most of my friends. I'd hang out with them, cut school, wander over to Carl Brown's house, where his mother let us drink beer and listen to her Moms Mabley, Redd Fox and other X-rated comedy albums. We'd go out back and smoke a joint, open more beers, laugh at the records and feel so grown up.

Carl and the other guys made Ds and Fs at school. Not me. I found ways to get my school work done. I wasn't an A-student like Erma. I got by with mostly Cs, an occasional A and B and a few Ds.

I knew I had to try to get a job at Safeway. I worked up my nerve and figured I'd have as good a chance as anyone, especially because the store now had a black manager. Mr. Henderson was one of the first black managers with Safeway Stores in Little Rock. I heard he made $50,000 a year, an incredible sum of money in 1969. Mr. Henderson was very short - about 4-foot-10 - dark skinned and walked with an air of authority through his store. The black customers viewed him as a wealthy man with a prestigious job.

Some people tried to undercut his accomplishments. Whispered he was an Uncle Tom. "No black man gets promoted by a supermarket chain unless he cow-tows to white people," they'd say. He knew my mother by name, and saw our family in the store all the time.

I rehearsed what I'd say. On a Saturday morning, I put on starched and creased black cotton pants, a white shirt and black tie, and headed to Safeway. I repeated my short speech in my mind and tried to calm the butterflies in my stomach. I walked to the back of the store, through the swinging, black rubber-faced doors and into the office where I'd once come with cheese in my underwear.

Mr. Henderson looked up from his clipboard of inventory sheets.

"Excuse me, Sir," I said, trying to overcome my timidness. "Can I talk to you for a minute?"

"Come in," Mr. Henderson replied and motioned to the chair. "How can I help you, Anderson?"

"Mr. Henderson, I got into trouble in this store a few years back. I know you weren't here, but I figured you'd heard about it. I took some cheese and got caught. I've always been real sorry about what I did.

Anyway, I was hoping you might consider hiring me part-time as stock clerk whenever you have an opening. I'd like to fill out an application, if you think you might consider me."

Mr. Henderson looked bigger in the small crowded office. He flipped a stack of papers pinned to the bulletin board behind him. He grabbed what looked like a work schedule and took it down.

"Well, Anderson," he said.

By his tone, I figured that I didn't have a chance.

"Tell me this first. Did you learn your lesson?"

"Yes, sir. I've never taken anything from a store again."

He leaned back and let my words hang in the air. He scratched the top of his head and remained quiet, like he was struggling with his decision.

"When could you start?"

The question startled me and took a few seconds to register. I jumped up from the chair, a big smile on my face, and looked like I was going to reach across the desk and hug Mr. Henderson.

"I can start whenever you want, Mr. Henderson."

"Well, come back tomorrow at noon. Wear a white short sleeved shirt and a black tie. I'll put you to work."

My big break. I bounced out of the store and climbed on my motorcycle. I couldn't wait to tell Momma and Erma. They wouldn't believe it.

As I pulled up, I saw Momma in the front yard, raking leaves, wearing her old stained work clothes - a once-white, long-sleeve, loose cotton shirt to shield her skin from the hot sun and a pair of baggy brown cotton pants. As I took off the helmet, she stopped raking and leaned on the wooden rake handle. She pulled a handkerchief from her pocket and wiped the sweat from her brow.

When she saw my face, her demeanor brightened. She could see the happiness and excitement on his face.

"Momma, guess what?"

"What, Brother?"

"I got a job at Safeway. Mr. Henderson gave me a job. I start tomorrow. I'm gonna be a stock clerk at Safeway."

She reached over and pulled me into her strong arms. I was as tall as she now, but being wrapped up in her embrace always made me feel smaller. I beamed at the thought of making my Momma proud of me.

I SET out to make a good impression at Safeway. I arrived early and avoided horsing around with the other stock boys. When Mr. Henderson called for stock boys to go bag groceries or fetch carts in the parking lot, I eagerly complied while some of the other stock boys dallied in the back and had to be called twice.

My attitude paid off. Within six months, Mr. Henderson called me into his office and asked if I wanted to start training as a cashier. I had told Mr. Henderson repeatedly that I was going to be the best stock boy and cashier that he'd ever had. It might have sounded like boyhood bravado. But Mr. Henderson could see the sincerity and ambition in my eyes. I was soon racing the other cashiers on busy Friday and Saturday nights to see who could clear their lines the fastest. I'd unload items from the cart with one hand and enter the amounts on the cash register with the other, fingers moving as fast as an accountant's on an adding machine. Sometimes, I'd look up and see Mr. Henderson standing at the front of the store, watching me.

Mr. Henderson knew I had the potential to succeed, where so many other young black men in town seemed to be constantly getting arrested by the Little Rock police. He encouraged me to become a full-time employee after my high school graduation. I dreamed one day I'd be a Safeway manager and earn lots of money like Mr. Henderson.

Our Safeway was the place to shop for the black community. A Saturday afternoon could feel like a social gathering with residents exchanging greetings and children racing to the toy aisle.

I always kept my eye out for one family in particular, the Myerses, one of the most prominent families in town. Mrs. Rachel Myers was a beautiful and petite woman with thick brown wavy hair, light complexion and a splash of freckles on her face. She was a teacher at Rightsell Elementary, where I once attended school. Like most of the boys then, I had a crush on her. In the intervening year, she had risen to become principal of Jefferson G. Ish Elementary School and later would be tapped as a Little Rock school system's Assistant Superintendent of Elementary Education, overseeing many of the elementary schools in the city.

Her husband, Rev. Lloyd Myers, was the pastor at Rose of Sharon Baptist Church. He also worked in the insurance business, starting out as a mail clerk for Blue Cross/Blue Shield and working his way up to Manager of Purchasing at the state headquarters in Little Rock. Rev. Myers was light-skinned with a wavy short afro and an athletic build. He kept fit since beginning to play tennis at Philander Smith College, a small black college near downtown Little Rock that was supported by the United Negro College Fund. The Reverend had even won a few championships in local tennis tournaments and kept the trophies shiny and polished in his office at Blue Cross/Blue Shield.

Lloyd had met Rachel while the two were students at Philander Smith in the early 1950s. Rachel was a quiet, soft-spoken debutante and Lloyd was a popular man on campus, a social and academic leader. They were instantly attracted to each other and married shortly after graduation. Good-looking, educated and hard-working, they made an ideal couple and produced four equally beautiful children, Deborah, the oldest, Sandra, Lloyd and lastly, John.

It was Deborah who caught my eye in Safeway. I couldn't help but admire such a prestigious and affluent family. I had passed by their house all my life. It was a large, three-bedroom ranch-style home built on a steep embankment at 1514 W. 21st St., not far from my house. But it was a world away, set in the nicest section of the black community. Rev. Myers' big shiny American made cars always sat parked along the street out front.

I'd walk by and see the three Myers children playing out front (the youngest, John, wasn't born until 1968, and as a young child use to always playfully attack me, like a wild animal, whenever we were left alone). I'd blushed with embarrassment at the thought of stopping to talk to them. I feared I would be shunned for I was from a poorer home, was dark-skinned and had parents who were divorced. I wished my family could be like the Myerses, happily together with professional jobs and a fine brick home.

Our home was clean and decent, and Momma provided well for my sister and I. But we were in a different social class. I felt too self-conscious to even attempt to befriend such a family as the Myerses. I did no more than occasionally make eye contact with Deborah or Sandra at school and demurely say "Hi".

As Mrs. Myers and Deborah came through the line at Safeway, I'd tell myself to slow down. Unloading their groceries gave me time to make idle chit-chat with them. Secretly, I longed for Deborah to notice me and fall madly in love with me. I would glance at her, hoping to see some indication on her face, some body language, that said she was attracted to me. I knew that I couldn't make the first move with a girl like her.

I was in that awkward stage of adolescence - tall and lanky physically and so unsure of myself emotionally. I tried to project a strong and confident identity, but I didn't really feel it inside. It was my curse from birth.

I'd heard the story of my birth countless times and thought it explained my maladroit demeanor. My mother gave birth to me on July 18, 1954, and named me Travis Lamar Hill. When father arrived - he had been en route to the hospital when I was born - he was furious at my name. He wanted me named after his father, Anderson Chester Hill. He rushed down to the hospital records office, where a young black lady sat typing birth certificates.

"There's been a mistake," he said, practically out of breath. "My wife gave my son the wrong name."

He persuaded her to pull out the baby's birth certificate. She fished around and pulled out one halfway at the bottom of the stack in front of her. Travis Lamar Hill had been typed in the blank space.

"Yes, Travis Lamar Hill," the lady said and saw the look of insolence on my father's face. "My wife got it mixed up. The boy's gonna be named Anderson Chester Hill, The Second." He drew out the words, "The Second", making it sound aristocratic and regal.

For a second, the woman debated what to do. Names on birth certificates were not supposed to be changed. She looked at this man and saw his hard-set jaw. He wasn't going to take "no" for an answer. She reached for a pencil and handed it to him.

"Here, you write it in. Just cross out the other name."

And so my identity changed within hours of birth. It was an omen of the confusion I would feel as a child.

Now at 15, I knew I didn't have a chance with Deborah Myers. But it was great to fantasize. I'd finish ringing up Mrs. Myers' groceries and checked out Deborah as often as I could without being conspicuous.

She was talking to her mother about a new pair of white tennis shoes she got on the way to the grocery store. She was planning to wear them to a friend's party next weekend. Maybe she'd wear that blue cotton skirt she got for her birthday. Chat...Chat...Chat.

She didn't even notice me.

Mr. Henderson was standing at the front of the store. He could tell what I was feeling. "Poor kid", I'm sure Mr. Henderson probably thought. He watched me watching Deborah, and could tell by my slower paced cashier actions, I was infatuated with her. "All those hormones", he probably chuckled to himself, "mingled with youthful optimism."

I didn't truly understand the depth of social barriers. Black boys didn't chase white girls. Poor boys didn't chase rich girls. And dark-skinned blacks usually kept to people of their same skin tone. Mr. Henderson, a dark chocolate-black man, like me, had learned that lesson.

Skin tone was a sensitive issue for blacks. Mr. Henderson once told me that he remembered reading a speech given by a man named Willie Lynch, in South Carolina, back in 1712. Lynch was giving tips to white plantation owners on how to keep their hordes of black slaves in submission. Lynch's secret: Exploit the differences among the slaves and keep them pitted against one another. Then, they'll never unite against whites.

It was a philosophy that took hold on plantations throughout the South. Dark-skinned slaves worked in the fields and light-skinned slaves, usually the offspring of forced sexual relations between white male overseers and their female slaves - enjoyed comfortable surroundings as house servants.

The distinction far outlived the institution of slavery and continued to divide blacks as deeply as the traits that separate whites, such as educational level, income and ethnic background. Light-skinned blacks usually sought out light-skinned blacks and this ensured their children would reap the same preferential treatment in both the black and white communities as they did.

Mr. Henderson told me about this societal rule to implicitly alert me to the fact that my chances with Deborah Myers did not bode well. I later read Lynch's speech and could see the far reaching effects Lynch's philosophy, as rigorously applied by the slave owners, has had on my people, to this very day. That still didn't stop me.

I OFTEN saw Deborah in the halls of Little Rock Central High when I started there my sophomore year. I'd say, "hi", but I wasn't getting anywhere with her. She was a year ahead of me, so we didn't have any classes together, which would have presented the chance for me to make a move. Nor did our paths cross outside of school because I hung with a different - and wilder - crowd.

That first year at Central High was so exciting for me. It felt good to leave junior high behind. But, even more than that, Central High held such a mystique for blacks. The school was at the center of the world's attention in 1957 during forced integration, three years after the landmark U.S. Supreme Court decision in *Brown v. Board of Education of Topeka.*

Following the ruling, the Little Rock School Board adopted a plan to comply with the high court's order. The first phase was to begin in the fall of 1957. Throughout the South and the State of Arkansas, however, politicians were devising a strategy of stall-tactics. On the day before schools opened that fall in Little Rock, the governor sent the Arkansas National Guard to block the Negro students from entering the school.

For three weeks, the guardsmen blocked the students' entrance. Mobs of both races formed outside the school to protest. The local police could barely stop them from attacking each other. Finally, the district court issued an injunction against the governor and the Arkansas National Guard, demanding they cease and desist with their human barricade around the school. The governor and guardsmen left. But the next day, when the students again attempted to attend school, a furious and vengeful mob of whites amassed outside the school. The students were barely whisked away to safety. Fearing another civil war, President Eisenhower dispatched federal troops to Little Rock. The Negro teenagers walked up the stairs to the school, surrounded by their own battering ram of armed soldiers.

I grew up with that story. Knew it by heart. Everyone in town knew about the "Little Rock Nine", as those first brave Negro students were called. Central High was the site of an epic battle for us and we viewed it as a monument to our victorious crusade for equality.

The place was huge, the crown jewel in the local public school system. It covered two city blocks, and looked more like a college campus than a high school, especially to us blacks who grew up near the smaller black high school, Horace Mann.

Central High stood five stories high in places and had a light aged-brown brick facade. In front was a concrete pool, called the Dunking Pond, because students were always throwing each other in the water. It was impressive to stand in front and take in its architecture and landscaped grounds. Attached in the rear was the school's own football stadium. In between the stadium and the school were many tennis and basketball courts. And a new library wing had recently been completed off to one side.

I arrived 12 years after the legendary battle. School integration hadn't yet trickled down to an integrated student body. Black kids and white kids stayed as distant as we had been at Westside Junior High. The black kids congregated at the southeastern edge of campus, corner of Sixteenth and Park streets. The white kids mingled all the way on the other side of campus. When the school bell rang, the two groups would join together and head to class. There might be a few black kids mixed in with the white kids, but for the most part, the two groups rarely spoke to each other.

As young men, desperate for some female attention, we prided ourselves on looking good. We all wore starched bell-bottom blue jeans, white and black tennis shoes, and snug-fitting polyester-knit shirts in wild, colorful prints. We spoke in a continuous stream of street slang and practiced our cool-guy limps.

Drugs were plentiful on campus, and we often smoked a joint before going to class. My use of marijuana and other street drugs increased throughout that year and by my junior year, getting high was a daily routine.

I started hanging with Frog Walker. Froggie was a year ahead of me, tall and handsome, with more girls than he could juggle. He drove a 1957 Chevrolet, two-door, jet black, and jacked way up in the back with big tires and shiny silver rims. The car had lifters in the back that made it bounce as it drove down the street, stereo blasting. In the car were Froggie, me and a couple guys in the backseat looking bored and unaffected by it all.

Being seen with Frog Walker greatly boosted my social status.

My new status required the proper image - an air of being tough, a fighter, street smart and wild. My guys and I would scout around for chemical drugs - mescaline and acid - and pop some before school. Or we would head to the liquor store, smoking pot on the way there and chugging beer on the way back. Many times, we wouldn't make it back to school, choosing instead to drive around town, listening to 8-track tapes of Jimmy Hendrix and Santana. Loud, and full-blast!

Mescaline, acid and speed heightened my senses, so that the music sounded crystal clear. I seemed to merge into the music. We'd sit around for hours without talking, lost in the guitar riffs and the pounding beat. We'd usually cruise through the rich white section of Pulaski Heights, bragging that one day we'd live in a fancy home. Next stop would be the neighborhood doughnut shop. We'd gorge on sweet dough-nuts and talk with the wild white students, who were also skipping school and taking drugs.

I was as wild as any of them. But unlike them, I managed to get through school with Cs. Bobby Thomas bragged about missing 160 days out of the 230-day school year. Somehow, Bobby T. managed to get promoted to the next grade. At that time, there weren't strict require-ments on school attendance.

Bobby T. also had his own car. He'd pull up to Sixteenth and Battery in his white 1963 Chevy, shiny rims on the wheels and muffled pipes that made the car hum and purr. "Hey, man," he'd shout to me and Otis Rayford. "Let's go hang!"

Otis and I would jump in the car. We'd cut school, and swing by the campus several times in the day - at class breaks, lunch time and after school. Drunk and high was our thing. We flaunted cutting school. We'd lean out of the car and talk to the guys who'd mingle around, finding out what was happening and what drugs were available and where. All the time, we'd be checking out girls and talking "much" trash.

It was during one of these bull sessions that I first spotted Sandra Myers.

She was a year younger than me. I had seen her back when I attended Westside Junior High School. She was just a cute little girl then. But now, Wow! She was standing on the stairs beside the big, double wooden doors on the right side of the school.

She had a cigarette in her hand, which surprised me. She was trying to appear nonchalant as she smoked. Her awkward movements and the tentative way she put the cigarette to her lips gave her away. I kept my eyes on her, studying the way this shy and quiet younger sister of Deborah's had blossomed into a real beauty. She was the loveliest girl I'd ever seen. An angel, I thought. She looked just like her mother, light-skinned with freckles, 5-foot-2 and a great body.

My heart stirred in a way that it hadn't before. This must be love at first sight, I thought, and decided to make my move. I got out of the car, leaving the guys behind. I walked toward her and watched her drop the cigarette on the concrete stairs and squish the butt with her shoe. She was talking to a group of girls and didn't notice me approaching. As I reached the bottom step, she looked down at me.

"Hey, Sandra," I said, my eyes trying to hold her gaze.

She smiled and returned the greeting. I had become experienced in the dance of sexual pursuit, and could see in her eyes that she would accept my gentlemanly advances. I kept walking, acting like I just happened to pass her by, and went into the school. As I walked through the school, out the front doors and back to Bobby T's car, I was plotting how I could win her over. All that time I'd spent pining away for Deborah. I was grateful nothing ever happened between us. Fate, I guess.

I started asking around. Was Sandra dating anyone?

I learned I had my work cut out for me. Sandra was seeing Gary Nunn, one of those all-around great guys who parents adore. Gary was tall and thin, well-groomed, with light skin and a big thick black Afro. He had his own new car, a rarity among 16-year-old boys. His family was well-respected, just like the Myers, and he was an excellent student, well-mannered and sure to be successful in life.

But Gary had one weakness. He wasn't a fighter. My strategy was to scare the hell out of him. That should be easy. Gary came from a sheltered home and knew nothing about the rough ways of the street. He'd cower if I showed up to fight.

I was riding around one night with Bobby T's younger brother, Larry, whose nickname was Bird. My nickname was Andy Capp. The guys started calling me that because I'd started wearing a cap just like a cartoon character that appeared in the daily newspaper, *The Arkansas*

Democrat. Otis Rayford was in the seat beside Bird. I was in the back.

"Hey, Andy Capp," Otis said. "There goes Gary and San."

The guys knew I was hot after Sandra. I looked ahead and recognized Gary's blue 1966 Mustang.

"Hey, follow them," I yelled.

We were two cars behind Gary. By the turns he took, I could tell he was taking Sandra home. As Gary pulled into her driveway, we parked a block away and waited. Sandra got out and walked inside. Gary backed out and headed across town to University Park, another affluent black section where he lived.

Gary must have recognized Bird's car in his rear-view mirror because when we stopped at a red light at the busy intersection of University and 12th Street, near Gary's house, he turned around and waved. We stayed close on his tail and parked behind him when he pulled into the driveway.

He got out and walked back to Bird's car. He was smiling. But I knew he had to be curious about why we followed him.

"Hey, what's up?" he said, walking to the driver's side of the car.

I climbed out through the other door and stormed up to him fast. He looked like an animal trapped in headlights. I moved closer, standing chest-to-chest with him, and got right-up in his face.

"I heard you been talking about me," I said, my chest puffed out and hands clenched in fists at my side. "You been saying shit about me and I don't appreciate it. Keep it up and I'll kick your ass."

"I...I...I don't know what you're talking about, Andy Capp."

He was bracing for a fight, unsure what to do. He couldn't have had any idea what brought this on. He turned timid and meek, afraid to incite me any further. Road kill, I figured, and really lit into him, on a roll, going strong.

"I'll kick your ass right here, Punk! If I hear anything else I'll flatten your sorry ass, you hear me?" I flexed at him one final time.

A door opened behind me.

"Gary, what's going on out here?" his mother called. "Are you okay?"

"It's nothing, Mom," Gary struggled in vain to sound nonchalant. It sounded like his stomach was in his throat. "I'll be right there."

His mother closed the door to the large, brick-faced ranch-style home. She went into the living room, pulled back the drapes on the front window and peered outside.

"Hey, Andy Capp. Let's roll," Bird yelled, seeing the mother at the window. She'd call the cops if I laid one hand on her precious boy. I looked at Gary and saw the fear in his eyes. Mission Accomplished! I turned and strutted my cool-guy limp back to the car.

Within two weeks, I was walking Sandra to classes. Gary would see us together. He'd look down as we walked by. He surely understood my motive now, yet, he was powerless to stop me.

I've often thought I should feel bad about bullying poor Gary. But I did what I had to do to win Sandra. I loved her from the beginning. I used to always tell her that I knew she'd be a beautiful old woman, just like she was in her youth.

GOING NOWHERE FAST

Running from the devastation that ruins my people.
Running to find a safe haven from the dirt and shame.
Running to show myself new.
Running to run nowhere.

I'm going faster to my grave.
I'm not ready to be shoveled.
I'm a young man, smart and maneuvering my way;
to the halls of academia to show you who I am.

I possess savvy.
I am suave.
I have a swift tongue.
I serve you.

4 THE COLOR DIVIDE

"Nothing in the world is more dangerous than a sincere ignorance and conscientious stupidity."

Rev. Martin Luther King, Jr. (1929-1968)

My school grades continued to slide. It was easy to do. The white teachers might yank aside a white kid if his grades took a dive. Call the parents; get the kid back on track. But they let the same behavior go unchallenged among black students.

It seemed to me the teachers didn't care if I attended class or not. My presence was tolerated, but certainly I did not feel welcomed. The deal had been cut years before. Black kids could attend Central High, but the school's most valuable resources - the attention and energies of its teachers and administrators - were reserved for the white students. Teachers would allow the black kids to sit in the back of class, their heads on their desk, not learning anything. The teachers didn't engage them in class discussions or demand that they perform up to their abilities.

We black students complained frequently among ourselves about the treatment. The civil rights movement had been waged all around us. But in our school, it felt like a socially accepted form of segregation still reigned.

In early March of my junior year, just when the weather warmed up enough for us to return to our morning hangout at the corner of Sixteenth and Park, several guys started yakking about the inferior treatment. I wasn't paying attention to them, because I was talking to a few of my friends. One of the guys started talking loud and angry. We all stopped and listened to him.

In hindsight, it seemed as if a kind of energy materialized around us in a matter of minutes. The molecules in the air began to accelerate, bumping into each other, until there was so much friction, a spontaneous combustion was inevitable. It may have been spring fever. Or simply the right place at the right time.

The guy who was yelling - a tall, gangly senior with a huge Afro; I didn't know his name - was saying we shouldn't take such neglect anymore. I turned to my boys. We were not the passionate-activist types. I was surprised to see in their eyes that they, too, were ready to make a stand, Right here, Right now!

The issues were easy to identify. There were no black students in the Student Government Association. Blacks were openly discouraged from participating in most school sports, except for football and basketball. The basketball team was almost all-black and had gone to the state championships every year I attended Central High. We all loved the basketball team and attended almost every home game.

The kid with the big Afro - I heard someone call him Jerome - said they should demand changes in the administration. All the administrators were white, with one exception: a black assistant principal named Mr. Powell. The students called him an Uncle Tom and the "spook who sat by the door." He never supported the black students or counseled or encouraged us. He was the school's "Doberman Pinscher," guarding against black disciplinary problems. He had a reputation of dealing even more harshly with black kids than with white ones. He'd suspend us in a heartbeat. I guess, he did what he had to do, in order to maintain his employment position.

A group of kids packed closely around Jerome, who was saying he'd taken too much crap during his three years at Central High. We needed to Unite, Demonstrate, Protest, March!

"The honkies don't care about us!" he yelled. "They treat us like dogs! Let's show them we won't take it anymore!"

Other students wandered over to the group. In a matter of minutes, a plan emerged. We would march up and down Park Street, the main drag that ran right in front of the school's front entranceway, the same spot where former Governor Orval Faubus had stood in the doorway, prohibiting the "Little Rock Nine" from entering. We would definitely get the attention of the administrators, probably even the whole city.

I had never participated in a protest or sit-in before. Of course, I knew all about the civil rights marches, the Black Panthers and the Black Muslims. But in the heydays of the civil rights movement, I was too young to participate. Now, I could redeem myself. Suddenly, I felt proud and emboldened at the thought of joining the ranks of young black militants.

The school bell buzzed loudly, signaling it was time for students to get to class. Our rowdy group stood motionless, everyone's eyes darting around to see which students would chicken out and go on to class. About five slithered away.

Those of us who remained seemed invigorated by our decision to stay. We pressed together into a pack. A girl began singing *We Shall Overcome*, and everyone joined in. A couple students wrote in big letters on notebook paper, Equality for All, and carried it over their heads.

With Jerome in front, we shuffled along the sidewalk of Park Street in front of the looming structure. Our demands crystallized: We wanted black representation on the SGA. We wanted more blacks to receive awards and commendations. We wanted black students to be named occasionally as Homecoming King and Queen. Blacks never stood a chance in the vote for the popular and good looking "Tiger Beau & Tiger Beauty" couple. That fortunate couple, would majestically reign over all homecoming activities. The white students voted for a white beauty and beau. We were so outnumbered, our votes carried little weight.

The school stretched for two blocks, so it took a while for us to march up and back. When we passed the front entrance the second time, the principal was waiting for us, arms akimbo and a bull-horn hanging from his right hand. Mr. Carter was a big white man, 6-foot-5, 300 pounds and bald. He stood at the top of the stairs leading up the main entrance. He put the bull-horn to his mouth and warned us to get to class or face immediate suspension.

"I'm giving you *one* warning." His amplified voice carried for blocks. We could see students inside the classrooms, faces pushed against the windows, straining to see what would happen. "The Little Rock police have been called and they're on their way. Ya'll better get to class. The police have been instructed to remove all troublemakers from the campus."

The dual threat of suspension and arrest wreaked havoc. Many students started sprinting across the grass. A few jumped through ground-floor windows to get inside, afraid, I suppose, to walk past the principal and in the front doors. Only a fraction of us - maybe one-tenth - stayed, including me. We stood firm in absolute defiance. When the police arrived, the group numbered 50.

Jerome strode confidently up to a white officer. He was the self-appointed leader and wanted to explain our grievances. The white officer responded brashly and loudly. He would only say this once. He spoke in a demanding voice, as trained in military tones, to make sure all the kids heard him the first time.

"I don't care what your problem is, boy. Ya'll are disturbing the peace. This is an unlawful demonstration. No discussions. No negotiations. Just arrests. Save the sob story for your parents when they bail you out of jail."

That's all I needed to hear. I wasn't going to jail, no matter how valid our cause. Just the summer before, five boys from Horace Mann High School ended up in jail and had their butts kicked, real bad.

The story around the neighborhood was that the guys went to a teen-age meeting place along the banks of the scenic Arkansas River, called the Sand Bar. It was a popular hangout for both black and white kids, although the two groups mostly stayed on opposite sides of the clearing, drinking, smoking pot and listening to music from their cars.

After hours of partying one steamy hot Saturday night, the five guys hooked up with a white girl. Several had intercourse with her. The others watched. The next morning, she went to the police station. Rape, she said, and the boys were arrested within an hour. They sat in jail all summer. Two weeks before school started, the girl recanted her story. The charges were dropped and the boys were released. Police had no choice. There was no official apology to the boys or their families. City leaders said the boys were lucky to be alive. "How dare they sleep with a white girl!"

Truth was the boys were lucky to be alive. Black folks knew that. So no one complained when the boys returned home with cuts and bruises. The boys said the white jail guards would hit them around whenever they felt like it.

Remembering the story, I knew we black boys would receive similar treatment for stirring up racial unrest in Little Rock. Several TV news crews had arrived and were filming our march. The cops were on good behavior now. But get us away from the camera's eye, and there'd be no saving our hides.

The students began dispersing and I walked away with them. The principal was yelling students' names in the bull-horn. Anyone whose name was called was immediately suspended for three days. "Anderson Hill." Oh, well, I shrugged and headed home.

When Momma heard the whole story, she half-heartedly scolded me. I returned to school the following Tuesday. The place was still buzzing with tales of our heroic action. The select group of us who had held firm became instant martyrs. Our fame increased when, in the next week, the administration announced a new policy to start designating both black and white Tiger Beau and Beauty, along with other coveted titles, such as Most Popular Student and Most Likely to Succeed.

I treasured my small role in bringing about the change. To my great pleasure, my beautiful girlfriend, Sandra Myers, was chosen as the school's first black Homecoming Queen the following year.

IN early May of that year, with my junior year drawing to a close, I was summoned to the guidance counselor's office for my annual evaluation and counseling session. The counselor reviewed students' grades and recommended what classes we should take the next year.

"Anderson, you're barely passing English and Science," she said. "I see you're doing well in Bookkeeping and Accounting. Looks like you'll get a B in those."

I was known as a whiz in accounting equations. Students regularly sought me out for help. "Andy Capp, how come you understand this bookkeeping so well?" they'd say. I didn't really know why. I grasped it right from the start. Courses involving "cash transactions" excited me.

My standardized test scores ranked me in the upper-mid range for my grade level. Clearly, I was performing far below my academic abilities.

Miss Beatrice White was the guidance counselor, a frail white old maid, who wore her graying hair up in a bun, glued together with lots of hair spray, and thick glasses with black rims, the kind that hung from her neck on a fake gold chain. Everyone had long ago given up hope that she might retire. She spoke in a high-pitched nasal tone, which kids imitated behind her back..

"Well, Anderson, you're going to be a senior next year. I was wondering what are your plans after graduation?" she asked as she flipped through my file.

I thought about my goals: Get my own car. Party with my friends. Keep working at Safeway and maybe someday work as a postman or lawyer. I wasn't sure what to tell her.

"Well, I guess I'll go to college."

My sister, Erma, was almost through with her freshman year at Langston University, a small, private black college in Langston, Oklahoma.

"My mother says if I go to college, I'll make a lot of money one day. That sounds good to me: Money."

I chuckled but stopped abruptly when I noticed Miss White hadn't cracked a smile. She kept flipping through the file. When she looked up at me, a frown had formed on her face.

"Young man, I don't think you'd do too well in college. Based upon your performance here at Central, I think you'd be best served to learn a trade. There is always a need for good tradesman."

Her face softened slightly as she looked me in the eyes and repeated, "Based on your grades, I seriously doubt you could succeed in any college."

I slumped in the chair. I wanted to protest and say, "You're Crazy!" But I was too unsure of myself. She was right. I hadn't done that well at Central. College probably wasn't for me.

"Whatever you think, Miss White."

"That's very wise, Anderson. We'll get you enrolled in something useful."

She busied herself with paperwork, signing me up to attend a half day of school in my senior year and work at a job for the other half. The cooperative-education program was designed to give mediocre students a head-start on finding full-time employment to support them after high school.

A buddy of mine, Al Burt, was in the cooperative-ed program. He worked as a messenger for the Arkansas Department of Revenue, in the state Capitol Mall. He'd probably be able to get me a job, too.

I put on my Sunday church suit, looking sharp as ever, and went down to the Capitol. After telling the department supervisor about my work experience at Safeway, he said, "sure, he'd hire me."

I stayed at Safeway through the summer and explained my plans to Mr. Henderson, who wished me well. I knew I'd miss Safeway, but I also looked forward to the new job. I'd earn more money and, better yet, I'd get nights and weekends off. That way I would have a lot more time to spend with Sandra and party with my boys.

I reported to work at 7:30 a.m. and stayed through lunch. Then I'd head to school for the basic classes needed to graduate: English, math and science. Basically, the job involved driving around, going to different government offices and dropping off memos and packages. I would swing by campus at every opportunity. In the four-door Ford sedan, dark-blue car with state tags, I looked like an undercover police officer. I noticed students checking out the car, wondering who was I working for.

My supervisor, Mr. Stevenson, a white guy in his early 40s with a friendly face and a good build, quickly noticed that I was the hardest worker among the cooperative-ed students. He started giving me more responsibility and more hours. I would leave the house before dawn and head to the big post office downtown to pick up all the mail for the Department of Revenue. I'd be busy sorting it when the other students arrived at 7:30.

With the extra hours, my paychecks grew fat. For the first time, I could afford my own car. I didn't have to look long. On my delivery route, I'd seen a car for-sale across from an insurance agency on Main Street where I frequently went for pickups and deliveries. It was a white two-door 1965 Chevy in great shape. It had white interior, white floor mats and all the original equipment. I must have stayed there 20 minutes walking around that car.

I couldn't wait to tell my mother. The next morning, I dragged her out there. I had called the owner. He met us and allowed me to take it for a test drive with my mother. After some whining, on the ride back, she agreed I should buy it. I had saved $200; she loaned me the other $300.

Life couldn't get any better. I was driving around with my own wheels. What freedom. I came and went as I pleased. I was close to graduation and felt like my own man. I put all my money into that car, buying wide tread tires, new silver rims and a great sound system. Soon, I was bouncing up and down the street just like my man, Froggie Walker.

ON June 2, 1972, I sat in a blue cap and gown in the air-conditioned Barton Coliseum, where high school graduation ceremonies were held. The place was crowded. My graduating class numbered 600 plus, and the bleachers were filled with proud families. I spotted Momma high up in the bleachers with Aunt Otha and Uncle Coleman. Erma would be home from college the next day. She had final exams and couldn't make the ceremony.

I slumped in my chair, looking bored as the tedious ceremony droned on for hours. Inside, I was glowing. It was my big day. A milestone in my life. No more hassles with school and Momma. I was done with my childhood; ready to be a man. No more being bossed around. I'd be living on easy street now. I remembered the fat bag of marijuana hidden under the driver's seat in my car. I couldn't wait to fire up a big one. Celebrate the moment. We were going to party hard tonight!

Bobby T had scored some acid. Otis had a case of our favorite beer, Schlitz Malt Liquor, waiting on ice.

Finally, the ceremony ended and I pushed through the crowd to find my family. Everyone had tossed their caps into the air. I kept a hold of mine and had it in my hand. I had hardly worn my mortarboard, because I didn't want it messing up my short, neatly combed afro. Momma was dressed in a bright yellow dress and was busy snapping pictures of me. She lifted up on her tip-toes and kissed me on the forehead. Her face beamed with pride. I enjoyed seeing her so happy, but was antsy to join my dogs. I didn't have to tell her I'd be home late.

There was a whirlwind of parties that night, drinking and carousing until 6 a.m. We crashed at Bobby T's house and I finally dragged my butt into the house the next morning at 11. Hung over all the way, I planned to spend the day in bed. Sandra and I had a date that night.

When I walked into the house, I could feel the tension in the air.

Erma was seated on the living room couch and called for me to come in and sit down.

"Child please," I said. " I need to go to bed."

Erma could see I was hung over. She and Momma had been talking about me for hours that morning. Nothing would derail their plans to confront me.

"Mom and I want to talk to you, Brother," Erma said.

She was dressed in blue jeans and a Langston U T-shirt. She had matured into a tall, slender woman, light-brown skin and long flowing thick black hair. She exuded an air of sophistication that she must have acquired at college, where she had earned one of the highest grade point averages among her class.

In contrast, I barely made it out of high school. My grade point average was a dismal 1.5, a D-plus. I had been hired full-time by the messenger service and planned to get my own place by the time my Honey Pie, Sandra, graduated from Central High the following year.

As Erma sat on the couch, my mother walked in from the kitchen. She was wearing a flowered house dress and terry-cloth slippers. We all sat looking at each other as the portable air-conditioning unit rattled in the front window.

"I applied for you to attend Langston," Erma said. "And I've even arranged for you to receive financial aid."

I was stunned.

Langston? What was she talking about?

My face must have given away my reaction. I wasn't going to Langston. My friends were here. Sandra was here. I wasn't college material, anyway. I was going to make it without that crap. Lots of other men had.

"Brother, now listen to me," my mother said.

"Don't ya'll start on me."

I sprung from the chair and headed for the front door. I reached in my front pants pockets for the keys to the souped-up Chevy. I was getting out of here. This was my life. I would make all the decisions that affected Andy Capp.

I had my hand on the door knob when Erma jumped on my back, knocking us both to the floor. She grabbed me around the neck and hung on for dear life.

"You're not going anywhere, Brother. You walk out that door and I know what'll happen. You'll end up in jail like all your other drugged-up friends. You aren't doing anything with your lives. You can do better than that, Brother. We don't want you to become another black man, falling victim to the streets, their lives wasted."

She was in tears. I wanted to punch her but felt bad for making her cry. She couldn't hold me down for long. I stood up, carrying her with me because her arms were so tightly wrapped around my neck.

"Stop it, you two. Stop it." Momma had tears in her eyes. "Both of you just sit down."

I was angry at Erma, but I couldn't stand to see my mother cry. It cut right through me, my layers of toughness peeling away like an onion and revealing a still vulnerable and scared kid. Tears welled in my eyes.

"You need to go to college," Momma said.

She sat beside me on the couch and put her hand on my cheek. "Brother, you know you need to go." I couldn't look away from her. I didn't want to go. But I knew she was dead right. I was going to go to Langston.

I reached over and hugged her. Erma came over and sat on the other side of my mother. We must have made quite a sight. The three of us hugging and crying.

Not long afterwards, a letter arrived from Langston University, awarding me full tuition, plus room and board. I couldn't back out now. "Erma Genie." That's what I started calling her. I couldn't believe my smart sister had made it all happen so easily. I laid in my twin bed at night, flipping through the college's brochures. I didn't read the text. I looked at the pictures, imagining myself in the campus scenes, surrounded by smart black people.

I WAS worried about starting college in the fall. With my poor grades and lack of college-prep courses in high school, I'd lag far behind the other students.

To get a head-start, I decided to enroll in summer classes at the University of Arkansas at Little Rock. I signed up for world civilization and freshman math. Not only would the credits transfer to Langston, but I also figured I could learn some self-discipline and study habits.

I walked nervously across campus on my first day of classes. I noticed right away that there weren't many black people around. The stately maroon brick buildings, manicured landscaping and sea of white faces made me wonder if college would be the right environment for me.

I found the right building and walked into an auditorium that served as the classroom. A few hundred students sat at small desks waiting for class to begin. The rows of seats slanted steeply down to the front where a small podium and microphone waited for the professor's arrival. I took a seat in the back and scanned the crowd.

I counted two black students, two girls.

At Central High, a solid third of the student body was black. It was easy to fall into a clique of kids and feel at ease, even in a predominantly white high school. I could tell there'd be none of that here.

The white students appeared so at ease. They leaned over and made fast friends with the people sitting next to them. I glanced at the students around me. They avoided my gaze. The chatty students fell silent as a 30-ish man walked in, wearing jeans, a tweed blazer and his long hair tied in a ponytail. "Cool," I thought.

I perked up in the seat. As the professor began asking questions, checking to see how much we knew about world civilization, I raised my hand again and again. I was eager to demonstrate my newfound positive attitude in class. He didn't call on me, though. I imagined the room from his vantage point. Surely, my black face stood out in all this whiteness.

The year was 1972. But higher education for blacks hadn't changed much in the South since the 1950s. I remember Gov. George Wallace had stood at the entrance to the University of Alabama, blocking the entrance of one black student not that many years before. Wallace shouted in the face of the Deputy Attorney General of the United States, who arrived to personally read an order from a U.S. District Court judge ordering the university to admit the black student. Wallace screamed, "Segregation in the past, segregation today, segregation forever!"

In 1969, for instance, the first black had broken the color barrier to play for the University of Arkansas' football team. The Razorbacks consistently landed a spot on the list of Top 25 college teams in America. It had been the dream of so many black boys to play ball for the Southern football powerhouses: the University of Mississippi, the University of Alabama, University of Georgia and the University of Tennessee. But they were flatly refused a chance to play.

John L. Richardson was the first black to play for the Razorbacks. He was a local kid, a star at the all-black Horace Mann High School. Erma went to school with him, although he was two years ahead of her. John was a legend in town, considered by the locals to be their own Jackie Robinson, the first black allowed to play Major League Baseball in the late 1940s. Every black in town cheered John Richardson on and followed his stats in the local paper like a proud parent.

I hadn't expected such a chilly reception at the University of Arkansas at Little Rock. My second day of world-civ class wasn't much better. The professor asked the students about Darwin's theory of evolution. I knew about that, although as a Christian, I didn't believe in it. I raised my hand. Again, only white students were called on to speak.

I felt my confidence slipping away.

The white students sounded so smart, so polished, with their perfectly enunciated words and grammar. I glanced at the other two black students. They looked nervous, too. I thought the three of us should have sat together. Safety in numbers. But it was an unwritten rule that when blacks were outnumbered by whites, we kept away from each other. Our survival depended on chumming around with white students. That was our only hope of gaining acceptance. Or so we thought.

As the summer wore on, I fell further and further behind in both classes. I psyched myself up for the first test in world-civ. I did all the reading and crammed until 1 a.m. The test came back. I had failed.

In my mind, I blamed the teacher for flunking me because I was black. I didn't realize how ill-prepared I was for college as a result of my party attitude at Central High. My writing skills were inadequate. My composition in essay questions was lacking.

I was doing just as poorly in math. The professor skimmed through much of the material, figuring the students had learned it in high school. I, the only black in the class, had not. I'd never seen algebraic equations and geometric theories. My high school guidance counselor figured it would be a waste of time for me to take such classes. Now, I was making straight Fs on the exams.

I felt myself straddling two worlds. Often, after class, I'd rush to my car and drive straight for my neighborhood. I'd drink a beer, smoke a joint and feel like I could finally relax and just be Andy Capp.

I didn't like the white college environment. But I told myself it was worth the struggle. I was a trailblazer, cutting a path for the blacks who would come after me. That made me feel special.

Despite my setbacks, college did make me feel special. I saw the faces of neighbors and Momma's friends light up when she told them her son was attending college. They were impressed. I stopped by Central High one day to get a copy of my high school records to take with me to Langston. I bumped into one of my former English teachers, Mrs. Bullock.

"What are you doing now, Anderson?" she asked.

"Taking classes at UALR. I'm going to Langston University next month."

Mrs. Bullock, one of the few black teachers at Central, looked surprised. She turned away her gaze.

"I thought you'd be in jail, Anderson. You were such a wild boy."

I thought about her words that night laying in bed. I wasn't sure if I could make it through college like Erma and Sandra's parents. I wanted to believe in my ability. But, as the summer drew to a close, I dropped the math class to avoid getting an F. I didn't need that on my college transcripts. In world civ, I eked out a C.

As I packed for Langston, I vowed to work harder.

LANGSTON was an all-black college with black professors and black administrators. It sat in an all-black town, Langston, Oklahoma. Population 300. Added to that was 2,000 students and 500 college employees..

After the summer at UALR, it felt like Utopia to me. I didn't have to worry about my diction. The professors took a personal interest in the students, especially in me, when they learned I was Erma's little brother.

Everywhere I went, people called me Erma's little brother. She was a starlet at the college - smart, pretty, socially connected, a leader. That year, she ran for treasurer of the Student Government Association, and won. Her name was everywhere. It seemed to hang over me like a cloud.

I wondered if I could carve out my own identity at Langston. A major in accounting, like Erma, I had many of her teachers. Erma was one of just three people on campus to maintain a continuous 4.0 grade point average, a perfect record of straight A's. I'd have a lot to prove. I studied hard and made the honor roll my first semester.

I restricted my partying to the times when I'd finished my class work. Then, my best friend, Ruel Green and I, would head off in Ruel's brand new blue Mustang. Ruel was from Tulsa. He was a quiet and cool guy. I hooked up right away with Ruel and his Tulsa friends. They liked to party and smoke pot.

Ruel and I would drive over to the University of Oklahoma, about an hour away in a city called Norman, and look for girls and drugs. The University of Oklahoma was a huge place with 30,000 students and an urban feel that appealed to me. In contrast, Langston sat in a rural area. Few of Langston's students dressed and acted hip like me. Most were from small towns themselves.

Ruel and I, were soon making plans to transfer. Once we finished all the paperwork, we found an apartment and enrolled in the state school in the fall of 1973. I found it very stimulating. The university's football team was ranked "No. 1" in the nation that fall, spreading football frenzy and a rowdy partying mood throughout the campus. On Saturdays, when the team played, we'd party all day and all night. During the week, I attended classes and studied until late into the night.

The routine was fun for three months. Then, I became homesick and disenchanted by the impersonal environment of such a big university. Ruel had found himself a girlfriend and was spending all his free time with her. I wasn't doing too good in my classes. And I was lonely for friends and missed Sandra something bad. She had started attending Hendrix College in Arkansas, a small private college where rich white parents sent their kids. It was a tough school to get into. Sandra was among a handful of black students there. She was a National Scholastic Finalist.

For me, life had settled into a boring routine. I went to class, dutifully took notes, returned to the apartment, studied a bit and went to work at Safeway as a stock boy and a cashier.

The job was more to give me something to do than to earn money. Between my financial aid, the money my mother sent and my Safeway paychecks, I had plenty of money. I bought another car - a red and white 1967 Pontiac Grand Prix.

The college environment felt much like the University of Arkansas. The professors seemed indifferent to me. I felt little of the camaraderie that usually develops among college students. After doing so well at Langston, where I made the honor roll throughout my freshman year, I was frustrated by my poor performance. I began to attribute it to my skin color.

By Christmas break, when I received my grades in the mail, disappointed to see straight Cs, I decided not to return. I had picked up a magazine in the grocery story and flipped through a story that listed the Top Places in America For Professional Blacks. In the South, only

Atlanta and Houston ranked high.

Atlanta, I thought. That's where I wanted to be.

I checked out the college directory in the Little Rock public library and saw that I'd have plenty of colleges to choose from. The city has a University System that is comprised of six historically black colleges clustered in one area: Morehouse College (all male), Spelman College (all female), Atlanta University (then a graduate school), Morris Brown, Interdenominational Theological College and Clark College (now Clark Atlanta University).

I had been bouncing around between schools and knew I needed to find a place where I felt comfortable and could thrive academically. One of the colleges in Atlanta would provide the best of the two worlds I had encountered - a black college where the professors took a personal interest in students like me, coupled with an urban setting.

I had excelled at Langston and lost ground at the University of Oklahoma. I remember once going to my professor's office to get help in a math course at the University of Oklahoma. I arrived during his designated office hours, those times that professors set aside to meet with students one on one. This professor grew irritated with my questions.

"Didn't you learn this in high school," he finally asked in a biting, impatient tone.

I understood his tone. He didn't want me wasting his time because I hadn't learned the material in high school. He figured I wasn't bright enough to handle the course work, and probably here only because of affirmative action. It seemed that his opinion was, I just took up space that could have gone to a more qualified white kid.

Black colleges were use to offering remedial courses for students. The need for those courses had nothing to do with the students' abilities. Lots of students, like me, were never encouraged to take college-prep classes in high school. We floundered academically at college due to our lack of exposure, not because of our IQs. I had no doubt that I was as bright as any white student. I just hadn't received the direction, guidance and appropriate classes in high school to prepare me for college.

ATLANTA was intoxicating. There was no other way to describe it.

I'd never seen so many well-dressed black people in my life. In Little Rock, there were only one or two black police officers on the force. In Atlanta, there were black officers in almost every patrol car. The number of professionals - lawyers, doctors, accountants, politicians, and bankers - was phenomenal. Back home, a black hospital had meant an inferior hospital. In Atlanta, the mostly black hospital had the best equipment and the best trained staff.

I chose Clark College and enrolled as a business and accounting major in the fall of 1974. My enthusiasm for academics returned. I was studying hard, doing well and socializing with all kinds of people.

In the college compound stood a wall, on the same side of the street as Atlanta University, where students would gather and watch people go by. We'd hang out there, or my dorm mates and I would wander over to Spelman to eye the gorgeous females. We'd stop by the parking lot, get high in one of our cars and return to the wall. We'd stand there for hours, day after day, relaxing in a pot-induced daze and chatting with people.

The place had a street festival atmosphere. Street vendors would try to sell us trinkets. And one man, a Muslim, known as "Black Man," would rant about the white man being the devil. I'd stand and listen, not because I wanted to convert to Islam (I'm a devout Christian), but because the man gave away slices of cream cheese pies. They sure tasted great when I had the munchies from getting high.

My competitive streak emerged in my classes. I'd talk trash with my classmates, bragging that I would make the highest grade in class. Most of the time, I did. I'd sit up all night with my friend, Victor Jackson, a tall slender black male, born and raised in Atlanta, studying for exams and taking breaks to play a game of chess.

I developed a reputation as being such a good student that the business department chair, Dr. Barbara Jones, asked me to become a student teaching assistant. Soon, I was filling in as a substitute teacher for the accounting professors. I most liked substituting for Mr. Drake, who became a role model for me.

Mr. Drake was a Certified Public Accountant, a flamboyant man, who wore tailor-made suits, and drove a 454 SEL Mercedes Benz. I'd watch him get in the two-seat car. One day I'd own one, too, I promised myself.

I liked Atlanta so much that I decided to stay in the city the following summer. Through a job co-op program at Clark College, I found a job as a ramp agent at Atlanta's enormous airport. I worked for Delta Airlines, loading and unloading baggage, and transferring baggage to other planes.

The place was loud. But the work wasn't bad. On a normal shift, each crew would handle baggage from five flights. The rest of the time we'd hang out in the break room next to the gates. We'd play cards on the long wooden benches and wile away the time.

Right away, I sensed a deep hostility from many of the white ramp agents. The white agents segregated themselves into one section of the break room. The blacks gathered on the other side. Every day, the supervisor would come in early and write people's names on a chalk-board, assigning them to certain crews.

After the supervisor left, the white ramp agents would go to the chalkboard and start switching around names. If I had been assigned to a white crew, a guy would erase my name and assign me to a black crew. At first, I didn't mind. It was more comfortable to work with black guys anyway. But as the summer wore on, I began to resent it.

I decided to take a stand. When a white agent moved my name, I'd get up and move my name right back. The first time I did it, boy, they were shocked. I could read their thoughts: How dare this "uppity nigger" challenge their authority. I realized I had erred by letting them get away with it for so long. I should have stood my ground the first time it happened.

Within a week, the white agents were complaining routinely to the white supervisor about me. Hard to work with. Difficult attitude. Not a team player. Racist against white people. Too hard to get our work done with that guy around.

I knew nothing about their complaints. On the last day of my summer internship, I was summoned to a top manager's office for my exit evaluation. The man asked how I liked the job. I noticed his facial expression changed as he flipped through my personnel file. He began to read off the complaints. I asked who had made the complaints and wasn't surprised when the manager listed the names of the white agents. I was candid with the manager, telling him I thought the white agents resented seeing a young black man who was enrolled in college and on his way to a professional career. The white agents, on the other hand, weren't going to college. This would be their job for life.

I told the administrator - a nondescript middle-aged white man - that I wanted to contest each and every entry. He looked pensive for a moment and then got up and went out through his glass door. Twenty minutes later, he returned. He sat down behind his desk and said he would make whatever changes were necessary in my file so that I could return to Delta after college, if I wanted to.

I was relieved. I did not need a reputation as being difficult in mixed racial groups. Whether the administrator feared a discrimination claim from me or truly believed that I'd been wronged, I don't know. But at least I'd now be able to use Delta Airlines as a reference.

The episode made me happy to return to the all-black setting at Clark College. Those kinds of prejudices never happened there. I was beginning to see how white men expect black men to act subservient in some situations, "To be A Steppin Fetchit." If I didn't play along, I could expect retribution.

That fall, I found myself rolling in money. I had received another scholarship for being the male with the highest grade point average on campus. That gave me more than enough money for tuition and fees. I moved into a luxury apartment, off-campus, complete with its own fire place and other amenities, and used the extra money to pay for a campus meal plan. Rather than having to worry about shopping and cooking, I ate three good meals a day on campus. Surprisingly, the college cafeteria had great food.

My academic performance was getting noticed. Two prestigious colleges, Harvard University and Massachusetts Institute of Technology, were trying to recruit me for graduate school. The two colleges had made arrangements to bring several high achieving black students to Boston for interviews. If all went well, I could receive full tuition and board.

I knew Harvard was one of the best colleges in America, even the world. But I didn't understand the opportunity that was being handed to me. After the trip to Boston, I turned down both offers and decided to work for a big accounting firm in Atlanta. Over the years, I've doubted my decision not to attend one of those colleges. I can only say that's what I wanted to do then.

I was interning for a big accounting firm, Main LeFrantz and Company, which had offices worldwide. As the internship was ending, I just happened to be selected as the class spokesman for the college's annual employer-internship banquet. The formal dinner was an impressive event. The college president and top administrators would attend, as well as representatives from some of the biggest companies in town. As spokesman, I would offer a student's perspectives on the opportunities presented by the internship program.

I prepared and practiced my speech for weeks, and delivered it with aplomb.

The banquet hall filled with applause and I received many compliments as I made my way back to my table. Afterward, while all the guests were mingling around, the main partner from Main LeFrantz came up and offered me a job. I accepted on the spot.

I was on a roll. Just before graduation, I was voted Most Outstanding Student in Accounting by the faculty and Most Outstanding Student in Business by college alumni.

After I started working full-time, I learned the main reason I had been hired: Main LeFrantz was the auditor for several colleges in the Atlanta University Center. To keep the contract, the colleges demanded the firm hire more minorities. I was their living proof that the firm was acting in good faith to comply. I was the second black professional in the firm.

OVERNIGHT, I moved into a higher level of professionalism. My mother took me shopping and bought me ten new suits. She knew the importance of dressing well. In the corporate world, appearance can count as much as 90 percent for the beginning of professional success.

I enjoyed moving beyond the menial work of an intern and was getting directly involved in audits. My first audit was back at Morris Brown College, within the Atlanta University System. During my undergraduate days at Clark College, the student interchange system among the schools, allowed me to take several classes on Brown's campus. I made an appointment and introduced myself to the college president and other administrators. They treated me with such respect and deference. They knew the power I wielded. Auditors don't just analyze numbers. They draw conclusions about whether an individual and a department are following proper internal procedures. No one wanted to be on the receiving end of a critical audit.

Unknown to me, a historically black college in Daytona Beach was demanding Main LeFrantz send a black auditor as part of its contract. I was called into the office of one of the firm's partners and told to pack some belongings. I was going to Bethune-Cookman College in Daytona Beach.

Two senior white auditors and I left on a late Sunday night flight for Daytona Beach. I'd never been to Florida and wondered if the pictures - sandy and clean beaches, palm trees and sunny blue skies - were for real. We checked into a hotel on the beach. I sat up late, listening to the sound of waves crashing ashore and reflecting on how far I'd come.

We had our work cut out for us. The college needed us to reconstruct many of its financial records. The college had purchased a new IBM computer system, entered all its financial information and threw away the precious hard copies of the documents. The system crashed. All their data was gibberish. And their old paperwork was gone.

It would be tedious work. I wasn't looking forward to starting work the next day.

But I was eager to see this historical institution. I had learned about the college's founder, Dr. Mary McLeod Bethune, while I attended Langston and Clark colleges. She was as prominent a figure in black history, as Thomas Edison was to white history.

We drove from the beach, across a bridge over the Halifax River and onto the mainland. We entered a small black business district on Mary McLeod Bethune Boulevard, then called Second Avenue. I could see the red brick buildings of the campus and its sign, designed in maroon and gold, the school's colors. We pulled into a drive, shaded by large oak trees, and parked in front of White Hall, the main administration building with its white columns, crisp white trim and air of authority.

The three of us piled out of the car and started to unload our equipment and files from the trunk. The senior member of the team, Jim Bell, pointed out a large, gray historical marker and said that was where Dr. Bethune was buried. Her grave sat behind the stately, two story, wooden white house where she had lived on campus. The house had been turned into a museum in her honor.

She was a legend. The 15th of 17 children born to freed slaves, Mary Jane McLeod was born July 10, 1875, near Mayesville, South Carolina. She arrived after Emancipation, but several of her older siblings were born into slavery. At the age of 7, she attended school for the first time and would say as an adult, "The whole world opened to me when I learned to read."

Her parents, dirt-poor farmers in South Carolina, encouraged her quest for learning but were unable to finance her dream of a college education. A teacher of hers introduced her to a white dressmaker, Mary Crissman from Colorado, who offered to pay for Mary Jane's schooling at Scotia Seminary, now known as Barber-Scotia College, in Concord, N.C.

Mary Jane's plan was to become a missionary to Africa. After receiving another scholarship, she attended the Bible Institute for Home and Foreign Missions. She studied diligently for two years to prepare herself for missionary work but was repeatedly told by the Presbyterian Board of Missions that there were no openings for "colored missionaries."

A strong, hard-willed young woman, she decided to shift her attention to educating African-Americans in this country. She spent years teaching at various black schools in the South. During that work, she learned about the deplorable conditions in which blacks were living while building the Florida East Coast Railroad.

At the age of 29, already married to Albert Bethune with a baby boy, she decided to open a school for girls in Daytona Beach. "$1.50 and faith in God," it would later be said, created the Daytona Normal and Industrial School for Training Negro Girls. It sat beside the railroad tracks in a wooden lean-to. When the doors opened in October 1904, she had five girl students, ages 8 to 10. The girls' families were to pay 50 cents for tuition. But it was always fund-raising, then and now, that would keep the place alive.

The school grew quickly through the years, adding more buildings on land that once had been used as the town dump. In 1923, it merged with the Cookman Institute for Boys, then located in Jacksonville, and became Bethune-Cookman College. She served as college president until 1942 and, even afterward, remained closely tied to the institution. She died at her desk in the two-story white wooden home in 1955 and was put to rest in the backyard.

Dr. Mary McLeod Bethune, a big-boned, tall imposing woman with masculine features and hair that turned snow white in her later years, was known for far more than her college. She served as an advisor to four U.S. presidents and was a close personal friend of Eleanor Roosevelt. The First Lady even spent the night on campus as a guest of Dr. Bethune's - a shockingly bold move for a wealthy white woman in the segregated South of the 1930s.

AS WE unloaded our equipment and files, we were greeted by a college administrator who led us into the front entrance of White Hall. Over the double, white wooden doors was painted Dr. Bethune's motto in black letters: "Enter to Learn, Depart to Serve."

As we walked into the cool dark building, I could see an auditorium straight ahead. The doors were open and I could see on the stage hung a huge picture of Dr. Bethune. She was older in the painting - white-haired and exuding an air of gentle nobility. I was surprised by the depth of racial pride that I suddenly felt so strongly. It was unlike anything I had felt at Langston or Clark. It was a high-voltage electrical charge because this college, just like so many blacks, had developed and flourished under the harshest of circumstances.

We were led into the office suite of the college president and sat down in an adjoining conference room. The president, Dr. Oswald P. Bronson, Sr., was traveling that day, raising money for the college. Behind the desk in his personal office also hung a picture of Dr. Bethune. I paused again and thought about what a determined spirit it took to create all of this.

We settled around the large conference table. On the wall behind my chair was an oil painting of a 50s-ish black man with dark-rimmed glasses, jet black wavy hair, a receding hairline, very pleasant and warm face and well dressed in a brown suit.

"That's Dr. Bronson," Jim Bell said, noticing me looking at the picture. "He travels a lot. But I'm sure you'll get to meet him before the audit is over."

I finally did two weeks later. Dr. Bronson seemed to take an immediate interest in me. I'm not sure why. I guess he saw me as a young, ambitious and educated black man. I didn't realize that Bronson and a few other college administrators were plotting a way to hire me away from Main LeFrantz. I was just who they needed in their business office.

When Dr. Bronson first mentioned the idea to me, I played hard to get. I had already decided I would jump at a chance to work at this college. But by holding out, I hoped to get a decent-sized raise out of the move.

This would be an ideal chance for me to return to a black environment, one that was filled with intellectuals. The place felt so vibrant and energetic. It drew me in on the first day. I could be safe in a place like this. Blacks are in charge and can thrive in various professional careers here. The whole mystique of the place and of Dr. Bethune was so contagious. I accepted the employment position. This was where I wanted to be.

Two of Dr. Bethune's grandchildren still worked on campus. Evelyn Bethune was a telephone operator in the main administration building. Albert Bethune worked in the library. I took every chance to talk to them, enchanted by the remaining family lineage.

The setting appeared to meet all my social and professional needs. No longer did I have to worry about splitting verbs every now and then. I knew my chances for advancement would be strong in such a small environment, where the leader of the institution had already taken a personal interest in me. I knew I would shine here.

Racial tensions and prejudices would not be able to scale the campus walls and reach me. My people will surely take care of me, and I will take care of them. Why suffer in the massive white world, when I don't even have to be exposed to it anymore?

Little did I know this environment would prove to be my downfall. A famous Native American named Chief Joseph, once said, "It does not require many words to speak the truth."

TWO

Shades of masculine beauty appear
crystal clear.

Brightly colored cosmic suitors gravitate
to the juices that overflow rivers.

Fascinated by the influence that the two
bring to the table.

No one else exists except us two.
We sponge to soak up what the others make up.

I want to be a part of you.
I want to remain in my own cover.
I like me too, but I want to be you.

I want to impress everybody with me being you.
I know you want to be me too.

5 GREED

"Love of money is the mother of all evils."
Diogenes, Greek philosopher (400-325 B.C.).

WELCOME HILL FAMILY was written in black letters on a sign held above the crowd by a man in a black polyester suit, white shirt, black bow-tie and black cap, the customary, crisp uniform for the drivers of an Atlanta limousine service. He was standing in the main terminal of Atlanta International Airport, waiting for a family of four, arriving on a 12:35 p.m. flight from Daytona Beach. I had now only known Bill Williams for a short "mind-blowing" period of time.

Our driver didn't know what we looked like and was busy scanning the faces of the people stepping off the escalator, leading up from the concourse walkway below, and heading to claim their luggage, get a rental car or meet family and friends.

Andy, my 6-year-old son, with sprouts of black curly hair on his head, spotted the driver first.

He and Lauren, his 4-year-old sister, her long sandy hair bouncing with a headful of colorful ribbons, took off running.

They were excited about riding in a dark gray stretch Cadillac, an indulgent assortment of accessories waiting in its cool interior, including a TV and a bar. During the flight, I told them we were treating ourselves to a limo ride to our hotel, instead of having a relative pick us up.

They had never ridden in a limo, although they had seen Bill Williams' dark blue Lincoln Continental limo pick me up at our home several times. Andy ran up to the young white driver and tugged on his trousers.

"We the Hills," Andy blurted incorrectly, but nevertheless proudly. "Where's your limo?"

The driver appeared surprised that he had been waiting for such a casually dressed family on a Tuesday afternoon. Usually, he was dispatched to pick up dignitaries and wealthy businessmen, especially during the work week. I doubted his reaction stemmed from seeing a black family. Atlanta, after all, is a black Mecca. He picked up affluent and powerful blacks all the time. But picking up a young family, with small children, was a rarity.

Our extravagance may have seemed like a waste of money. But I had quickly adopted the pampered lifestyle of Bill Williams. Luxury transportation was the only way to travel. Limos and first-class airfare. Not only was it more comfortable, but I reveled in smugness as I watched the people pass by me in the first-class cabin on their way back to those cramped coach seats or as they saw me step from a limo onto the sidewalk. "Must be nice," their glances seemed to say. "Yeah. It is," my eyes replied.

Lauren and Andy walked over to the baggage carousel with the limo driver. The man gathered our luggage as Lauren pointed to our belongings. The driver wheeled the baggage cart through the high-ceilinged airport and outside to a cloudless, blue sky and muggy, hot day.

He immediately went to the passenger door of the limo, opened it and stood attentively as we climbed in, kids first, then Sandra and finally, me. The kids squealed in delight as they saw all the amenities contained inside of the automobile. Telephones, television, bar, and all types of remote controls. The smoked glass window, between the driver and passenger compartment, started going up and down, which was being playfully controlled by our children's curious fingers. Sandra and I, romantically looked at each other and smiled, before we told the kids to stop.

Off we went to the Marriott Marquis, a 50-story hotel in downtown Atlanta. The interior of the hotel was breathtaking with an atrium and glass elevators that we could watch traveling up and down the 50 floors.

"We have been expecting you, Mr. Hill," one of the bellmen said as he led us to the check-in desk. "Mister McGrath said to treat you well doing your stay with us."

David McGrath was my neighbor in Daytona Beach, living right across the street from me in Pelican Bay. He was a managing partner in the Daytona Beach Marriott, an oceanfront high-rise hotel, the only one to receive five-stars in the Daytona Beach area. He was well-known throughout the Marriott chain and had taken care of our hotel arrangements in Atlanta. Judging by our room, he had some pull. We were given a sprawling suite on the 49th floor of the hotel.

I remember when I first met David. We had just moved into Pelican Bay. He saw me in my yard and came over. He stood 5-foot-10 with an average build, wire-rimmed glasses, graying hair and an Izod golf shirt.

"It must be nice for black folks to be able to afford a home like this," he said in a pleasant Southern voice, smiling at me. "What type of work do you do?"

My voice reverberated with an affluent indignation as I replied.

"Excuse me, are you implying that black people can't live on Pelican Bay Drive?"

"Of course not," he said. "Would you get real? I just want to know who you are!" I filled him in and we became friends on the spot. Our children played together, we attended some social events together, and we crossed paths at business functions.

We were in Atlanta for the grand opening of Underground Atlanta, a collection of shops and eateries under the downtown area of Atlanta. My younger brother-in-law, Lloyd (who, I should note, was the first black Student Government Association President at Central High) served as the tenant design architect for Rouse Company on the renovation of the historic complex. He invited us to celebrate the opening with him.

I had visited Underground Atlanta when I was a student at Clark College. Back then, it was in a down-turn, struggling economically and structurally. Now, it sparkled with fountains, glass walls, vendor carts, crowded stores and people everywhere.

The trip seemed to be filled with pleasant surprises at every turn. In the hotel elevator, I ran into Deion Sanders, the number one draft pick for the Atlanta Falcons pro football team, who was accompanied by an attractive young lady.

On another night, when Sandra and the kids had plans of their own, I decided to walk over to a hot nightspot, called Atlanta Nights, and meet an old friend from college for drinks. As I walked out of the hotel, I noticed a new black BMW at the curb. Behind the wheel sat Dominique Wilkins, superstar basketball player with the Atlanta Hawks pro team. I had watched him play in many games.

"Hey, will you give me a ride over to Atlanta Nights," I asked him through his rolled-down window. I expected him to say, no.

"Get in, I'm going that way," he said and started up the car.

We talked basketball on the 10-minute ride to the club, mostly about whether the Hawks could win an NBA championship. Then his cell phone rang and interrupted our conversation.

"Hey, brother," he said into the phone. I eavesdropped on his conversation and could tell he was talking to his brother, Gerald Wilkins, who then played for the New York Knicks and now with the Orlando Magic.

As we pulled up to the club, I noticed a long line wrapping around the block. I was about to walk to the back of the line when Dominique called out to me and pointed to the bouncer at the front door. The bouncer was waving me in. No one in the line even grumbled at my special treatment. They were too busy talking about seeing Dominique. I must be important to be chauffeured by the "human highlight film," as the star player was known in the NBA.

Could all of this be happening to me? I thought as I walked into the club. I chalked it up to my Midas Touch. Lucky, Anderson, that's who I was. Bob Billingslea had introduced me to a developer named Bill Williams just two weeks earlier. The guy was promising to send all sorts of business my way. My financial outlook was looking brighter by the minute. Singer and former Television Entertainer Melba Moore had performed for the college President's Ball at our club. We also had recently entertained Edward Patten and William Guest, formerly of *Gladys Knight & The Pips,* at our home. The dinner lead us to create a new corporation called *Pips II,* for investment and speculation, in the Mirage.

I HAD visited Williams' office in Orlando for the first time, two days before departing for Atlanta.

I drove to the far side of Orlando, took the Kirkman exit off Interstate 4 and passed Universal Studios Florida, which was then under construction. I turned into the parking lot of the 10-story Orange Bank building - framed in solid glass, darkly tinted. Bill must be paying a fortune in rent, I thought.

When I stepped off the elevator on the sixth floor, I saw the wooden door with a gold plate, engraved with black letters, Renselear

Development Corporation. An attractive, young, light-skinned secretary was seated at a desk inside the door. She buzzed Bill, who came right out and shook my hand.

I again admired his taste in clothes; he always seemed to wear a different tailor-made suit. I don't think I ever saw him wear the same one twice. We walked back to his office and, as we passed through the corporate headquarters, he introduced me to various staff members, including his corporate executive administrator, O.J. Tate. At the time, I thought Tate was a well-tanned white guy but later learned he was African-American.

Of course, Bill's personal office was impressive. The walls were covered with snapshots of him with famous people, including President Reagan and President Bush. There was another one of him with heavy-weight boxing champion, Mike Tyson.

This guy has some serious contacts, I thought. I studied each picture to make sure it was real. I knew a few people who had their pictures taken with life-sized cut-outs of famous people.

The office was twice the size of mine, which I had always con-sidered large, and sat in a corner of the building. Ceiling to floor win-dows, covered the two outside walls, which gave a view of the large-scale construction taking place at the future Universal Studios.

"That is going to be quite a development," Bill said, noticing me watching the construction crews and heavy equipment moving around the site.

"How do you like that car?" he asked, pointing below to an isolated section of the parking lot where a drop-top, powder blue, brand new Rolls Royce was parked. "I just got it."

"Nice, '' I replied. "I've never driven a Rolls. I bet it's quite a machine."

"I'll have to take you for a ride sometime."

We turned back to his office. An oversized, dark wooden desk sat in one corner with three telephones on top. Two plush chairs sat facing the desk. And in the far end of the office, there was a small, intimate sitting area with a brown leather couch, matching love seat and wooden coffee table. That's where we sat down as Bill started talking about the stories behind his pictures with certain dignitaries and his contacts in town. Bill always was a name-dropper.

"I've had all sorts of people here to see me," he said. "The governor. The mayor. Congressmen. State representatives."

I noticed a model blimp on a side table. It was anchored to a bronze pedestal and sat under a thick glass enclosure. When I showed an interest in the curio, Bill said it was a prototype for one of his companies which sold advertising nationally on the sides of blimps.

"I have a strong interest in air travel and air advertisements," he said. "I'm even a ten percent stockholder in TWA, you know, Trans World Airlines.

"I'm sure you are short on time, Anderson," he continued. "But I was hoping, if your schedule permits, that I could show you the Grand National Office Park. The one Bob Billingslea mentioned I'm trying to buy. It's 10 minutes away off International Drive. I'd like to have you look at the property."

"It will be my pleasure to ride with you, Big-timer," I said with a chuckle. I wanted to break up the formalities that Bill was putting on me, now that I was in his nest.

"I'm about to close the deal on the office park. I'll want you to meet with my tax attorney, Ken Freeman from Ohio," Bill said, maintaining his formal tone. "Ken will be flying down, hopefully this week to finalize the transaction with the sellers. I can use you as the escrow agent to handle the funding for the $13 million deal. Your fee will be $100,000, if you think that's acceptable."

I could tell it wasn't really a question. Bill knew I was salivating at the thought of $100,000. That money could finally lift me out of my hole. I'd known this man only a few days and he was already promising me some serious money.

I hadn't replied to his question when the door to his office opened without a knock and in strolled Tate.

"Anderson, we're glad to have you involved. As you no doubt have noticed, Bill is a very well-known person," he motioned to the photos on the wall. "He's had inquires from *Ebony* magazine and other national publications wanting to do stories about his success, but Bill's policy is to decline interviews. He says he wants to keep his good fortunes quiet."

"By working with Bill, you will make all sorts of contacts," Tate continued. "The mayor of Orlando, Bill Frederick, is a regular visitor.

Gov. Bob Martinez recently came in. And Bill is close friends with Jacob Stuart, the executive director of the Greater Orlando Area Chamber of Commerce. Jacob has been assisting Bill with introductions around town. It's been a big help. Bill, for instance, was just appointed to the prestigious United Arts Council. No black man has ever sat on that board."

All the bragging was getting a bit much for me. My head was bobbing up and down, acknowledging that I recognized the big names. These guys are slick and extremely self-promoting, I thought. In business, it's all about sales, even selling yourself.

Bill and I left for the office park and later I followed him to his home in Bay Hills, an upscale, gated, golfing community on the same side of town. As we pulled into his driveway - me in my Benz; him in the light blue Rolls - he hit the automatic garage door opener. Inside I could see a four-door, candy apple red Rolls Royce.

I was looking at it when Bill got out of his car.

"I don't drive that Rolls around much. With Orlando being such a small community, anytime people see a big black man like me in a Rolls, it attracts a lot of attention. If it became common knowledge that I had a du-wop (two), the very thought would kill them white folks." "Brother man, its killing me," I quickly replied.

Besides the two Rolls Royces, Bill also had a dark blue limousine that he said he kept at the office. He gave me a brief tour of his stately home and then I said I had to get going home.

"I think you should meet Dr. Bronson," I said. "If Bob Billingslea hasn't set something up already, I'll arrange a meeting for Dr. Bronson, you and myself."

Bill flashed me his charming smile. "Great, Anderson! That would be great."

TWO days later, I took Bill to Dr. Bronson's personal residence, in Daytona Beach.

"Brother Williams, one of my trustees told me about your meeting the other day with Brother Hill. He said it went quite well. I understand you're from Cleveland and have extensive construction experience. Can you get the necessary bonding? That's the major problem with almost all our minority contractors. They just can't get the bonding. Am I right Brother Hill?"

"Yes, sir."

"My company receives that kind of bonding all the time, Dr. Bronson," Bill said. "Although I agree that it's unfortunate that more minority contractors can't do the same. It stops them from getting ahead in this business."

Bill began telling Dr. Bronson about his affiliation with the Church of Christ. He sat on the national board and listed several prominent people in the church whom he knew. Dr. Bronson, whose background was as a minister, loved such church talk.

"I've tried to bring some of those very people here to speak to our students," Dr. Bronson said. "They are hard to get. Would you be able to help us secure any speakers?"

"Of course, Dr. Bronson," Bill answered. "That is why I'm here. To be of any assistance I can."

After working with Dr. Bronson for years, I could easily read his body language. I could tell he was impressed with Bill and wanted to do business with him. With the introductions out of the way, we sat down to talk business. Dr. Bronson outlined the construction plans for the two upcoming buildings and his long-term dreams of future college expansions. Bill told him about his work with Walt Disney World and other business ventures, and said Dr. Bronson could check with Bob Billingslea to confirm his experience.

As we concluded the meeting, Bill suggested we offer a prayer. The three of us joined hands.

"Lord, we have come here today in your spirit," Bill said in a heartfelt tone. "We need you, most Heavenly Father. Let this new relationship be fruitful and help it to unfold the way that it should in your eyes."

"Amen," Dr. Bronson and I said simultaneously. We opened our eyes and looked across at each other. Bill still had his eyes shut tight and appeared to be praying fervently. Several minutes elapsed. I bowed my head and waited. I knew Dr. Bronson was thinking the same thing I was: We finally found our man. He was exactly what the Board of Trustees had been demanding.

I WAS standing in my law office, looking out a window of my second-floor office, when I saw the light blue Rolls pull into the parking lot.

I jumped from my desk and ran down the stairs like a kid. I was secretly hoping he'd take me for a ride in the Rolls. He hadn't brought it up again since the meeting at his office.

"Let's get busy," he said, his usual greeting as we shook hands in the parking lot.

"That is one beautiful car," I said, walking over to it for a closer look. It had a brightly polished wood-grain dashboard and console, and white leather cushion seats.

"I had it shipped in from overseas," he said proudly. "You might have seen it featured in *The Orlando Sentinel*. Not too many of these cars around."

In the car's backseat brazenly sat the newspaper's transportation section with a big color photo of the light-blue Rolls. I looked over at my Benz and, for the first time ever, thought it was an inferior car. My standards were moving up.

"I should have called you," Bill was saying. "I wanted to come over and tell you how close the deal is on the Grand National Office Park. My tax attorney is coming to town and I want you to meet him at the attorney's office for the seller. It's on Magnolia Avenue downtown."

"When do you want me there?"

"Can you make it tomorrow?"

I had other appointments scheduled but would clear my calendar on a moment's notice for him.

"Sure."

When I arrived at the attorney's office the next day at 1:30 p.m., Bill introduced me to Ken Freeman, the tax attorney from Cleveland. He was a slender man who carried a very large black leather briefcase. Bill told Ken that I was acting as the escrow agent and was authorized to review the proposed contracts after the two sides agreed on the details.

We spent the rest of the afternoon finalizing the agreement. After we concluded the negotiations with the team of attorneys, bankers and real-estate brokers, Bill asked me to ride with him in his limo to the airport. Ken and one of his financial officers were taking his private jet back to Cleveland.

Private jet? This guy owns a private jet, too, I thought.

I expected it to be a small prop plane. As we arrived at Herndon Airport (only commercial carriers use the bigger Orlando International Airport), the limo driver pulled up to the private-executive flight center.

Bill pointed out the window. "That's my jet over there on the tarmac. Get out for a moment and take a closer look."

I had only been in one other private jet. It was owned by Kodak Corp. and used by entertainment giant Bill Cosby. Two years earlier, Dr. Bronson had persuaded the Cosbys to donate $750,000 to Bethune-Cookman College's science program. Cosby allowed Dr. Bronson to return home in the jet. Doc called me from the jet as it was on its way from New York to Daytona Beach.

"Brother Hill, I'm very happy to tell you the Cosbys have given a significant contribution to the college," he said over a phone line crackling with static. "This is a great day for the college."

"Do you want us to meet you at the airport? We could round up the band for a celebration."

"Good idea, Brother Hill. This does call for a celebration."

Unfortunately, I couldn't locate the band director. Instead, Tommy Huger and I drove to the airport. When the green and white Lear jet arrived, I felt butterflies in my stomach. I was nervous at the thought of meeting Bill Cosby.

When we climbed into the plane, I saw that Dr. Bronson was alone. He said Cosby couldn't make the trip. But he sure was happy with the $750,000 check signed by Camille Cosby. He kept waving it around all the way back to the campus.

Now, I was standing in the doorway of a similar Lear jet. I poked my head in and two pilots greeted me with a smile. I knew Bill didn't have the same kind of money as the Cosbys. I wasn't sure how much money it took to maintain such a lifestyle, but it was far beyond my reach, and I thought I was doing well.

Never exposed to such wealth, I was overwhelmed with Bill's material possessions. My goodness, I thought. This man has to be sent from God. What timing that he should arrive just when I was struggling to keep up with the significant debt payments on the Mirage, as well as my home and cars.

I knew Ken Freeman handled most of Bill's legal work. But the two of them had agreed that Bill needed an attorney in Florida. I was overjoyed at the opportunity. I had already mentioned the business arrangement to Dr. Bronson, who gave his approval for me to work for Bill as long as no conflicts arose with my duties for the college.

Because so much of Bill's work would involve real-estate trans-actions in Orlando, Dr. Bronson and I figured there would be little chance of a conflict of interest. I did explain to Bill, however, that if there ever were a perceived conflict, I would always defer to the college. About the same time, Dr. Bronson also gave his approval for Tommy Huger, the college's construction expert, to work for Bill. Tommy had been cool to Bill at the beginning. But after I told him about the possi-bilities of making big money, Tommy became excited about joining our team.

While I was working on the Grand National office park sale, Bill also took me to a vacant site on the southeastern edge of Orlando and explained that he was in a joint venture with a Chinese businessman from New York City to build a Great China tourist attraction (now called Splendid China). Expected cost: $34 million.

I had talked several times with the Chinese businessman, and had faxed back and forth the contracts that spelled out Renselear Develop-ment Corp.'s involvement in the project. Bill hoped not only to construct the theme park, he also wanted to go in as an investor. The blueprints called for a replica of the Great Wall, elaborate gardens, performers and Chinese food and gifts.

"Work hard on this one, Anderson," Bill had told me. "If we can get the numbers right, we'll make quite a sum of money off this project."

I pinched myself to make sure I wasn't dreaming.

My debts were mounting. I needed money badly. Besides paying my bills, I now owed the $35,000 that I had taken from the college's escrow account. Plus, I had recently borrowed $50,000 from the college's Executive Vice President, Dr. R.J. Gainous.

Dr. Gainous was a dear friend to me. Whenever I felt down or needed advice, I sought out his counsel. I would stop by his funeral home, where he divided his time with the college, and sit down for a chat.

I had gone there looking for money. I was tapped out at my bank. My line of credit was full and the bank refused to increase my limit.

"Come on in, Brother Hill," Dr. Gainous said. He was very handsome, slightly balding. His office was decorated in remnants from the early 1970s - avocado and gold tones. It seemed wasteful to Dr. Gainous to replace perfectly good furnishings only in the name of fashion.

"What's going on tonight?" he asked as I sat down in a leather green chair across from his desk. "How are things at the Mirage?"

"Well, Doc. I really need some help."

"Let me tell you something, Brother Hill. When you had your grand opening down there, you sent out a bunch of invitations. But you didn't send one to me and my wife. There were a lot of people in town who weren't invited - people who know you and Sandra. You hurt a lot of feelings by doing that. No wonder business is slow down there. I know people who swear they'll never set foot in the place."

He was right. At the time of the Mirage's grand opening, Sandra and I made up an invitation list that included people in their 20s and 30s, like us. We had assumed older people wouldn't want to come. But we failed to realize our purchase of the Mirage was a major event in Daytona Beach's black community. Both Sandra and I later learned how snubbed many people felt.

I bent over in the seat and buried my head in my hands.

"I know I've made some mistakes," I said. "I really need your help, Doc. I'm in tremendous straits."

I told him about the condominium plans and how they had fallen apart. I explained my overdue payments on the Mirage and that it wasn't making enough to cover the overhead. I had refused to put up a for-sale sign outside, but I was quietly looking for a buyer. A Venezuelan couple had promised to take it off my hands. They made two payments and split town, and once again the club was an albatross around my neck.

"What do you need, Brother Hill?"

"Money, Doc."

"How much?"

"Fifty thousand."

He leaned back in his chair for a few moments.

"Okay, Brother Hill. Come by tomorrow afternoon at one and we'll go to the bank."

I used the money to catch up on my past-due bills. Soon, I regressed to my wasteful-spending ways. I had developed a reputation, for example, of handing out $100 bills at parties and at my club during my episodes of grandeur, which were fueled by tequila and cocaine. Sometimes I'd give out more than $1,000 a night. I told people that I wanted to share my wealth. And partly, that was true. But mainly, it was my out-of-control ego that was running amok, looking for a crowd to idolize me.

My drug and alcohol abuse continued to be a source of worry for Sandra. To celebrate our 10th wedding anniversary, we decided to take a cruise to the Bahamas, where I would speak at an alumni convention held on board the luxury liner. It was a relaxing trip - with no kids around - and Sandra and I rekindled the strong and passionate love that we had shared for so long.

As we sailed back to Miami, Sandra and I stood on the deck of the ship.

"Anderson, I want you to stop drinking and using cocaine," she said.

"I know San. I'm trying to quit."

"I want you to do it for your physical health, Anderson. But also, the kids are getting older and I don't want them exposed to that kind of behavior."

"Yeah, I've thought about that, too. I guess it is time to quit."

"You're jeopardizing so much, Anderson."

I had recently received the Business of the Year Award from the Central Florida Community Development Corp. The Volusia County Area Chamber of Commerce also had honored us with the Outstanding Community Business and Service Award.

I promised Sandra that I would clean up during an upcoming trip to China with the Honorable Joseph W. Hatchett, a judge on the federal 11th Circuit Court of Appeal in Atlanta. We were to be part of a delegation in the fall that included the judge and other dignitaries. I certainly couldn't be drinking and tooting coke with them, especially when traveling overseas.

"We'll be gone almost a month. That will be the perfect time for me to sober up," I told Sandra.

Sandra accepted my promise without an argument. Quietly to herself, she prayed I wouldn't self-destruct before our scheduled departure.

TOMMY HUGER was busy at the college making sure Bill Williams received a major role in the construction of the Living Learning Center dorm, the first of the two new buildings going up on campus.

The college had hired Allen Green Construction as the construction manager and primary contractor on the project. Tommy told Allen Green to give Bill whatever subcontracting work had not yet been awarded. Allen Green Construction, a white-owned company, needed to hire minority subs to fulfill the Board of Trustee's directive. Tommy said Bill's company could handle the brick work on the building's facade, the roofing, painting and other tasks. Bill promised to immediately mobilize the needed crews because the building was under a rigid timetable for completion by September 1, 1989, five months away.

It didn't take long for Allen Green and Bill Williams to start fighting. On many occasions, Allen was forced to make payments on Bill's behalf to his suppliers and crews. Bill said he was having cash-flow trouble. As the person responsible for completing the building on time, Allen had no choice but to make the payments to keep the project on track. Allen complained to Tommy and me that Bill wasn't qualified for the job. Bill's irresponsible financial practices were becoming common knowledge around town.

Bill countered that Allen, a white man, was trying to make it hard for a black man to succeed. Allen was jealous that Bill would soon win all the college's construction work and was spreading vicious rumors about Bill because he threatened to take away business from white-owned companies.

I agreed with Bill and thought Allen was making things sound far worse than they were. In my opinion, any black person, who appeared successful, might receive some opposition from white people. To me, Bill performed better than any minority contractor we had found in our nationwide searches.

Bill admitted that he was having trouble meeting his payroll from time to time. As a businessman myself, I understood cash-flow problems. Bill was a black man with enormous talents. He just needed someone, such as me, to support him.

Bill began dropping hints that he wanted to serve as construction manager on the next big project, the Mary McLeod Fine Arts Center. Dr. Bronson and I had already promised the job to Tommy Huger.

"Tommy will not be able to mobilize the forces needed. Nor will he be able to receive the bonding required by the feds," Bill said.

I agreed. Despite the complaints from Allen Green, Bill was completing his assigned work on the Living Learning Center. Before long, Bill and I were planning for him to also handle other future projects - the Wildcat Student Center and the second phase of the fine arts center.

"I can use my lobbying firm in Washington, D.C. to assist with the movement of legislation through Congress to get the college the political funding," Bill promised.

When I recounted the conversation to Dr. Bronson, he agreed that we should give Bill as much work as possible.

IN JUNE 1989, while construction of the Living Learning Center was progressing, Bill signed a contract with the college to become construction manager for the Fine Arts Center. The project architect, Bill Faust, objected to the decision and argued for Allen Green to get the job. Allen assumed he would get the job if he did a good job on the Living Learning Center.

But Dr. Bronson and I had made up our minds. We wanted a black construction manager on a campus project, especially one undertaken in Mary McLeod Bethune's honor. Given the historical development of the college, it was long past due for black companies to start getting the lion's share of our business.

Tommy, of course, was upset, too. But Bill quickly smoothed

things over by promising Tommy a significant amount of work on his other projects throughout the Southeast. Tommy agreed to Bill's involvement and began drawing up the necessary documents on the fine arts center for my review and submittal to the federal government, which was footing the bill for the approximate 3 million dollar building.

I soon agreed to modify the documents to give Bill more upfront money, upon his request. The money was payment for working with the architect to ensure the building could be constructed within budget and within the allotted timeframe.

Bill Faust, the project architect, had received the job on the recommendation of Congressman Bill Chappell, who helped push through the federal appropriation to pay for the building. Within weeks of the project starting, Bill Faust and Bill Williams were at each other's throats. Faust echoed the same complaints as Allen Green. Williams again explained them away as racism.

In all honesty, my judgment was too clouded by greed to effectively evaluate the merits of the complaints. The day before Williams signed the contract to act as construction manager, he gave me a check for $10,000 from his upfront money. He said the money was payment for my fees on the Grand National and Splendid China projects. Both deals had fallen through.

He grew more bold in his dealings with me. I went to his office in Orlando one afternoon and he suggested we go out to dinner at the Peabody Hotel, a high-rise hotel near Orange County's sprawling convention center and the Sea World theme park. The Peabody would become our regular meeting place in the coming months.

I followed Bill in his light blue Rolls on the 20-minute drive from his office. As we pulled up, I saw that the bellmen recognized Bill's car and hustled over to open his car door. I pulled up behind in my black Benz. As Bill stepped from the car, he handed the valet attendant a $20 bill. He walked back to my car and told me to do the same. The guys treat your cars better that way, he said.

We walked into the restaurant and were immediately seated. The waiter came and I ordered my usual - straight tequila and a little water. Bill didn't drink alcohol. He had his usual Coke. After my third drink, as I ate an appetizer of duck and waited for my prime rib dinner to arrive, Bill said he wanted me to have the $40,000 payment he was about to receive from the college.

"What for?" I asked.

"You and I are partners. I want to be sure that you're taken care of. I need you to be satisfied with our business partnership because if we play this game right, we'll both make a lot of money. I'll be able to pay you $50,000 a month if things work out right."

"You want to give me your full payment?" I asked again, incredulously. I knew I should politely decline his offer, but I needed the money. Just a couple months ago, he had promised $100,000 in fees for the Grand National deal. Turned out I'd only received $10,000 so far.

"You need it, Anderson. Take it."

"We need to be careful about how we transfer this money. If people start seeing all this money coming from me to you, there'll be trouble," I said.

"My thoughts exactly," Bill said. "I'll tell you how we'll do it. We will create a corporation. Then we can move money between us and disguise it as corporate business. No one could tell a thing."

He took the paper napkin under his Coke glass, took a pen out of his inside suit pocket and wrote the words, Equal Dux.

"That is what we'll call it. You can handle all the details - filing the necessary paperwork with the state. This will be the deal: Whatever you bring in for me and the company, I'll give you half. Sound good?"

I nodded, busy eating my duck.

"Remember to cut Huger in for something," Bill said. "We have got to keep him happy. If he starts to feeling jealous about our business relationship, he could cause trouble. Huger is hungry, I can tell. Give him some money and he'll be fine. You don't have to give him a lot. I want you to have most of the $40,000. Just a little money, keep him hoping for more."

The next day, the college cut Williams a check for $40,000. He stopped by my law office and gave me a cashier's check for $40,000. From this, I wrote a check to Tommy for $7,500 and spent my share of the money that day catching up on my payments for the Mirage.

I was straddling two worlds. To the community, I appeared as a pillar, a role model. Dr. Bronson was placing more and more responsibility on me. I had just received the Faculty's Outstanding Community Services Award, a prestigious annual award voted on by the entire faculty. When Dr. Bronson presented me the award at a banquet at the Daytona Beach Hilton on the beach, he seemed to glow. There had been people over the years who had warned him about me being too ambitious and not loyal enough. As he stood there, I could tell he felt comfortable with the trust he had placed in me. He had groomed me, paying part of my way through law school and encouraging me to seek an internship with the Central Intelligence Agency in Washington, D.C. People whispered that I wouldn't return to Bethune-Cookman College. That I had just been using the college for my own advancement, but I had proudly returned.

My life looked good to the outside world. But inside, I knew I was following a dangerous and immoral path. I was accepting payments from Bill that weren't right. His financial net was pulling me in and I wasn't even putting up a struggle. Sure, I rationalized the payment as fees for all the time I spent on Bill's projects. But I didn't believe it. The sick feeling in my gut told me otherwise. I was gambling with my law career and could be disbarred by the Florida Bar Association, if I got caught.

I was at a crossroads and I decided to take the low road. All the money could solve any problems that come up, I reasoned. With my legal expertise and Bill's connections, if there's any trouble, we'll be able to wiggle right out of it.

A few days after I received the $40,000 check, Bill came by and gave me a corporate check for $15,000. He said I should use it however I needed. I deposited the check that same afternoon and wrote out several checks of my own to pay bills.

My bank called the following afternoon. Bill's check had bounced. "Oh No!" I thought as I hung up the phone. What's this guy pulling on me? Now wait a minute, just call him, maybe he's just having a temporary problem with cash flow. It happens to every businessman now and again.

When I reached Bill, he sounded very apologetic and said he didn't know what caused the mix-up in his account. He'd stop by the next day with a cashier's check. Within the same week, he also gave another $5,000 to Tommy.

The money was flowing. Two weeks later, Bill gave me a cashier's check for $25,000. With my newfound source of wealth, I was partying hard, buying all the cocaine I could pack in my nose, plus the noses of some friends. I had caught up on my past due bills and felt such a sense of relief at not having banks politely and relentlessly hounding me for money.

The partying became a regular event. Tommy and Bill called me from his private jet on their way back from a business trip. They had been lining up new clients out of state. Tommy told me to get my butt down to the Daytona Beach airport, so they could stop and pick me up. We could all party on the way to Orlando, where Tommy had his truck and he would drive me back.

Bill had bought a bottle of Jose Cuervo tequila just for me. I poured myself a big glass and went up to the cockpit after the pilots reached cruising altitude. I'd done a few lines of cocaine while I waited for them to arrive in Daytona Beach. Now, I was cranked on high, asking the two pilots to explain all the instruments and knobs. At one point, I happened to glance back into the cabin of the plane and caught Bill, leaning back in a captain's chair, watching me. He had such a look of superiority on his face, like he had manipulated me right where he wanted me.

You fool, I thought. I'm the one manipulating you!

I was beginning to have doubts though. Once we landed, Bill's limo took us back to his office to get Tommy's car. On the ride back to Daytona Beach, I quizzed Tommy to make sure Bill was completing the fine arts center on schedule.

Problems were arising, we both knew. Bill wasn't paying his suppliers and subcontractors, so they were threatening to stop work. Suppliers were refusing to deliver any more construction materials to the college until they were paid. Dr. Bronson and I had developed a payment system where the college paid those people directly and gave Bill payments for his fees, only.

I told Tommy that we had an obligation to protect the college, and he agreed. We were both earning salaries from the college. I, in particular, was earning good money from the college.

I received a tidy sum for negotiating the multi-million-dollar purchase of the future site of the Mary McLeod Bethune Fine Arts Center. The college bought the prime property from a local natural gas company and the Volusia County School Board. It would eventually become home to both phase 1 and phase 2 of the fine arts center.

The college's decision meant Bill's cash flow was shrinking. He came by and asked me to again modify his contract to give him more money. The contract called for him to receive $40,000 for reviewing the architectural plans. That was the money he gave me. Now he wanted another $90,000 for the same work. He assured me there would be sufficient money to cover the added expense without going over budget on the project.

I talked to Tommy and we agreed to do it. I rewrote the contract and Bill received a check for $86,447 from the college. Just like clockwork, as soon as he picked up the check, he stopped by and gave me roughly half - $41,000.

This was in early August of 1989. Construction had not yet started on the fine arts center. Completion of the Living Learning Center was scheduled for Sept. 1, when students began arriving for the fall semester.

Tommy and Craig Watson, the architect on the Living Learning Center, informed me that Allen Green was trying to submit various change orders on the building. I guess Allen wasn't making the profit he had expected and wanted to substitute inferior work in some areas to cut his overhead.

I had no idea these change orders had been submitted to the college's accounting office and was furious at Allen Green for not bringing them directly to me for approval. I felt he was trying to sneak one by me and grew even angrier when I recalled all his complaining about Bill being an unethical businessman.

I got him on the phone immediately. Tensions had built up between us during the course of the project and we quickly began shouting at each other. I told him he would complete the project, as designed, for the agreed upon price and within the agreed upon schedule. Otherwise, his company would be fined $1,000 a day, that would be taken out of his final payment.

Allen became infuriated and told me, unless I approved the change orders, he wouldn't have the building completed on time and the college could figure out where they'd house the hundreds of students planning to move into the complex.

After I slammed down the phone with him, I immediately contacted Dr. Bronson to let him know of the trouble. I recommended, and he agreed, that we should fire Allen Green and hire Bill Williams to complete the project.

I KNEW Bill would be pleased to hear the news. When I called him, he said he had some good news, too. Dr. Bronson had arranged for Bill and me to attend a luncheon with all of the college presidents of the United Negro College Fund in New York City. Renselear Development Corp. was sponsoring the meal, which would be an opportunity for us to offer our construction services to colleges nationwide.

At the time, Dr. Bronson was Chairman of the President's Council. He promised to whole-heartedly endorse our company. I didn't know anything about the plans. Bill had worked out the arrangements with Dr. Bronson, unbeknownst to me.

We worked hard on the presentation, which outlined our expertise and the ability of our team to prepare all the documents to receive federal grants and low-interest loans, as well as handle the actual construction of campus buildings.

I was excited about this trip. Bill's secretary handled all the travel arrangements and Bill kept saying he was going to introduce me to all sorts of important people. We both needed this trip to work.

I had recently pledged my signature to an unauthorized loan at United American Bank for $200,000 on Bill's behalf. If we failed to repay it in 90 days, the college would be liable. I had pledged the college's permission and good credit with my signature as its attorney. My signature constituted bank fraud. To commit this federal crime, I received $5,000 from the loan proceeds.

Bill said we'd pay the loan back before anyone found out about it from other loan proceeds from the blimp company.

We landed at LaGuardia Airport and got into a waiting limo for the ride into Manhattan. I stared at the skyscrapers and imagined being involved with big-time Wall Street transactions. Manhattan was built on big-money deals. We were here hoping to get our own.

The next day we made our presentation to the college presidents. Bill looked impressive as usual, 6-foot-5 and impeccably dressed and groomed. After his opening remarks, O.J. Tate set up architectural renderings of Bill's projects on several easels. Tate said these were the projects in which Bill had served as a construction manager.

I was surprised to see only drawings of the two buildings at Bethune-Cookman College. I had assumed Bill handled college construction all over the country. Yet, his only examples were from our college. And, technically, he hadn't served as construction manager on the Living Learning Center. Well, he did for the last month of the project, but Allen Green Construction had overseen the vast majority of the work.

After Tate finished his presentation, Dr. Bronson walked to the podium. He said he personally wanted to introduce the next speaker because this was a young man who rose through the ranks of the college, and received a joint law degree and master's of business administration - the first minority at The University of Florida to do so.

Dr. Bronson reminded the presidents that they already knew this young man. He had given a presentation to the Presidents' Council a few years before on campus security.

Today, this young man wouldn't be speaking on behalf of Bethune-Cookman but as a joint partner and associate of Renselear Development Corp. The college, and Dr. Bronson, personally, had agreed to allow him to work as the company's attorney.

"My friends," Dr. Bronson said in conclusion, using the salutation that he often used in public addresses and with the college presidents, "I want you to know these two young men are the premiere black construction team in the country. They can, if you give them the opportunity, meet all your construction needs."

As I stood up, there was a flutter of applause.

"First I must say that it was Dr. Bronson who saw more in me than I saw in myself. He encouraged my educational and professional development. I owe everything I've accomplished to Dr. Bronson."

My comments drew another round of applause for Dr. Bronson, who basked in the attention and my kind words.

I launched into my sales pitch for Bill Williams.

"Mr. Williams has the unique capability of finishing the job he starts. When we needed him to come to our rescue with the Living Learning Center complex, which he showed you in the rendering, his expertise saved Bethune-Cookman College from embarrassment in terms of having hundreds of students without housing."

"Mr. Williams also has been engaged to construct phase one of the Mary McLeod Bethune Fine Arts Center, which Dr. Bronson convinced Congress to fund with a fifteen million dollar grant. I want you to know that Bill and I will be able to assist you from the inception to the completion, if you will give us the opportunity. Thank You."

Later that night, we attended a social gathering for the presidents. Many of the presidents wanted to know more about Bill's work at the college. I told them about our struggle to find minority contractors who could receive bonds, a type of insurance policy required on federally-funded projects to ensure the work is completed. I personally had seen the bonding documents from Renselear Development Corp. He was the only minority contractor I had ever seen who was able to obtain such documentation, which requires a stellar credit rating and solid financial foundation.

Bill sent the rest of his staff back to Orlando, but he and I had a big night on the town ahead of us. Bill and I were going to "do" the Big Apple. We sat in the restaurant on the top floor of the Marriott Marquis, which rotated around the Manhattan skyline.

"Bill, I sincerely hope what you said today and showed those presidents can come true. You have the capability to perform. I know you can do it. So, in your words, let's get busy," I said.

"Brother Hill, that's not a problem. All we need to do is get the contracts."

We left the restaurant and climbed in Bill's limo. We said we wanted to go to the hottest black nightspots in Manhattan. We dashed from club to club all night. We'd pull up in the limo, and the doormen, assuming we were someone important, would wave us right in ahead of the long lines. We acted like royalty and we were treated that way by the employees of the clubs.

The phone rang non-stop in my law office for the next few weeks. Administrators from black colleges nationwide were calling at the request of their presidents to get more information about our company. They wanted us to submit proposals and bids on various construction projects - dormitories, administration buildings, student centers, lecture halls.

We ended up signing contracts with Jarvis Christian College in Hawkins Texas; Johnson C. Smith University in Charlotte, North Carolina; and Rust College in Holly Springs, Mississippi.

Given all of the new ventures, I was feeling pretty comfortable with Bill. The three contracts totaled about $15 million in work in the near future. Within a week of finalizing the agreements in late November/early December 1989, Bill stopped by with $77,000 in cash for me.

I'm not sure where he got the money. Because over the coming months, all the contracts with the college would fall through. Bill got sidetracked with work in the Virgin Islands and dropped the college projects. He had heard there was big money to be made in the islands after Hurricane Hugo.

Unlike Miami, which cracked down on unscrupulous builders and construction practices after the hurricane, no such restrictions existed in the Virgin Islands. Builders could still get by with quick, shoddy - and extremely profitable - work. Bill and Tommy rushed off to start bidding on projects.

And I...well, I was given the task of calling the United Negro Fund colleges and informing them to look elsewhere for a construction company.

GONE TOO FAR

Reaching to touch the sky
I slip past the clouds.

The blue canvas pulls me
closer.

The magnet's force is stronger
than I anticipated.

I go past my destination into
a place that escapes my map.

I am lost.

6 TAILSPIN

"Oftentimes have I heard you speak of one who commits a wrong as though he were not one of you, but a stranger unto you and an intruder upon your world. But I say that even as the holy and the righteous cannot rise beyond the highest which is in each of you, so the wicked and the weak cannot fall lower than the lowest, which is in you also."
Kahlil Gibran, Lebanese mystic (1881-1931).

Maroon and white streamers hung from ceiling of the Mirage, and layers of confetti covered the glossed, parquet dance floor, as well as the maroon carpeting and the white table-clothed dinner tables.

About 1,000 people were jammed elbow-to-elbow for New Year's Eve. Tuxedos and evening gowns were the attire of choice. I stood eight feet above the crowd on a stage, dressed in black tails, a white shirt and black bow-tie. A colorful party hat was cocked to the side of my head. I gazed down at Sandra, looking sexy in a sequin and lace black gown, seated at a table with 10 close friends. She looked nervous and mouthed the words to me, "You can do it."

In seven minutes, a new decade would start. The 1980s had begun with so much promise for me. My children were born; I received my law degree and MBA; interned for the CIA; moved up quickly at Bethune-Cookman College; acquired our dream home; and bought more material possessions than I had ever dreamed possible, but my future looked bleak as I braced for 1990 to begin.

As I stood watching the revelry, I wanted to run and hide where no one could find me. This club felt like two strong hands wrapped around my neck, squeezing tightly. Buying the place had been a dreadful mistake, I thought, recalling the Mirage's checking account was $60,000 overdrawn and growing daily. Pips II was not working out as I had hoped for.

"And now ladies and gentlemen, we have a special treat. Something to really end your year with a bang. LIVE FROM THE MIRAGE, ANDERSON HILL and the MIRAGE PLAYERS!"

The MC handed me the microphone as five, slender black men began to swirl and move in synchronized steps behind me. The guys, dressed in tuxes and top hats, began to harmonize one by one, and blend with the live band's blaring music.

I started to sing in my unrehearsed, off-key voice: "Thank You. I just want to thank you. Thank You, Daytona for supporting the Mirage."

The guys behind me chimed in, doing a Motown/Temptations kind of thing: "Thank You. Thank You. Thank You."

The song continued for several minutes to the hoots and hollers of the crowd.

"My involvement up here is really a comedy act," I said when the band stopped playing. "But this backup group has extreme talent. They're students from Bethune-Cookman College and you'll be hearing a lot more from them."

With that, the MC grabbed the microphone and started counting down the final seconds of 1989. The place erupted in cheers, hugs and kisses; 1990 had begun, bringing with it the most wretched days of my life. I desperately tried to recapitulate where things had gone wrong. I started to remember the following horrible facts of joint scienter...

ALL OF us had invited the devil into our house but were surprised when he refused to leave politely.

Dr. Bronson phoned my law office and said he needed me to handle a delicate situation concerning the college's Chairman of the Board of Trustees, Dr. Wendell Holmes, the first black to serve in that high post.

Dr. Holmes was a regal looking man, tall with a slight paunch under his characteristic pinstripe suits. He owned and served as funeral home director in Jacksonville, a position that made him instrumental in the lives of black residents. He had once served as chairman of the Duval County School Board in Jacksonville, along with Vice Chairman of the Board of Trustees at the historically black college, Hampton Institute.

I had been pivotal in his election to chairman, a feat that required a Napoleonic strategy. As ironic as it sounds, the Bethune-Cookman board never had a black chairman since the college started in 1923.

The day of the election, after I argued persuasively and intensely for Dr. Holmes to become chairman, several white trustees attempted to delay the election to give them time to come up with another candidate, most likely a white one. I cut them off and convinced the remaining members into voting right then and there for Dr. Holmes.

It was a historical moment for the college, and Dr. Bronson, Dr. Holmes and I savored the milestone for months.

"Dr. Holmes has experienced substantial financial difficulties," Dr. Bronson was telling me on the phone. "The College needs to assist him, if possible, Brother Hill. He has a major problem that could destroy him and undermine all we have done to get him elected as our chairman."

"What happened, Doc?" I asked nervously.

"It involves a loan from the Small Business Administration, that is a federal agency, which had become delinquent. Wendell has been engaged in litigation over this delinquent loan and it appears his attorney cannot negotiate a favorable resolution of the federal government's judgment. I believe it's for $115,000. I need you to confer with Bill Williams and see if his connections in Washington can work this out. Wendell is very distressed about his financial situation. I told him you'd try to take care of it."

"I'm sure Bill will be happy to be of assistance, but don't you think this poses a conflict of interest?" I asked.

"Well, Brother Hill," Dr. Bronson replied. "The college has allowed you to work for Bill and that is a conflict of interest. Don't you agree, Brother Hill?"

"Yes, it is an ethical conflict. And there's no way I could work for his company without your approval, Doc. I'll speak to Bill and let you know what he says."

"Thank you, Brother Hill. I'm sure Wendell will be grateful."

We hung up, and I rose to my feet and slammed my office door in disgust. I was angry about having to ask Bill for such a dirty, little favor and I wanted my office staff to know they should leave me alone for the rest of the afternoon.

I knew Bill well enough to know he'd jump at the chance to fix Dr. Holmes' loan trouble. We were all becoming more and more indebted to this man. I knew one day Bill would play his trump card. He already had enough dirt on me, but now this.

For a brief second, I thought about going to the Board of Trustees and laying out this political scheme to fix Dr. Holmes' judgment. The white trustees would grab onto this like the Koh-i-noor diamond. They'd be only too happy to bounce the first black chairman from office. But what would I say? In order to tell them about Dr. Holmes, I'd have to fill them in on all my unethical dealings with Bill.

"Teresa," I called over my intercom. "Can you get Bill on the telephone for me?"

"Right away,"

Not a minute later, and she was back on the intercom.

"Bill Williams, line 1."

Bill didn't hesitate when I asked for his assistance. "Sure," he said. He just needed to contact his retained D.C. law firm to get the ball rolling.

The next day, a lobbyist named Steve Pruitt with the law firm, called. I explained the scenario, and gave him the case number for the civil judgment and a contact person with the Counsel for the Small Business Administration in Jacksonville.

Not an hour later, an attorney with the federal agency called me. He asked how he could help. I said Dr. Holmes needed a more favorable judgment. He said he'd check into the matter and get back with me.

After a several days, the attorney called back. The Small Business Administration was willing to accept $50,000 to pay off the $112,852.85 delinquent loan. They could set up a payment schedule for Dr. Holmes. Probably $5,000 down and $483.75 a month.

The paperwork was signed and Dr. Holmes paid the $5,000.

"Dr. Holmes, line 2," Teresa announced over the intercom.

"Attorney Hill, I called to personally thank you and Bill Williams for your invaluable assistance. As you know I contacted congressmen and U.S. senators and they couldn't get anything done. Whatever you need to do for our man, Bill Williams, don't hesitate to accommodate him."

Dr. Bronson called me a few minutes later and also expressed his gratitude. I hit the speed dial on my phone to pass along the praises to Bill. I recounted the men's comments to him and was surprised when Bill responded in a sarcastic and cutting way.

"I already know about all that, Big Andy. Do you think they

would tell you before they told me?"

It surprised me because I had thought I was the special envoy between all these men, that they needed me to talk to each other. But they obviously were taking to each other all the time. I was just their do-boy.

I sat silent, embarrassed by my naiveté. "Talk with you later, Bill," I said and hung up.

TOMMY Huger came into my office first thing one morning and said we had trouble. We had paid Bill Williams $200,000 to complete the Living Learning Center after Allen Green was fired. We had been told by the college's accounting office that's how much money was left in the construction account and if we didn't spend it, we'd have to ship it back to the federal government.

Now, two months later, Tommy just learned there had been an error in calculating the balance in the account. The project was more than $600,000 over budget, and Bill was still owed one final payment.

"What did you just say to me Tommy?" I heard what he said regarding the massive over-expenditures, but wanted him to repeat it, as my shoulders sagged, as I sat in my burgundy leather chair. "How in the hell did we let that happen?"

"It's all my fault, Anderson. Here." He handed me a letter with several typed paragraphs. He was resigning.

"Oh, Tommy. Don't do this."

I went over and shared the bad news with Dr. Bronson. He also refused to accept Tommy's resignation. But he was furious.

Bethune-Cookman College doesn't have a few hundred thousand dollars sitting around, waiting to be used. This deficit would hurt the college. Tuition and fees pay only 55 percent of the college's annual budget. The rest comes from donations.

Although Tommy accepted the blame for the mistake, it was clear Dr. Bronson was holding me responsible. After all, Tommy reported to me. It was my job to supervise the construction projects.

Dr. Bronson ordered Tommy to immediately vacate my law office and return to campus. And I would no longer have any role in construction projects.

Dr. Bronson was growing ever weary of the Hill-Williams duo.

I had been to see him not long ago to recommend the college co-sign for a $250,000 loan for Bill at South Trust Bank. The loan would be guaranteed based on an assignment of future invoices on the upcoming fine arts centers. In other words, the bank would rely on the good faith of the college in paying Bill his future fees, which then would be used to repay the loan.

In all of the college's history of construction projects, we had never given such approval before. Bill told me it was no big deal; the money would provide him with gap-financing to help with short-term cash-flow problems as he began the construction of the fine arts center in mid-September 1989. Remember, at this point, the college was paying very little money directly to Bill's company. The college had taken over the responsibility of paying Bill's suppliers and subcontractors to ensure they were paid.

Dr. Bronson was leery of this loan. I had gone to his home to talk to him about the deal. He was sitting in a plaid, easy chair in his living room.

"Brother Hill, are you sure we're on a sound legal basis with this transaction?"

"Yes, Doc," I replied. "We will make out all of Bill's future payments jointly to his company and the bank. Then, the bank can make whatever deductions are required to fulfill the loan obligation and give Bill the difference. We actually owe Bill this money pursuant to the fine arts center contract. I think that we should help him. He's been very good to me, to Dr. Holmes and to the college. He has performed adequately. And also Doc, he has the capabilities of doing great things for the college."

So, Bronson signed the loan documents. Of course, it didn't take long for the bank to start calling us. Bill wasn't delivering the payments to the bank. Somehow he was cashing the checks even though they were made payable to both Renselear Development and South Trust Bank, and, therefore, the checks should have required a bank signature to cash them.

During the time South Trust was calling us to get its money, one day Dr. Bronson received a telephone call while I was sitting in his office. The call was from a member of the college's Board of Trustees, John Bustamonte.

Bustamonte had been appointed as a trustee a year and a half earlier. An attorney and president of a Cleveland bank, Bustamonte had substantial holdings and was thought to be a potential large benefactor for the college. For some reason, lately, he had stopped attending trustee meetings. We didn't know why, well, at least I didn't. Dr. Bronson could have had prior knowledge about this gentleman's absence from meetings and he did not share the reason with me.

When Dr. Bronson picked up the phone, I couldn't tell what the call was about. Dr. Bronson said only, "Mmm-hmmm. Mmm-hmmm. I see. Mmm-hmmm."

After a few minutes, he said: "Mister Bustamonte, can I let the college's attorney listen in on this call? He's sitting right here. You know Brother Hill, our internal attorney."

"Brother Hill, go pick up the telephone in the outer office."

I picked up the phone and offered a cordial greeting.

"I just wanted to let you gentlemen know," Bustamonte started. "I cannot remain involved with the Board of Trustees because of the college's association with Bill Williams."

"Bill Williams defrauded this bank. He borrowed money from us and never repaid it. He left town with a Roll Royce that was financed by our bank, but he had not made any payments on it. I just want you gentlemen to know that Bill Williams should not be trusted. Thank you for your time and good-bye."

Dr. Bronson and I stared at each other for a few moments. He dropped his head and shook it back and forth. I walked over to his desk, put my hands on the edge and leaned closer to him.

"Brother Hill, Bill Williams obviously has had some serious problems. You would agree with that, wouldn't you?" Dr. Bronson said.

"Yes, I'd agree with that, Doc. He's had some financial difficulties like any businessman does. I've had problems myself with the Mirage and the large amount of money that I have to pay out," I said. Thinking to myself as I looked at him, Bronson appeared somewhat determined to ignore the Bustamonte's clear and concise warning. An uneasy feeling was all over me. But why wouldn't he tell me to terminate Bill's ties with the college immediately, after a telephone call like that from a trustee? Was Dr. Bronson linked to Bill Williams in illegal ways that I did not know about?

"Well, do you think we should stick with him or should we cut him loose?"

Lord knows, I should have answered that question honestly. With Bill's recent payment to me of $77,000 cash, I had received more than $300,000 from him in seven months. Even as I gave my answer, I knew I was lying. We should have cut Bill loose right that instant, but I didn't say that.

"We need to stick with him, Doc. I think Bill is coming out of his problems. We've got some good leads that may eventually materialize with some of the presidents from the UNCF luncheon."

"I've heard some complaints from the presidents that Bill isn't following up," Dr. Bronson replied.

"Well, you know, he and Tommy have been involved in this Virgin Islands project. Bill thinks there's an opportunity to engage in additional business from the hurricane. I still think we should stick with him."

"You think he's trying to get his life back on track?"

"Yeah, Doc, I really do."

"Well, okay then. We need to do all we can to help struggling black males. Our race doesn't have an abundance of black males with the training and skills that you two gentlemen have. I'll do whatever I can to help you two be successful."

Bill, at that time, had signed contracts with the college to act as construction manager on the future second phase of the fine arts center, estimated to cost $8 million, as well as construction manager on the future $6 million Wildcat Student Center.

I'm sure Dr. Bronson had to be alarmed about the growing problems with Bill. First, the Living Learning Center construction budget faced a more than $600,000 deficit, then the South Trust loan, and now Bustamonte's resignation. However, despite the problems, I was still angry with him for yanking me out of my role in college construction projects. At the time, I thought he wanted to eliminate me because I was becoming too powerful and threatened to ascend to the president's office someday. Only in hindsight do I see that he must have been worried about where my loyalties lay. After receiving such a call from Bustamonte, I should have advised him to severe ties with Bill. That was my duty as college attorney. But I had argued on Bill's behalf. No wonder Dr. Bronson was re-evaluating the Hill-Williams partnership.

TROUBLE moved in fast, like a thunderstorm on a hot Florida afternoon. My life was turning into a mad dash from one crisis to another.

Months earlier, right before we attended the United Negro College Fund luncheon, I co-signed for Bill to receive another loan for $200,000 from United American Bank. This was just after Bill's first loan to South Trust. Judging by Dr. Bronson's hesitancy to sign that loan, I knew he would never agree to sign a second one. So I signed my name as college attorney, and obligated the college to repay the debt, without its proper permission.

I had been sitting in my office that day when Teresa came over the intercom and said a Mr. Sid Cash, President of United American Bank, was on the phone.

I'd never heard of Sid Cash nor United American Bank. I picked up the phone, unsure what this was about.

"Hey, Anderson. This is Sid Cash. I'm sitting over here at the bank with Bill Williams. Bill is a good customer with our bank. He told me he's doing significant amounts of work for you guys over at Bethune-Cookman College. He's been incurring quite a bit of debt waiting for his payments to come from Washington. You know, those damn feds never pay people in a timely fashion. Anyway, Bill came in looking for some help from us and I'm glad to help."

"Of course, we'll need the college to co-sign for the loan. Bill said Dr. Bronson is ailing and wouldn't be able to drive over here to Orlando to sign the papers. Bill asked if you, as college attorney, could sign for the college. We will accept your signature to finalize this transaction."

What was this guy talking about?

"Excuse me, could you put Bill on the phone," I asked.

I heard a rustling in the background and Bill came on the line.

"Bill, What is going on?"

"Sid and I are good friends, Anderson. So I came down here to see if Sid could help me out. He's willing to extend me two hundred thousand. I'll bring the assignment papers over later today. See you then."

He hung up. By the time he arrived a few hours later, I was worked up. The college had only recently agreed to sign at South Trust Bank. How could Bill have gone through all that money? Work wasn't moving that fast on the fine arts center. I didn't have any more invoices. We had pledged them all to South Trust as collateral for its loan.

"Just use the same invoices," Bill said. "They'll never know."

"I don't know, Bill. This doesn't sound good."

"You heard what Sid said. If you sign on behalf of the college, the loan will go through. There will be some money in it for you. Don't worry."

"Bill, I need to think about this."

"Oh, I see. Ole Bill helps everybody. Now who is going to help ole Bill? Bill has helped you. Bill has to think about enlarging Dr. Bronson's house. Look at what ole Bill did for Dr. Holmes. Ole Bill has been working hard ever since he came to Bethune-Cookman. Can anybody help ole Bill? Come on, you can do this for me Anderson."

He pulled out what appeared to be loan documents, showing he would receive more than $5 million from some bank within 30 days. The documents appeared legit, although it did not specifically say, Bill Williams or Renselear Development. I guess I saw what I wanted to believe.

"I've got all the money to repay these loans right here," he said, waving the documents in my face. "Look at how much money you've gotten from me already. I need this money, so that we can keep working and pay everybody. I've got to pay you. I've got to pay Tommy. Now, are you going to help ole Bill or not?"

I dug through my files and found the same assignment papers the college had used for an earlier loan with South Trust. I whited out the name of that bank and faxed them to United American Bank. The next day, Bill brought the new loan documents for me to sign.

It was Sept. 22, 1989. I remember sitting and looking at those documents. I absolutely, totally, did not want to sign them.

"Go ahead and sign the thing, Anderson," Bill said. "Quit messing around. We've got to get busy. Let's get busy, Anderson."

So I signed my name. I made copies and gave the originals back to Bill. When he put the originals into his portfolio, I wanted to reach in and grab them back. Tear them up. But I didn't. Bill left without even saying "thank you."

It was that easy. Bank robbery. No weapon needed. No getaway car. No high-speed escape to freedom. It was a sophisticated scam, so sophisticated in fact that it caught me off-guard. A few trumped-up invoices and Bill's promise that there would be a forthcoming invoice. Voila, cash. The bank never received any invoice from me or Bill as collateral for the new loan.

I would have never thought up such a scheme. I don't know how Bill learned it. But, darn, what a powerful scam. You know a bunch of bank presidents weren't sitting around eager to loan hundreds of thousands of dollars to a couple black men.

I've relived that moment a million times, turning it and twisting it to see it from every angle, playing and replaying the scene with different endings. My downfall was set in motion that day. In all honesty, I had no idea how that one event would snowball, spiraling out of control over the coming 18 months.

I agree I should have known, given my extensive education and training. All I can say is that I truly thought we were going to repay the loan before anyone found out. I might have been a naive country fool, but I knew to sign and not repay would amount to professional suicide.

What was my cut for committing this federal crime? Bill gave me a cashier's check for $5,000 from the loan proceeds of $200,000.

THE United American Bank loan came due in February 1990. In the six months since we received the loan, we didn't make one payment. A partial payment probably would have stalled the bank for a few more months. Bill paid zip.

With Sid and his attorney hounding me all the time, I had become a nervous wreck. I wasn't sleeping nights. I was drinking larger and larger quantities of tequila and snorting more and more coke. I was spending almost every night at the club, surrounding myself with barflies who fawned all over me.

When I looked at my wife and two kids, I knew I existed on

borrowed time. I made a huge mistake and would be caught.. I discussed my worries with no one. With the feelings bottled up inside me, I vacillated between coke-induced heights of grandeur, where all the problems would be solved, to deep lows of self-loathing. It was just a matter of time before I became publicly humiliated before my family, my mother and my sister, my in-laws, Dr. Bronson, Bethune-Cookman College and the rest of my community.

I told myself I would fight for my own survival. I turned desperate, clutching at straws, and digging myself in deeper.

I rarely saw Bill these days. In the first few months of 1990, I received $15,000 from him. The money quickly went to stay current on my bills. My income from the college was drying up. An internal college committee, which studied what other colleges paid their attorneys, had reported I was grossly overpaid. The college started scaling back my pay. A second internal committee also recommended the elimination of the Executive Vice President post, after Dr. Gainous retired, denying me the promotion and added income. And I had been relieved of overseeing college construction.

I was out of the loop at the college. I'd drive by the main administration building, White Hall, and see Bill's car parked where mine had once parked. Bill appeared to be meeting with Dr. Bronson on a regular basis these days. I had been the go-between for the two men. Now, I wasn't even invited to their meetings.

With my income dwindling, I played the Lotto with fervor. I heard on the TV news one Sunday that two tickets purchased in Volusia County would share the $30 million jackpot. I just knew I had one of the tickets. I was scared to look. I had purchased 500 hundred tickets - at $1 a piece. When I finally checked, reality soaked in because I didn't have that winning ticket.

Bill and I began to argue more. I remember on one occasion he told me Bob Billingslea was a wolf in sheep's clothing. I asked what he meant. Bob was a drunk, he said.

So, what? I knew that.

Bob also had received large sums of money from Bill.

For what? I asked.

For introducing me to you.

Bob was paid for that first meeting in my office with Bill?

Yep. $5,000. And Bill made several more payments because Bob was always crying about being broke.

I was mad as hell. Bob had used his position as college trustee to practically force Bill Williams on me and on the college. I thought Bob had recommended Bill because he believed in his abilities. Everyone around here is on the take.

So far, I had been able to keep the United American Bank loan a secret. When the bank's attorney, Bill Lawton, filed suit against us for failure to pay, I persuaded him to serve me with all the legal documents. Usually, those documents went to the college's registered agent, Ernest Cook, Vice President for Fiscal Affairs.

In the early spring of 1990, Bill Williams, myself and Dr. Bronson were meeting in his office when Dr. Bronson got a call from Bill Lawton. As soon as his secretary announced the caller, I knew we were in trouble.

Dr. Bronson listened for several minutes and then he put the attorney on hold.

"There's an attorney on the phone who says you two obligated the college to a loan at his bank. I don't want to know anything about this. I want you two to work out this matter immediately. You two talk to this man and tell him you're going to take care of this."

Bill and I got on the phone. We promised Bill Lawton we would repay the money if he just gave us more time. He agreed to prepare a motion to abate the lawsuit to give us additional time.

Dr. Bronson never mentioned this matter to me again. Shortly after that, Dr. Bronson called and asked me to draw up a contract for Bill Williams to purchase Dr. and Mrs. Bronson's shopping center in Ormond Beach, just north of Daytona Beach, that he had been trying to sell for years.

When I talked to Bill about the details, he bemoaned the fact that Dr. Bronson "was dumping a pink elephant" on him. Bill said Dr. Bronson felt he had done many things for Bill, and now it was time for Bill to repay his graciousness.

Bill agreed to purchase the shopping center for $135,000. The Bronsons owed $79,583.66 on it. I was to contact Florida National Bank to see if Bill could assume the first mortgage. The bank said Bill could assume the Bronson's mortgage, if he had satisfactory credit. Dr.

Bronson wanted $10,000 at closing and would accept a short-term note on the remaining $45,416.34.

I prepared the contract. Dr. Bronson and his wife, Helen, signed it on February 28, 1990. I then later delivered it to Bill, who reluctantly signed on March 2, 1990, as president of Renselear. Bill said he didn't like being forced into the deal. But he didn't have a choice. Bill had to come up with the money by the closing date, set for March 30, and he was not going to use personal or corporate funding.

It hadn't taken Bill long, in the "interim" of the signings, to come up with a financing plan.

He called me in a huff on March 1, 1990, and said he just learned from a "little bird" that Tommy Huger and Craig Watson had signed a contract with the college to build a classroom building that would serve as a branch campus. It was called the Spuds Educational Center Building, located in Spuds, Florida. Bill had figured he and I would get the contract.

"You know, Bill, I'm out of the loop," I said. "I don't know what you guys are doing in terms of construction. I just don't know anymore. They now treat me like I have the plague, when it comes to construction decisions!"

"You know, Anderson, I need that money. I know you need money, too. And I've got this obligation with Dr. Bronson. We need to get paid."

"How are we going to do that?"

"Well, you've always helped ole Tommy. Now, Tommy is trying to deal you out. You need to get busy. Go talk to Dr. Bronson and see what can be worked out." I took Bill's advice.

I drove to the president's office and told Dr. Bronson that I needed some money. My expenses were continuing to mount and I was receiving only my $32,397 annual salary from the college. I needed to get in on the Spuds project. Bill had thought that he convinced me to believe that the project should not have been awarded to Tommy and Craig without my knowledge. I knew better. I was no longer involved in construction, because of the cost overruns on the dormitory, but I played along. I could tell that Bill had received specific directions from someone, and I could be one of the beneficiaries, if I played my cards right. I am sure that Tommy had not mentioned the project to him. Tommy probably knew that Bill might want a substantial piece of it.

Dr. Bronson buzzed Tommy, who now had an office on campus, and Tommy came over. I told Tommy, as soon as he entered the door, that I couldn't believe he would enter into such a contract without telling me. He and Craig Watson had gone behind my back and convinced Dr. Bronson to give them the deal and cut me out. Tommy was confused because he had no professional responsibility to tell me about any college construction, since Dr. Bronson had removed him from my office. Tommy probably wondered why Dr. Bronson would not speak up in his defense, as I continued to assert my "lines-of-authority" mis-representations. Nevertheless, I kept the pressure on.

Tommy felt badly about the charades. He told Dr. Bronson he didn't want the Spuds project and that I could have it. After he stormed out of the office, Dr. Bronson said I should prepare the paperwork for Bill Williams to receive an immediate payment of about $100,000 to handle the Spuds project. "Whatever Bill does with his money, is up to him, Brother Hill. I hope that he will take care of you and his other responsibilities."

I went back and called Bill. It seemed like he already knew what I was going to say. He told me that I should prepare a contract and get Dr. Bronson to sign it. The total value of the contract was for $450,000. He'd then mobilize a crew and move some dirt around up at the site. Finally, he'd submit an invoice for $103,500 for site work, and we'd all get paid.

Dr. Bronson signed the contract on March 1, 1990. Several short days later, I took over a requisition for payment, and Dr. Bronson signed off on that. The next day, I went by the college's business office and picked up the check.

I delivered it to Bill, and we cashed it at his bank. He gave me $65,000 out of the proceeds. I had hoped for more. I hadn't received any money from him in months. I told Bill I needed more to keep up my payments on the Mirage and my law office. Bill refused to give me any more. He said there were other people who had to be taken care of, too.

I figured Bill needed the money to complete the deal with Dr. Bronson. But the shopping-center deal fell apart. First National Bank had refused to allow Bill to assume the mortgage. It turned out Bill had horrible credit.

By that time, Dr. Bronson had turned squirrelly about the trans-actions. I can't remember when Dr. Bronson told me - but it was before the bank advised me that they had turned down Bill for the mortgage - he said he didn't want to go through with either deal, not the one on the shopping center or to have his private residence enlarged by Bill. I would later find out that sometime in March '90, Dr. Bronson had been told by Jake Ross, the college's Director of Security and also an investi-gator for the State Attorney's office, that Bill and his company were under investigation. The investigation was based on an anonymous tip, that Bill had submitted a worthless performance bond to the college and the federal government for construction of the fine arts center. I was unaware of Jake's conversation with Dr. Bronson, until I read a deposi-tion of Dr. Bronson, taken in July '91. I assumed this was the primary reason that Dr. Bronson backed out of the transaction, because Bill was under criminal investigation. Nevertheless, the wheels of deception had been set in motion, and were not stopped. God knows, if I had known about the investigation, I would have backed off of Bill, too!

With that $103,500 from the Spuds project, neither Bill nor I paid any money on the loan with United American Bank. The attorney was hounding us again. As that litigation proceeded, the college was served with a tax lien from the Internal Revenue Service for Renselear Development Corp. The college was required to send all of the company's payments to the IRS for unpaid federal income taxes. The IRS also seized the office of Renselear Development Corp. in Orlando. Bill was effectively shut down, unable to conduct any business.

This latest turn put the college in an awkward position, because at the same time in May 1990, U.S. Congressman Craig James (who had replaced Bill Chappell) announced he would sponsor legislation to get the college a $9.2 million federal grant for the second phase of the fine arts center.

The college held a big groundbreaking ceremony on the parcel to celebrate the good news. Dr. Bronson and Craig James made speeches, and so did Bill, who was introduced as construction manager for the second phase. But the college had already been served with the tax lien so Bill's hands were tied.

Dr. Bronson seemed worried about including Bill in the cer-emony. A story about Bill's tax trouble had appeared in the local paper which made Dr. Bronson nervous. I told him that despite Bill's financial trouble, work was running on schedule on phase one of the fine arts center. The college couldn't be criticized for that.

Bill was close to tears after the news conference. He told me the IRS had closed his office and he could no longer receive any money from the college. I had never seen him act in such humble and humiliated fashion. After all we had done wrong, this was the first time I heard distress in his voice.

He told me I had to help him out of this hole. If he didn't get the IRS off his back, he couldn't finish phase one, much less start phase two. He'd be ruined, and I would not receive another dime from him.

He said Sid Cash from United American Bank was willing to help him. "What would UAB do for us?" I asked. "They have pending litigation against us."

Bill said Sid would help. I needed to attend a meeting with them at the bank in Orlando the next day. I sincerely hoped Sid would help us. It was June 11 and I hadn't received any money from Bill since March.

The bank was located in a renovated Victorian house, close to the heart of downtown Orlando, right off I-4 at the busy Colonial Drive. Sid Cash and Bill were waiting for me in a second floor office. It was the first time I had met Sid face to face. He looked like the typical bank president - upper, middle class white guy who played golf every weekend and whose wife belonged to the Junior League.

"Bill needs some help," Sid said. "I'm willing to lend him another $90,000. Mr. Hill, you can negotiate the transaction on his behalf. But this time, I need President Bronson's signature to secure the loan."

I thought I saw Sid wink at me as he said this. I guess he knew exactly what we were up to.

Bill and I took the papers, left and drove around the corner. Within 10 minutes, we returned and handed Sid the papers. He gave me a check for $44,462.16, which I immediately took across town to the IRS Orlando office. Sid gave the rest of the money to Bill. I don't know what he did with it. I didn't get a dime.

After giving the check to the IRS, I received a Release of Levy document that I took back to the college. Bill could once again receive payments from the college. The IRS turned his Orlando office back over to him.

My relief was short-lived. The next morning, Dr. Bronson called and said he was getting calls from reporters with the *News-Journal*, the black-owned *Daytona Times* and other media wanting to know about the college's relationship with Bill Williams and Renselear Development Corp.

Turns out a local supplier, Whiteside Supplier, was complaining publicly about Bill receiving the fine arts contract without going out for competitive bids. The supplier also said it wasn't right that Tommy and I were on this Bill Williams' payroll. "The whole thing over there stinks," the supplier was quoted as saying. This coupled with the recent stories about Bill's IRS trouble, the reporters smelled a front-page story.

The college's public relations department scheduled a news conference for that afternoon to handle all the reporters' questions at one time. Dr. Bronson told Tommy and me to be there.

Most of the questions were directed at me:

Q: How did Renselear Development become involved with the college?

A: A college trustee brought him to us.

Q: Which trustee?

A: I'd rather not disclose that at this time.

Q: Did you conduct a thorough background check on the company?

A: No, I did not.

Q: Why?

A: Because Mr. Williams came with a very high recommendation from a respected member of our Board of Trustees.

Q: Still, weren't you required to check out his credentials?

A: Not necessarily.

Q: What is the college's position on all the financial trouble Bill Williams is having?

A: Mr. Williams' financial trouble is his own business. The College hired him to build the fine arts center. Work is continuing on schedule, without problems, without delays. The college is pleased with his work.

I tried to sound self-confident. But the questions were nails in Bill's and my coffin. Like all people in charge of big institutions, Dr. Bronson hated - absolutely hated - bad publicity.

The next day or so, Dr. Bronson on June 15, 1990 terminated Bill's contracts on the second phase of the fine arts center and on the Wildcat Student Center. Dr. Bronson, however, waited until August 7, 1990, and then called me to draft a similar letter, for his signature, canceling Renselear's contract for the Spuds Educational Center. This was ironic for him to request that I draft the letter, because Dr. Bronson had one of the college's other attorneys, send a letter to Bill on June 12th, advising him to expeditiously complete the Spuds construction. "Why did he want me involved in the termination process for this project and not the others? Was this a loyalty check?", I wondered to myself.

I sent the letter over to Bill by certified mail, but he didn't seem too concerned about it. Perhaps, he already knew what was coming.

A college employee had warned me that another committee was going to recommend the elimination of the college's internal attorney position. I knew Dr. Bronson had to be behind such a move and was surprised he hadn't told me. I was a long-term employee of the college and surely would receive formal notice of my termination.

When I went over to the president's office and confronted Dr. Bronson. He told me not to worry. The college was going to drop my contract until the controversy blew over. I would keep receiving pay-checks and college insurance coverage, and would help represent him and the college. I would just drop out of sight for a while.

Rumors of my alleged firing spread quickly through the community. Sun Bank, which held the mortgage on my home, called and asked me point-blank if I still had a job. When I conveyed this to Dr. Bronson, he told me to schedule a luncheon with Sun Bank in the executive dining room of the bank. He also wrote a letter to Sun Bank, saying I remained the college's attorney in good standing..

At the luncheon, Dr. Bronson sang praises for me. On the ride back to campus, he told me everything would be all right. At that time, he knew he was about to get rid of me, for good. I'm not sure why he didn't tell me.

This nether world couldn't last for much longer. I clutched the little pieces that remained of my once prosperous life. I needed to take quick action if I were to salvage what was left. Desperate times call for desperate measures.

BILL HAD CALLED on June 22nd and said he found a young bank officer with North Carolina National Bank, NCNB, in Orlando, who was willing to give us another loan.

"Not another loan," I groaned.

"Now, Anderson, I want out of this mess as badly as you do. I've been doing some finagling and I've got it worked out. Let me tell you, I'm losing business every day because of all this bad publicity. I need to take care of all these debts quickly and get back to business."

He came over the next day with a loan commitment in his hands from First Equity Combined Capital Corp. of Dallas. It was a commitment to loan Renselear Development Corp. for $1,350,000. Bill said he was going to put up his TWA stock and his stake in Airship, the blimp advertising company, to secure the loan with a Dallas bank. That would take a few weeks. In the meantime, NCNB would do a loan that we could use to pay off the $300,000 to United American Bank.

Bill said he'd submit to the college an invoice for $350,000, showing he had already done work on the Spuds educational center. With the invoice and my approval signature as college attorney, the bank should extend us the loan. Bill promised that he would timely repay the bank.

It was too late for me to argue. We were on the edge of disaster. I needed to buy time until I could figure out what to do, such as start selling off my assets; liquidate everything I owned.

I faxed the info over to Mr. Gill, the loan officer. Bill called an hour later and said the $250,000 loan went through. The bank's attorney would be calling me about the closing date. The attorney called. All the paperwork was in order. Oh, just one thing, he said. On the letter I sent over, verifying Bill's work for the college, the attorney added Dr. Bronson's name under my signature. I would need to get his signature, too.

Bill brought over the original documents for me to sign. We sat down in my office and I told him I just couldn't forge Dr. Bronson's signature again. I wanted to tell him to sign Dr. Bronson's name. I didn't say it. I knew this criminal act was my part of the bargain.

"Anderson, we need to do whatever it takes so this ship doesn't sink. Now, sign the damn thing."

"This ship is already taking on a whole lot of water, Bill. A whole lot. I doubt it can be saved." I shook my head and signed Dr. Bronson's name.

"Oooh, ooh. You write Dr. Bronson's name better than the Doc. Yeah, everything will be all right."

After the loan closing, Bill gave me a cashier's check for $152,000. He told me to do whatever I wanted with it. Keep it all or give some of it to United American Bank. This new loan with NCNB came due in 60 days. I told Bill we didn't have much time to repay this new loan. Not a problem, he said. He'd have the loan from Dallas, and possibly a big payment for work he was doing at Rust College in Mississippi.

I didn't believe any of it. I just looked at it as a stay of execution for 60 days. After that, who knew what would happen.

From my $152,000 cashier's check, I went to United American Bank and gave Sid Cash a payment of $120,000. I told him I wanted this money applied to our first loan for $200,000, which had been past-due the longest. But Sid used $100,000 of the money to pay off the second loan for $90,000, plus interest and fees. I think he did that because he knew all along Dr. Bronson hadn't signed the documents.

THAT summer of 1990 was the worst time in my life. I telephoned Bill at least 25 times between the time we received the NCNB loan in June and when it came due in August. Half the time, Bill didn't take my calls. He had stopped visiting me at my office. When I did reach him, he'd tell me to calm down, don't worry.

I exploded in a phone conversation with him in early August. "You have got to do something, Bill. What in the hell have you been doing all summer? My life is about to go down the damn drain and you're sitting over there jerking me around."

"Anderson, you have always been such a weakling. You're just a punk. I can take you down anytime I want to. Remember that before you start screaming at me again. I've got more than enough to hurt you and the college. Sit tight and shut up."

"I have gone out on a limb for you, Bill, time and time again. I need you to do something for me. Get me out of this mess."

"I've done plenty for you and the college already. Don't think I won't use that information if necessary."

"Bill, we can't be messing around with NCNB. Sid Cash knew we were up to no good. But NCNB thinks this is a legal and appropriate transaction. If they find out otherwise, they're going to go to the police. The p-o-l-i-c-e, Bill. Our asses will end up in prison."

"Anderson, you're a wreck. I don't have time for this. All the drugs and alcohol are making you crazy."

"Bill, I want you to give me a check for $350,000 so I can repay NCNB. Come over tomorrow with it. Make me out a check for $350,000 and you won't have to worry about me again."

"Anderson ..."

"Just bring me the check, Bill. And you can kiss my black ass."

I slammed down the phone, figuring I'd never hear from him again. But he arrived the next day and handed me a corporate check for $350,000.

"Is this check good?" I asked.

"Of course, Anderson." He smirked and as he walked out and added, "See you later."

"Just get out of my office."

I deposited the check in my account the next day. Oh, Lord, how I prayed that the check would clear the bank. I even called Bill and asked again if the check was good. He said he had checked with his bank and the money was there.

I had it all calculated: $250,000 to NCNB and $100,000 to pay down the remaining $180,000 debt with United American Bank. That should keep UAB quiet for awhile. Get everyone off my back, so I can think clearly.

The same day, my banker called and said the check bounced. I called Bill right away and he started moaning about problems with the Dallas loan and his payment from Rust College. He told me to call Mr. Gill at NCNB and explain that we needed more time because the federal government was taking longer than expected to process our payment request.

Mr. Gill was polite after I laid out the story. I said we needed just a little bit more time. I didn't hear from him again for quite some time.

I knew I was on my own. I scraped together $20,000 and had my law office manager take it to Sid Cash. I was extremely broke. I didn't know what I was going to do to survive. It was useless to count on Bill to come through. But that was my only hope.

SHOVELING my way out of quicksand. That's how it felt.

Bill came by and said he had made contact with a wealthy, Jewish developer from New York City who was willing to extend him a $1 million line of credit. He told the man, Lou Wenger, that he was about to start on phase two of the Fine Arts Center and needed some upfront money to get started.

Mr. Wenger called me and I verified that Bill was the construction manager on the project, even though he had been terminated months before.

I told Bill this was the last time I was going to lie for him. I was exhausted from all these games and needed to salvage whatever relationship I had left with Dr. Bronson and the college.

"Dr. Bronson and the college don't care about you, Anderson," Bill said.

"I could tell that right away. When the shit hits the fan, what did they do? They brought Tommy back into the fold, but they left you hanging out to dry. Dr. Bronson and the college are only going to save their home boys. You, Anderson, are an outsider."

This rang true to me because I did feel like an outsider for the 14 years I worked there. Special consideration was always given to people who graduated from the college, such as Tommy. Tommy knew that there was a problem with the bond Bill had submitted for the fine arts center, but I didn't until more than a year later, when I read Dr. Bronson's deposition.

I grew increasingly distant from everyone around me. My wife and family didn't know the details of my trouble but sensed I was careening out of control. I stopped talking so much to Bill, who had messed me up over time and time again. And I rarely stopped by Bethune-Cookman College. I knew the employees were gossiping non-stop about my demise.

An attorney with NCNB called and demanded its money back immediately.

Bill and I were told to meet with the bank's executive vice president at the attorney's office in Orlando. The meeting was a week away. I was having trouble reaching Bill these days and told the attorney so. I couldn't guarantee Bill would be there, but I'd try to find him.

I couldn't, so I went alone to the meeting. The bank officials said they didn't know what was going on, but they were willing to renew the loan for a short period if we thought we could repay it.

I was honest with them and said I didn't think that would be a good idea. Bill was not trustworthy anymore, in my opinion. I left him numerous messages about this meeting and he obviously refused to show. I thought it best to just level with these bank guys. I wanted them to see my good faith by coming alone. And I admitted I made a terrible mistake with this transaction.

The bank attorney said he didn't care what the circumstances were behind the loan. At this point, the bank just wanted its money back. I said I doubted Bill or I could repay them anytime soon. The bank attorney said he's give me a few more days to locate Bill and try to convince him to repay the loan.

I tried to reach Bill. He didn't return my calls. Eventually, both he and I were served with court papers in a lawsuit filed by the NCNB. Both of us were scheduled to give depositions at the bank attorney's office on the same morning.

BILL kept ducking my calls. He didn't seem to care that I was twisting in the wind. My whole career going down the tubes and he was, Lord knows where. All of his promises about future loans and payments. He wasn't going to repay a dime of the outstanding loans. He had led me around by the nose. And now I was going to be the fall-guy while he moved on to the next big scam.

As I looked back on our 18 months together, I saw so many warning signs of his fallacious nature. I consciously, or unconsciously, had ignored them, partly out of greed and partly out of my desire for the enormous success that had seemed so close at hand.

I couldn't believe I had been taken in. A two-bit hustler was about to destroy my life. Did he care? Not one bit. He had used me. He had threatened me, threatened to hurt my family and threatened to disclose embarrassing information about Drs. Holmes and Bronson.

I felt so powerless and angry. As I sat, late the night before the depositions, drinking tequila and doing cocaine, my anger turned to rage. By 3 a.m., I had concocted a plan.

I would kill him!

I'm going down anyway. Might as well have the satisfaction of putting a bullet in his head. My family and everyone will be able to make it without me. What difference does it make if I go to prison for bank fraud or murder? My life is ruined anyway.

I stayed up all night, loading and reloading the pistol which I kept in my bedroom closet in case of a burglary.

This was my plan: In the morning, when Bill and I arrived at the attorney's office, I would provoke him into a fight. When he started swinging at me, I would reach in my briefcase, grab the pistol and shoot him. A jury just might buy self-defense because Bill is a big guy.

I continued drinking and doing cocaine all night. I left the house before Sandra and the kids awoke. I arrived in Orlando early and drove around aimlessly for an hour. When I arrived at the attorney's office at 9 a.m., I was drunk and high.

The bank attorney led Bill and me into a conference room with a long table. We were told to wait until the stenographer arrived and the attorney finished preparing for our questioning. As soon as the secretary closed the door, leaving us alone, I turned on Bill like a rabid animal.

"You aren't worth a SHIT! You've messed up everybody's life! And now, you're not even returning my calls. You don't have time for me anymore. You ain't no good. You're a punk. All you do is take advantage of people. You ain't worth shit!"

I waited for Bill to spring from the chair and start swinging. I thought for sure he was the fighting-type. Maybe he read the wildness in my eyes because he turned calm and passive.

"Come on, man. Everything's going to be all right, Anderson. We're going to work this thing out. Let's go and get something to eat." Bill knew this was one of my favorite activities. I weighed 250 and loved to eat.

"Let's go to our favorite spot," he continued, referring to the

Howard Johnson's Inn right across from United American Bank. "Come on, man. Let's go down there and eat and work this thing out."

I never took the weapon out of my briefcase. Bill never knew how close he came to his own death that morning. Thank God it didn't happen!

THE UAB attorneys had us sign a settlement agreement that called for us to make two equal payments on the loan. Sure, what the hell! I thought as I signed the papers.

We missed the first payment, of course. Then the bank attorneys got really mad.

Immediately, they served a subpoena on Dr. Bronson to give a deposition in the matter. When Dr. Bronson received the notice, he had the college's outside legal counsel call the bank to see what was up. The bank attorneys said Bethune-Cookman College was being held liable for repaying a $250,000 loan to NCNB and a $200,000 loan to United American Bank.

Dr. Bronson just about fell out of his chair when the attorney relayed the information. He told the attorney to call both banks and tell them the college never authorized these transactions.

He called me next and told me to come over right away. When I arrived, he gave me a letter from Dr. Holmes, dated Nov. 26, 1990, clarifying my relationship with the college. It said I was to perform legal work for the college on an as-needed basis.

I wasn't sure what the letter meant and Dr. Bronson was vague about the whole matter. The next day, I picked up the college's internal phone line, which was connected to my law office. The line was dead. My relationship with Bethune-Cookman College was officially over.

I went to the campus to see Dr. Bronson. He was packing up some paperwork in his office and appeared to be on his way out.

"Brother Hill, when I first heard about all this, I thought Bill Williams had committed the college to all these fraudulent loans. I couldn't believe the extent of your involvement in this. I trusted you, Brother Hill and would have never thought you were capable of such misdeeds. All this time, you've been loyal to Bill Williams, not to me, and not to Bethune-Cookman College."

There was nothing I could say.

He was walking out of his office and he turned around at the door and said: "Somebody is going to jail." And then he was gone.

I stood there after he left. I could feel it in my bones, a powerful premonition. After all I had accomplished, I was just like my father, heading off to prison.

I DIDN'T see Bill again for almost two months. I called him regularly to find out if he had the money to repay the loans. He was always yakking about some big plans to come up with money. But so far, he had zilch. I was not receiving any more money from him, and basically was living hand to mouth. I derived a small pittance from my private law practice. With the rampant rumors about me being a crook, my clients were taking their business elsewhere.

I had given the Mirage back to its original owners because I was so far behind in mortgage payments. I was being hounded by bill collectors and routinely served with lawsuits demanding payments for the cars, the house, credit cards and personal lines of credit.

In early January 1991, Bill called and asked me to meet him in downtown Orlando. He said he had $10,000 to tide me over for a while. I told him I didn't want any more of his money. Whatever cash he had, we should immediately turn over to the banks. Even if we gave the bank a token payment of $5,000 or $10,000, at least it would show we hadn't intentionally set out to defraud them.

"Man, you better think about your family first and forget about those banks," Bill said. We were standing at the intersection of Magnolia and Robinson streets in downtown Orlando in front of a Barnett Bank.

"Bill, I don't want any of your money. I do not want any more of it. Keep it."

He handed me a cashier's check for $10,000 and told me to do with it whatever I wanted. I told him I was taking the check to Bill Lawton, the attorney for United American Bank, and I would hand-deliver it to him.

By refusing to take his money for myself, Bill knew I was no longer an ally. If he could string me along with small payments, he could trust me to keep my mouth shut when the police became involved. And that could be any day now. I knew the only way to save myself was to keep making whatever small payments I could to the banks.

Bill realized I was breaking free of his control. He was through with me. After that Jan. 6 meeting on the street corner, I didn't hear from him or see him for a long, long time.

WITH all my business and professional ties severed, I truly was on my own.

My nature is to fight and stay determined in the face of adversity. That helped me succeed as a black man in a white world. Now, that trait would sink me further.

I should have surrendered, faced my mistakes, let go of all my belongings, filed bankruptcy.

Stupid me! I thought if I could buy more time, I'd figure a way to extract myself from all of it. But my mindset had become corrupted by drugs and alcohol, and my exposure to a master criminal. Stressed to the hilt and desperate, I adopted the tactics of my devious mentor.

In my law office, I spotted a file sitting on the conference room table. One of my associates, an attorney named Joan Lowe, was handling probate work for a client. A woman had died and Joan was distributing the woman's assets to the heirs. On top of the file was paper-clipped a check for $16,000. I took it and cashed it. I used $8,000 to cover payroll and bills for my home and law office, and $8,000 as payment on my line of credit.

I told Joan I had deposited the check into the office's escrow account. She immediately grew suspicious and, not long after, left my employ to start her own law office in town. When she finished handling the paperwork for estate taxes and other matters, she asked for the money back.

I put her off until the following Monday morning, hoping one of my Lottery tickets would hit big over the weekend. None did. One of the heirs came by my office after hours and banged on my door, demanding the money. I hid upstairs in my office and refused to open the door, even though the man knocked for 30 minutes. I know he saw my car in the parking lot and knew I was there.

Joan took me to court, and got a motion from a judge to compel me to release the funds from my escrow account. The order gave me 36 hours to come up with the money. I didn't have it. Joan filed another motion. She asked the judge to hold me in contempt for failing to comply with the court order.

After the hearing, she and I happened to ride down in the same elevator. One of the heirs also was with her. Joan screamed and yelled at me all the way down, calling me a crook and saying she wouldn't rest until I was sitting in jail. I didn't know it at the time, but Joan went straight to the State Attorney's Office and requested criminal charges be filed against me.

Jake Ross, called me at my law office not long after and asked if he could come by and see me. Jake was head of campus security at Bethune-Cookman College and also worked as an investigator for the State Attorney's Office.

I said, "sure, come on by."

By this time, all of my law office staff had left because I was unable to pay them. My wife, Sandra, was filling in as the receptionist. She was downstairs and buzzed me over the intercom to let me know Jake had arrived.

The next thing Sandra knew, I was being led down the staircase and telling her I was under arrest. Jake had allowed me to make a call before we left, so I called a bail bondsman and told him to meet me at the Volusia County branch jail.

At 36 years old, I was being arrested for the first time. It wouldn't have been so humiliating to be arrested in another town, but Daytona Beach is a small community, especially for people who work in the criminal justice system, like I did. Everyone knows everyone. I had to face people I had dealt with for years from a position of authority. Now, I was a lowly criminal.

I was locked up in jail for only a few hours before the bail bondsman got me released. As I walked out, a news reporter was waiting for me. I didn't say anything, just climbed into the car with the bail bondsman to take me back to my law office.

Sure enough, the next morning when I picked up the paper, there was my face and a headline saying, Attorney Hill Arrested on Theft

Charge.

This still was not the end of it. I was bouncing from one bad decision to another.

Next, I used the credit card machine in my office to get money. The machine allowed me to charge people's Mastercards and Visas for law services. I started using it to ring up cash advances on my credit cards. Once I rang up the transaction through the credit card machine, I would have a credit card deposit slip that could be tendered for cash at any bank.

I had available credit on my cards to carry me for a little while. But I went way over my limits, eventually charging more than $75,000. The bank finally caught on. A bank security officer called and told me to stop the activity. The security office said I must immediately repay the amount above my authorized credit limit. I told him I'd been living solely on the credit card slips for three months. I didn't have any other income.

So, again the police called me. This time, I went to the South Daytona Police Station. My bank branch was located in the city of South Daytona. In less than an hour, I was released on bail. The judge had set my bond at just $1,000. And there I was again in the next day's paper, "Attorney Hill Arrested 2nd Time on Theft Charge."

BILL WAS the next one to be arrested. It turned out the surety bond, which he had received to start doing work for Bethune-Cookman College in November 1989, was indeed a fake. Jake Ross had been right concerning his warnings about Bill, to Dr. Bronson, in March of '90.

The investigators tried to tie me to the crime. I was as surprised as everyone else. The one thing (a valid performance bond) which supposedly set Bill apart from all the other minority contractors, was a fraud. I had to shake my head. The whole thing was a sham from day one.

I read about it all in the local papers. The story said Bill was in the hotel business in the Tampa Bay area. He purchased an interest, and renovated the Admiral Benbow Inn, and was enjoying a bustling business in hotel rooms and a restaurant. Bill sat back while a young enthusiastic general manager, named Kevin Clayton, created the successful lodging environment. Kevin later established, a now defunct jazz night-club in Orlando, named *Pinkie Lee's*, with Robert Billingslea, as one of Clayton's major investors.

I couldn't believe it. All this time, when Bill supposedly was so broke, he was sinking big money into the hotel. He could have easily repaid our bank loans, given all the money he put into the hotel. It really hurt me to read that story. Such a brutal betrayal. How pained I felt for days knowing Bill could easily have saved me from such torment.

Only a few people extended a helping hand to me when I was down. One was a sweet semi-retired lady, who had worked in my law office for about a year and stayed on as a volunteer when I could no longer pay her.

Lee Lambert and her husband, Artie, who were white, even loaned me money several times when I was struggling to meet my payroll at the law office. Lee was in the office during my hard times and knew what was happening in my life.

"This too shall pass," were Lee's constant words of reassurance.

After a court hearing one day on my criminal charges, a local attorney came up and said how sorry he was to hear about all my troubles. His name was Paul Dubbeld. He was a well known criminal attorney, a white guy, 6-foot-3 and blonde hair. He had handled a few high-profile cases and had earned a reputation as a being a sharp, calcu-lating lawyer in the courtroom.

"Anderson, if you need my help, I'd be glad to represent you," he said that day in the courthouse hallway. I hadn't thought about hiring a lawyer. Didn't have the money.

"I won't charge you anything either," he said. "I know you've got a lot of different cases facing you. Whatever I can do, I'm willing to do it. You don't have to pay me a dime."

Oh, thank you God, I thought. Thank you so very much for sending me someone who thinks enough of me to volunteer their time to help me. I could have never afforded Paul. I bet he charged $200 an hour.

Paul took over my criminal cases, filing motions and handling questions from the media. I was glad to see him at least get some free publicity for all his efforts. I wished I could have given him so much more. I knew dozens and dozens of attorneys throughout Central

Florida. Paul was the only one who ever offered to help me.

And I sure needed help. It was only a matter of time before the banks went to the authorities. I searched through the U.S. Code books in my law office and learned that bank fraud carried a maximum penalty of 30 years in federal prison. As a first-time criminal, I wouldn't face the maximum. But, I did know the crime required some mandatory prison time.

THE FLORIDA Bar Association, the licensing body for lawyers, was the next to contact me. The Bar had learned about the theft of the $16,000 from my escrow account.

Lawyers can get arrested for doing cocaine, drinking and driving, and a host of other crimes and not lose their licenses. But stealing a client's funds is a sure way to get kicked out of the Bar. How can the public trust lawyers to handle their money if some of them steal funds and aren't dealt with harshly?

I knew I had other strikes against me. I had been a lawyer for only eight years, and I was black. That wouldn't help. A few years earlier, I had a $2 check on my law office account returned by my bank for insufficient funds. The bank acknowledged it had made a mistake and the matter was promptly resolved. But the Bar's disciplinary arm still sent an investigator to review all of my files and financial books. The investigator nosed around even after the bank backed up my version of the story.

In the end, I received a non-public censure from the Bar for not exercising due care for the returned check, even though bank officials fully admitted it was their error.

This time, no investigator came to my law office. All the statements and paperwork were exchanged via the mail. I picked up the newspaper one morning in April 1991 and read a story that said the Florida Supreme Court had issued an order temporarily suspending my license. The story said the Bar would petition the state Supreme Court to permanently disbar me.

It was an emotional blow to be stripped of my professional title. But it also meant I had no way to earn a living. The lawsuits were coming in a torrent. The banks wanted the cars back, the law office and my residence. The civil process servers knew me by name. "Hey, Anderson, got another one for you," they'd say.

I applied for various jobs around town, hoping to use my masters of business administration. But my name was dirt around Central Florida. So many news stories had appeared that it was as if I was a mass murderer. Friends and acquaintances were bailing out on me like crazy.

I hocked everything I could. I pawned my and my wife's Rolex watches, a bunch of her jewelry, stereo equipment and other possessions. I ran ads in the local newspaper to sell off furniture, our piano and other household goods.

Our church, Greater Friendship Baptist Church, also helped us survive. Pastor J.C. Bentley surprised the congregation and me one Sunday morning when he said unexpectedly, "The Hill family has been very supportive of this church. Now, it's time for the church to be supportive of them."

The collection plates were passed for us that morning and raised $3,000. Pastor Bentley and the congregation donated more on other Sundays. Dr. and Mrs. Gainous, along with other friends, also helped me and my family, whenever they could.

THE PHONE rang at the house one afternoon (I was spending all my days at home now; had no place else to go), and a man on the other end of the line said he was Special Agent Steven Lanser. FBI.

My heart stopped, let me tell you, "The FBI," that gets your attention!

"Mister Hill, I wanted to talk to you about an assignment from Bethune-Cookman College to NCNB."

For a second, I thought the call was a prank. Didn't the FBI knock on your door, flash a badge in your face and then start asking questions? I didn't think they conducted business over the phone. My mind raced to figure out who might play such a joke on me.

"North Carolina National Bank has turned over to us the assignment from Bethune-Cookman College that was used to secure a

$250,000 loan for Renselear Development. The college denies the existence of such an assignment. The college also denies the authenticity of the signature of President Oswald Bronson on the loan document. I know you were involved in this transaction. I'd like to know what your position is on the matter."

Before I could answer, he interjected, "Of course, Mister Hill, you have the right to remain silent. Anything you say, can, and will, be used against you."

I struggled to come up with an answer.

"It was never my intent to defraud a bank," I stammered. "I thought for sure Bill Williams and I would be able to repay them. I even received a check from Bill Williams to repay the loan. But the check - it was for $350,000 - bounced."

"We believe you signed President Bronson's name to these documents. Were you authorized to do so?" Agent Lanser asked.

"Well, you can check the files over there at the college. I was authorized to sign Dr. Bronson's name in legal correspondence, and often, I did. So, yes, I do believe I was authorized to sign his name."

"I see."

"I know you're investigating the case, but let me tell you I didn't do anything wrong. I am diligently trying to repay the loan and I have every intention of doing so as quickly as I possibly can."

"Yes, Mister Hill. We are investigating this case and we're investigating you as well."

"Well, if you're planning to file criminal charges against me, I'll fight them. I didn't do anything wrong."

"Okay. We can either deal with you or deal with Bill Williams. We thought you would be more cooperative in this matter than Bill Williams. If you want me to talk to Mr. Williams and see if he is inter-ested in cooperating with the government, then so be it. Have a great day, Mister Hill," and he hung up.

I had a lot of time to sit around thinking about that call. I didn't know what to do: - cooperate or fight to the end. I was buoyed by a recent victory in the foreclosure action over my house. By using an arcane legal principle, I had blocked the mortgage company from evict-ing us, at least for the time being.

Maybe I could beat a criminal charge. I had Bill's $350,000

bounced check, which would prove my good intentions. I could call several college employees as witnesses to verify that I was allowed to sign Dr. Bronson's name. Some of those same witnesses had signed his name on college correspondence, too. I could talk about Bill's sweetheart deal for Dr. Holmes. And I had a copy of the contract between Dr. Bronson and Bill Williams to buy the shopping center. I had read Dr. Bronson's sworn deposition in the criminal case involving Bill's fraudulent surety bond. Dr. Bronson said he never initiated or conducted personal business with Bill. The contract would show otherwise.

If I could kick up enough dust, I just might walk away scot-free. I talked it over with Paul Dubbeld, my attorney, and he agreed we might have a viable defense.

To convict me, prosecutors would have to prove two elements to a jury: The act itself, which would be easy to do because I did sign Dr. Bronson's name; and secondly, intent to commit a crime. Bill's check was dated Aug. 16, 1991 - the day the NCNB loan came due. That would prove I intended to repay the loan.

I needed only to plant a seed of doubt in the jurors' minds. That's all I needed: reasonable doubt.

I CAME to truly respect the power of the press. They knew more about my life than I did. I picked up the newspaper one morning and saw the headline through the plastic baggy. "Former B-CC Attorney and Contractor Indicted for Bank Fraud." I took the paper inside and sat at the breakfast table in a nook off the kitchen. The seating area was surrounded by wrapped glass windows. Outside, I could see a handful of golfers getting an early start on 18 holes.

I started reading. A federal grand jury, meeting in Orlando, returned a three-count indictment against Anderson Hill, Bill Williams Jr. and Renselear Development Corp. Count one was for bank fraud, maximum penalty of 30 years in prison. Count two was for conspiracy to commit bank fraud, a lesser degree felony carrying a maximum sentence of five years in prison. And count three was to forfeit any assets that had been obtained and remained from the illegal transaction.

I set the paper down and told Sandra about the charges. I never told her about problems until they showed up in the paper. I didn't want her worrying. She was sitting across from me, frowning but quiet as I explained. She wanted to know what this would mean for me and for us as a family.

The phone rang. It was FBI Agent Lanser. He needed to work out a plan to bring me in on the charges. He said he'd trust me to surrender myself at the federal courthouse in Orlando. I told him I'd be in the next morning. I asked if I would need a bondsman. No, he said. The government would recommend to the U.S. Magistrate that I be released on a signature bond, meaning I could sign some paperwork and be released right away.

Although I stayed confined to my house by day, I was still going out regularly at night to party with my friends. After the events of that day, I felt I needed to party hard! I stayed at the clubs till 3 a.m., drinking and doing coke. After I got home, I stayed awake till 5 a.m., doing every last bit of coke I had. I really overindulged that night, worrying about the latest turn of events..

Sandra and I arrived at the federal courthouse promptly at 10 a.m. This was the first time Sandra had accompanied me to a court hearing. The kids were in school, and I guess I needed some extra moral support.

Agent Lanser was waiting in the lobby. He did not look like a gun-toting FBI agent. He looked like an accountant with dark-rimmed glasses and dark hair. He was slightly heavyset. He introduced himself to Sandra and asked if we were ready to go upstairs to the U.S. Marshall's office. On the elevator ride up, he explained to Sandra that the Marshall's office would do a short intake on me, then I would go to my first appearance in the courtroom. She could wait in the hallway until she heard my name called.

The Marshall's office had a steel locked door like in a jail. Agent Lancer showed his I.D. and they buzzed open the door. He turned me over to a clerk who fingerprinted me and placed me in a holding cell. I had worn a white shirt and dark gray suit. The clerk took my tie, belt and shoes.

I sat in the small cell with steel bars for maybe 15 minutes, just long enough to start reflecting on all my mistakes - my stupidity, my greed, my being suckered in by Bill Williams.

A middle-aged, blonde, lady came named Mrs. Fields had some simple questions for me: My address, Where my nearest relatives lived, Previous criminal history. Then she picked up a small plastic cup and said I needed to give a urine sample after my arraignment.

I focused all my concentration on keeping a poker face. Sure, Yeah, A urine sample. No problem!

Inside, I was in a panic. I had enough cocaine in my blood stream to be charged with drug trafficking. How could I have not known about a requirement for a urine sample? As an attorney, I thought I was familiar with these procedures. Damnit! They'll revoke my bond and keep me locked up until my trial. I felt close to throwing up.

"Mister Hill...Mister Hill. It's time for your arraignment."

As Mrs. Fields walked away, two U.S. Marshall's agents came towards me with chains in their hands. They put chains around my hands, waist and feet, and then they ran chains linking all three. I couldn't walk and had to shuffle along to keep from tumbling over. I felt like a slave being led to auction, with the two white marshals on each side of me. All that was left to be done, was to strip off my shirt. Barechest and hobbling, with the chains clacking, it would have then been a classic scene, straight-out of the television epic, *Roots*.

The courtroom was small, barely big enough for maybe 20 lawyers, marshals, clerks and defendants. Spectators and the defendants' relatives had to wait in the hallway until their case was called. I spotted Sandra as they led me into the courtroom. I hated for her to see me this way. I looked like a criminal and felt like one, too.

A court clerk announced my name and case number. The U.S. Magistrate, Donald Dietrich, asked what I had to say about the charges. I wondered if he remembered me. I had been in his courtroom before, representing clients.

"I'm a former attorney, your Honor, and now I find myself at the mercy of the court. I respectfully enter a plea of not guilty."

"Yes, Mr. Hill. I remember you. I'm sorry to see you in this situation. But the government and grand jury have brought some rather serious charges against you. I will set a signature bond at fifty thousand."

The judge banged the gavel, everyone rose and he walked out.

A black assistant public defender walked up and patted me on the shoulder. I was standing there, head hung, looking at the floor. "Hey, be strong, be honest and things will work out," the young black man said.

I mustered a smile.

The Marshall's agents led me over to the court clerk. The young lady handed me some papers, told me to read and to sign them. Then, the agents led me back to the cell to wait until the paperwork was processed and I could be released.

As I walked out, I saw Sandra waiting in the hallway. I started to ask her to give a urine sample for me. I knew she didn't drink alcohol or do drugs. But I changed my mind, fearing the lab would be able to tell the person's sex by their urine. Sandra could end up in trouble with the law. I wasn't going to take that chance.

I went into the men's room and urinated as little as possible into the cup. Then I filled the rest of it up with water. I had no idea if it would hide my cocaine use. But it was the best I could do.

I took the sample back to Mrs. Fields and left it with her. I knew it wouldn't take long for me to hear about my sample.

That afternoon, Mrs. Fields called me at my home and said I had tested positive for cocaine use. I sounded shocked and kept saying there must be some kind of mistake. I've never used cocaine. Did my sample get mixed up with someone else's? Blah, blah, blah.

She'd probably heard it a hundred times before. She said I could be retested if I believed a mistake had been made. I told her I'd be back first thing in the morning. That gave me about 18 hours. Time to drink fluids. Lots of fluids. So much water and juices, I thought I'd burst.

But next time, my urine was clear. I tested negative.

Mrs. Fields said I still had to submit to a random drug-testing program. I said I'd happily comply because I never used illegal drugs.

I had decided to finally give up drugs and alcohol. After all the craziness and all the wasted money, I was finally going clean.

I couldn't risk it. One more bad urine sample and my butt would be sitting in jail. I needed to sober up anyway. Clear my head, especially if I wanted to find a way out of all these criminal charges. Cocaine and alcohol had caused me to lose my focus. I decided from that point on, I would never drink or do drugs again.

It would be for the best. Sandra was losing hope with me and surely was thinking about going back to her mother in Little Rock and taking the kids. I was on thin ice with her. My actions had disgraced her among her own circle of friends, not to mention, I had forced us into virtual poverty. Even our electricity and water service had been disconnected several times for failure to pay our bills. We had to dip water from the swimming pool to flush the toilets, when the water was shut-off. She had never lived like that in her life. Now, she'd finally get what she had been asking for years: Me to sober up.

My plan was coming into sharp focus. I'd defend myself in the criminal matters, no matter what it took. Why worry about saving Bill Williams or protecting Dr. Bronson? They weren't doing anything to help me now. I needed to protect myself and keep my family intact, circle the wagons.

I thought about Bill. He had been in trouble time and time again. Yet, he managed to stay out of prison. I had learned more from him than I realized. I, too, could escape this mess. I'd take down Dr. Bronson, Dr. Holmes and anyone else, if necessary. None of them care about me. Why should I care about them?

COME BY EARLY

You should have come by earlier
and I could have been better for you.
I could have acknowledged your presence
without much ado.
You should have come by earlier
and you would have seen me in my heyday.
I could have taught you a few things.

But you so late.
I can't do a thing for you.
You see I have failed to preserve a picture
for you.
You see me in my solemn clothes.

You should have come by earlier my son.

7 THE FORGOTTEN SON

"There are no illegitimate children - only illegitimate parents."
U.S. District Court Judge Leon R. Yankwich in a 1928 court decision.

THE stadium overflowed with 5,000 screaming parents and students, cheering for their team to win the 1991 Oklahoma state regional high-school football championship. The scoreboard read 28-24, Guthrie High over Stillwater High. Ten seconds remained on the game clock. Stillwater had the ball on Guthrie's eight-yard line.

The team needed a touchdown; a field goal would mean nothing.

The quarterback snapped the ball, rolled to the right, faked a pass into the end zone and handed off to a beefy running back - his bright orange uniform caked with clay from the constant pounding of four quarters. The running back found a hole and accelerated as he dodged a few hapless tackles. The end zone was in sight. A mere seven yards away. Run, baby. Run.

A Guthrie middle linebacker was the only thing standing between him and the game-winning touchdown. The running back danced right, then left, trying to shake off the linebacker. He looked like a big guy in his navy blue jersey and clay-covered white pants; he was 5-foot-10, 180 pounds. And he wasn't falling for the fake.

Crack.

The two players butted their helmets like rams and dropped onto the muddy field. Stopped at the four yard line. Game over.

The jubilant Guthrie team ran from the sideline to congratulate their teammates on the field. Their star linebacker lay motionless, face down, after the furious hit.

"C'mon, Greg. Get up. Get up." A couple of members of the defensive squad bent down and touched the Most Valuable Defensive Player of the Year on the shoulder. "C'mon Greg. We won. Get up."

Greg had been stunned by the hit, but he wasn't in pain. He lay still with his eyes open, savoring the moment. His last high school game. The cheering crowd. All his teammates around him. He knew he was the game hero.

Sad for Greg that his father did not witness his moment of glory. And even sadder for his father for missing one of those moments that produce a well-spring of pride in a parent. Another lost opportunity to beam and say, "That's my boy."

THE year was 1972. I was starting the second semester of my freshman year at Langston University in Oklahoma. I was dashing from one red brick classroom building to another, covered in a green parka to try and keep me dry in a cold, blowing downpour.

I noticed an attractive young woman - a petite 5-foot-5 with a short afro and sparkling eyes, and a figure right out of a centerfold of *Jet* magazine - running towards me from another building.

"Here," I said, taking off my parka. "This will match your lovely eyes."

She smiled and put the parka over her head. I could barely see her underneath all the fabric.

"I'm Anderson Hill, Erma's brother. What's your name?"

She appeared shy and said, in a barely audible voice, "Esther Coleman."

I followed her into a building and tried to keep a conversation going as she walked to her next class. She was a sophomore and a sociology major who lived in a dorm on campus.

I was thrilled to meet such a sweet girl. Sandra and I had broken up several months earlier. A girlfriend would be nice. I didn't have a steady girl at Langston.

Esther and I were soon seen walking together around campus. We made a good couple. Even my sister, Erma, approved. She said Esther was one of the nicest girls on campus, so shy and cute.

When I left Langston for the University of Oklahoma in Norman, about 50 miles away, I continued to see her.

I'd drive over to her parents house in Guthrie, just outside of Langston. Esther had nine siblings, and the family's small white, two-story, wooden-frame house bustled with non-stop activity. Her father was a minister at a local church. With so many kids to raise, the Colemans' economic status appeared to be similar to my own family's.

Esther and I would sit around and talk to her brothers and sisters for hours. Then we'd take my 1965 Chevy back to Norman. I had an apartment then with Ruel Green, but Ruel was out quite often, so Esther and I had plenty of privacy.

I was genuinely fond of her, but my heart belonged to Sandra. I was dazzled by Sandra in a way that I never felt for Esther. In retrospect, I realized I had let Sandra go too easily. We had gotten into a big blow-up and, with me going off to college, a break-up seemed the right thing to do. I had been stupid, letting my foolish pride stop me from getting her back.

During Christmas break, when I returned home to Little Rock, discouraged about my poor progress at the University of Oklahoma, I called Sandra and asked her out. Our relationship was always comfortable and easy-going in that way some couples instinctively take to one another.

My plan was to reunite with Sandra for good. And I was thinking about leaving the University of Oklahoma. During the three week Christmas break, I did some research and decided to return to a historically black college. This time, though, as I said earlier, I chose one in an urban setting - Atlanta.

I called Ruel and said I wouldn't be returning to Oklahoma. I'd stay in Little Rock for the spring, working, close enough to visit Hendrix College where Sandra was attending her freshman year. I'd get my paperwork together to apply to the Atlanta University system and enroll that summer.

Esther had no place in these plans.

The next thing I knew, my sister had me on the phone from Langston, yelling at me.

"Brother, what have you done to Esther? I saw her on campus, and she's fat, really fat. Boy, you better get your butt back up here and take care of her and your baby."

"What?"

"Your baby! Esther is pregnant! Now, don't tell me you're going to do like all these other niggers and run away from your responsibilities! I know why you didn't come back to Oklahoma. You're running away! Well, I'm telling Momma."

"I didn't know Esther was pregnant. I haven't seen her in months. You don't know if that baby's mine or not. Why are you blaming me when you don't know for sure?"

"I do know, Brother. Esther told me she never slept with anybody else, before or after you. She said you are that baby's daddy. Now, what you going to do?"

"I don't know."

I was 20 years old, too young and self-centered to think about Esther or a baby. My only worries were whether Sandra and her parents would find out. If so, Sandra would surely break off our relationship for good. I was certain of that. And I didn't want to give up my exciting plans of going to live in Atlanta.

Returning to Langston, marrying Esther, doing the responsible thing. Well, I never even considered that path.

I didn't call Esther nor did I offer any financial support. From that point forth, I ignored the situation. I know Erma and my Momma talked about the pregnancy and, from time to time, Erma contacted Esther about the baby boy. They passed on news about him, but they didn't pressure me to see him.

It was easy for me not to think about the baby, named Gregory Yhonce Coleman. I heard Esther married a man after graduating from Langston. Her husband probably loved Gregory and treated him like his own son. I rationalized that Greg was being cared for and didn't need me. I'd have my own family to worry about.

TWELVE years later, not long after I graduated from law school, I was sitting in my first law office, four blocks east of the Bethune-Cookman College campus. I rented a small storefront. L&D Electric was on one side, a sandwich shop on the other and railroad tracks were across the street. Upstairs was a three-bedroom apartment, shared by what seemed to be a dozen Bethune-Cookman students.

I was the college's "in-training" attorney and also taught undergraduate business classes. I had walked back in from one of my classes when the phone rang. I picked it up and immediately recognized the voice.

"Anderson? Anderson? Is that you."

"Esther?"

"Yes, it's Esther Coleman. Remember me?"

"Sure, I do. How ya' doing?"

I sounded friendly but was nervous. I hadn't talked to her since 1973. What did she want after all this time?

"I'm okay. I know this call is a surprise. You're probably wondering how I even found you. Well I saw Ruel, you remember Ruel Green, your old roommate, Ruel said you're an attorney now in Daytona Beach. I just called information and got your number."

"Yeah, I'm working for Bethune-Cookman College down here. I'm married and got a couple kids."

"I was married, too, but we've split up. I've still got just the one kid. Which is why I'm calling, Anderson."

"Uh, huh."

"Throughout the years, Greg has always asked about his real father. He keeps asking me to find you. I promised him this time I would. He'd like to speak to you and get to know you. I hope that's all right."

"Sure."

I could hear Esther whispering to Greg. He came on the line.

"Hello, Dad. This is Greg."

He had a sweet, high young boy's voice.

"Hi, there, young man."

"I know you don't know me. I do good in school and I like football. Momma says I look like you. She says I have your smile. Do I have any brothers and sisters? Can you come and see me?"

I was rocked by conflicting emotions. His little voice warmed my heart. But my head struggled to figure out how to deal with this situation. Sandra and my two children knew nothing about Greg. I had thought about telling Sandra many times, but I never did. That's the trouble with lies. Once you tell a lie, you can't seem to get out of it until life shoves the truth right in your face.

"Greg. I am sorry that I never contacted you. I am proud that you wanted to find me and talk to me. I've missed being your father. And sure, I'd love to come see you. You can come visit me, too, and meet your brother and sister."

"Yippee! I knew you'd want to see me, Dad."

I asked him to put Esther back on the line. Once she returned, I asked her to go to a phone where Greg couldn't hear our conversation.

"Esther, I'm sorry I abandoned you and Greg. I know it must

have been difficult for you all these years. He sounds like a very well-mannered and sweet kid. You've done a good job raising him. I feel real bad about my conduct. At the least, I should have been helping you financially."

"I'm not calling for money, Anderson, and I don't want child-support payments. We're doing fine. I'm calling for Gregory. He loves you, even though he's never seen you. I would like you and him to start building a relationship. It's not too late for that, Anderson."

"I agree, Esther. I'd like him to come spend the summer with us. There's a problem I need to deal with first. I ... ahh ... I never told my wife about Greg. She doesn't know anything. I should have told her but I never did. I'm not sure what to do now."

"Oh, Anderson. I'm sorry. I assumed your family knew about us. I don't mean to put you in an awkward position. I guess I shouldn't have called out of the blue. Why don't you think about all this and call me back sometime? I'll give you our phone number. I'll explain to Greg that this will take a little more time."

"No, Esther. That's not what I'm saying. I want to see Greg. I just need to handle this delicately at my end. I don't want to hurt Sandra and I definitely don't want to jeopardize my marriage."

"Yeah."

"How about this? Let me give you my address and you write me a letter, saying you decided to contact me after all these years to tell me I have a son. Send along a picture of Greg and your address and phone number. I'll show it to Sandra and tell her this is the first I knew of it. Yeah, do that. And I'll still plan for Greg to come this summer."

Sure enough, Esther wrote the letter. It appeared in our mailbox the following week. I showed it to Sandra, acting all shocked and anxious about the news. I lied, lied, lied to her. Of course, she said I should do the right thing and bring Greg down for a visit as soon as possible.

He was 10 when he arrived at the Daytona Beach Airport that summer, a tall, lanky kid with hazel cat-like eyes and caramel-colored skin that reminded me of his mother. I did recognize in him my wide-tooth smile and a body frame that one day would sprout as big as mine.

I went alone to get him at the airport, figuring we could spend some father-son time on the drive back to our home. We lived in Port

Orange then, about 15 minutes south of Daytona Beach, in a starter home, a three-bedroom, two-bath, concrete stucco house in a rather non-descript, middle-class neighborhood.

Greg was on his best behavior that summer. He was quiet and obedient. He took right away to his little sister, Lauren, then 1. But I noticed a rub with Andy, then 3. If Sandra and I weren't in the room, Greg would treat Andy badly, grabbing things out of his hand or simply ignoring him.

Based on my feelings of rejection from my father's absence as a child, I knew Greg was feeling abandoned. He was jealous and angry that Andy had received my full-time attention. I hoped time would help heal his wound.

When Greg returned to Oklahoma, I tried to compensate for lost time by sending his mother hundreds of dollars at a time. I bought him a motorcycle, just like the one I had as a boy. And beginning in that summer of 1985, Greg made it a habit to come stay with us every summer.

I talked often about him attending Bethune-Cookman College. I said I'd pay all his tuition and expenses. He was a good student in school and would have no trouble getting accepted to the college.

IN late 1991, when Greg was named Most Valuable Defensive Player of the Year and made the game-saving tackle at the state championship, I had already been arrested for stealing the escrow account money, for running up $75,000 in credit-card advances and for federal bank fraud.

I had told Greg the preceding summer not to visit us. Our lives were too chaotic, fighting bill collectors and surviving day to day with no steady income.

Greg knew none of these details. I put off telling him for as long as possible.

He was planning to attend Bethune-Cookman College the following fall. For years, he had looked forward to being a student on campus while his father was the college's star attorney, a top administrator and possibly its future president.

He needed to know his future had changed. I'd been fired from the college and could be in prison when he arrived to start college.

He was quiet after I told him over the phone, giving him the barest details of my crimes.

"Dad. I don't understand. How could you do those things when you always tell me to stay out of trouble?"

He sounded even more disappointed when I explained that I wouldn't be able to attend his high school graduation that spring. I urged him to continue his plans to attend Bethune-Cookman in the fall. I would try to work out financial arrangements with the college.

"I still love Bethune-Cookman and think you'll get a great education there," I told him. "Had I known the type of school it was, with its inspiring heritage, I would have attended college there.

"I don't want to let my mistakes stand in your way, Greg. It seems like it's becoming a cycle in our family. Men going to prison. First my father, now maybe me. I tried hard to avoid trouble, but I didn't. You've got to go to college and make something of your life, Greg."

I made arrangements at Bethune-Cookman for him to enroll in the fall of 1992. I didn't have money for his tuition, but luckily, he didn't need it. The college helped him obtain a variety of grants and scholarships. As the fall drew nearer, I warned Greg that he may encounter negative comments on campus, once the staff and students learned he was my son.

Even I did not foresee how vicious they would be. It hurt me deeply for Greg, who was only a kid. He was innocent in the whole matter and had no control over my actions. But he received the blame and the punishment.

A couple of times, professors even brought up the whole nasty affair during classes, going to great pains to tell the class that Greg's father, Anderson C. Hill, stole hundreds of thousands of dollars from the college and brought more shame upon the great institution than any other person in its 90-plus year history.

Dr. Bronson had fully supported Greg's enrollment, but his influence stopped at the presidential door. In classes and around campus, Greg took a verbal beating. He felt like a kid against the rest of the world.

I saw such sadness in his eyes. I asked him once if he could forgive me. I had caused him great pain, twice in his life: By abandoning him as a baby and by abandoning him again now after I promised to provide for him in college..

He said I was still his father and he would always love me. I thought, after hearing those gracious words from his heart, "He is a great son!" God blessed me to have him in my life.

I said he could transfer to another college if the treatment at Bethune-Cookman grew too bad. I also said he should stay in touch with Dr. Bronson and Dr. Gainous, who could help look after him.

"Yeah, Dad. I'm friends with Chip Bronson."

"You are?"

Chip was Dr. Bronson's son. When he was a teenager and I was the college attorney, I helped get him out of a drug possession charge.

"Chip was telling me about you and his father. He said Doctor Bronson used to be jealous of you and your success before you got into trouble. He said his father couldn't stand your Benzes and your big house in Pelican Bay."

"What caused that conversation to come up?"

"Chip said you helped him when he was arrested for possession of drugs. Chip really appreciated that and he thinks you're a good person. He wanted me to know that. I guess his father was talking bad about you before you got into trouble."

Years later, I would learn of similar statements. My sister, Erma, had called Dr. Bronson once, worried about my mounting debt and stress. He wouldn't talk to her, but he put his wife, Helen, on the phone. Helen said she and Dr. Bronson should have been living in that big house at Pelican Bay, not the Hills. This concluded their conversation.

Greg couldn't survive much longer at Bethune-Cookman. He moved back to Oklahoma and said he would attend a college closer to his mother. I continued to talk to him by phone and would see him whenever possible. But he was a man now; leading his own life.

Not too long ago, he rode from Oklahoma to Houston with a childhood friend. They were going to get a hotel room in Houston, hit the clubs and kick around a bit. On the way back, they were pulled over by police, while Greg was asleep in the front passenger's seat. When the officer questioned the two young men about the reason for their trip, they gave different answers. Greg told the officers, that unexpectedly, his friend's car, was driven away for a short period of time, by another man. The two of them stayed at the hotel, until the car was returned. Greg did not know the man, nor the reason that the car was driven away. The cop called in a dog, which alerted on an inside panel of the car.

The cops ripped apart the interior and discovered inside, several specially-made, secret compartments. The search netted $2 million (street value) worth of cocaine.

Greg called me from a Texas jailhouse. He swore he didn't know anything about the drugs. He was along for the ride. I then talked to one of the detectives, and he agreed that it appeared Greg knew nothing about the stash and said that he would include this fact in his police report. I believed Greg, too, and I felt very badly about my son's circumstances.

I don't believe in jinxes or black magic. But with the third generation of my blood line spending time in jail, I struggle to understand why we cannot break free of this vicious imprisonment cycle. Any amount of jail time, whether long or short, is a certain loss, to the individual and to our society. Maybe we have failed because we lacked a caring, supportive, male role model. My Momma was always there for me and Greg's mother for him, but a child needs a full-time father, too! Proper guidance and love are very important to all children, regardless of race. If so, who will be the first one of my children, and of the children of millions of other African-American men, blessed enough to break this regrettable cycle? *The Sentencing Project*, issued a report, co-authored by a Marc Mauer in October 1995, which firmly stated, based on U.S. Justice Department statistics, that almost one in every three young black men, are either in prison, on probation or parole.

And until then, as Momma would always say, are large numbers of black men destined to end up as "more bait for the white folks?" Unfortunately, I did!

FACE THE TRUTH AND BE DONE WITH A LIE

Slipped, and dipped
slided and glided.
The star falls to the ground.

Founded on the principle of truth and justice.
Gridlocked by the affirmative.
Surrounded by realities of infinite wisdom.

There is no shaking of firm foundations.
Mommas don't lie.
They snatch their babies from the lion's den.

Face the truth and be done with a lie.

8 SLICK WILLY

"You will know the truth, and the truth will make you free."
Holy Bible, New Testament, John 8:32

THE steel guardrail was slippery from the gusty rain. I wrapped my left arm around an antique-style light post to keep my balance on the edge of the high-rise bridge, 500 feet above the Halifax River.

From my perch, I could see the neon sign on the building that once had been my Mirage nightclub. The new sign said, Billy Bobs, a country-western restaurant and bar, which had attracted big crowds ever since it opened.

As I stared into the night-time sky, the rain pelting my face, I found it fittingly ironic. Not long ago, I was pulling up to the Mirage in my big Benz, handing out cash and partying non-stop. Tonight, I parked near the Port Orange bridge in a 6-year-old Buick Century (the Benzes had been repossessed) and climbed onto the railing to commit suicide.

I heard footsteps coming my way and, turning around, was surprised to see Bill Williams. Before I could react, he leapt toward me, his arms outstretched. "Too late, sucker," he said as he pushed me off of the bridge. I tumbled in super-slow-motion, waiting for what seemed like an eternity to hit the chilly water. I screamed in the loudest cry I had ever uttered.

"Anderson! Anderson! Wake up!" I opened my eyes and saw Sandra leaning over me, shaking my shoulder. "You were having a nightmare."

I gasped for breath. The anxiety of the dream had triggered an asthma attack - my first one in years - and I felt panicked as my lungs struggled for oxygen. Sandra ran to the bathroom to get my asthma inhaler.

I didn't know if I wanted to live or die. The path I had chosen was becoming increasingly stressful, spending my days and nights scheming, scheming, scheming to get out of the criminal charges that faced me. My lies were supposed to weave a cocoon to keep me safe. Instead, they were strung so taut, they were choking the life out of me.

The evening before, I had spoken candidly and honestly with my mother about my problems. Up until then, I parceled out only little pieces of information about what was happening, in an attempt to shield her from worry, and also to protect myself from the shame and humiliation of my actions.

"Brother," she had said on the phone. "These are the hardest words a mother ever says, but I told you so. I warned you about that man, Bill Williams. I knew he was up to no good. You let him lead you down the wrong path. You need to pull yourself together right now and do what's right. You didn't go to school all of those years for nothing. Use your good sense and think about your wife and kids."

I hated to admit it, but she was right. She had warned me a year and a half before. At the time, I had just started working with Bill. Momma came for a visit from Little Rock. We all went to dinner with Bill at one of the nicest restaurants in town, The Chart House, built alongside the Daytona Beach Marina with plenty of windows to enjoy the relaxing view of sail boats rocking graciously in their moorings.

"Your son and I are going to conquer the world, Mrs. Hill. He is going to be the president of the college. I know you're proud of him. You sure did a good job of raising him," Bill said that night.

He talked incessantly during the entire meal, outlining our construction plans at Bethune-Cookman College, his other business ventures and all his material possessions. I noticed Momma didn't say much. She politely listened and nodded her head.

When we got back home, I asked her if she was feeling okay.

"Momma, what's wrong? You didn't seem to enjoy your meal."

She placed her hand on my shoulder and a frown came across her face, reminding me of all the times she had scolded me as a boy.

"Brother, anytime a man talks as much as Bill Williams does, he's a liar. You should not trust him, son. I didn't understand everything he was saying about your business dealings, but I understood the gist of it. All those big projects - this and that - highfalutin good-for-nothing. You need to distance yourself from him before it's too late. The people at your college aren't going to like you fooling around with him."

"Oh, Momma, Bill's all right. He's a rich man and has a lot on the ball. I'm fortunate to be associated with him."

"Son, you're not listening to me. You're too old for me to be telling you what to do. All I can do is offer my advice. Whatever that man is doing, it can lead to no good."

I hadn't listened to Momma, nor had I heeded the warnings of Sandra and my sister, Erma. Sandra and Erma had confronted me about my drug abuse numerous times over the years and the dangers of my mounting debt, but I didn't listen. I told myself I was the shrewd and savvy professional man who was taking life by storm. What did those women know?

Now, they were all I had left. My income, my professional stature, and the vast majority of my friends were gone.

Momma, Erma and Sandra were talking all the time by phone these days, preferably when I was not around. They decided they were going to pound some sense in my head, and get me back on the right track, if it was the last thing they did.

"San," Erma told Sandra on the phone. "You need to talk with Anderson. Tell him he better not mess up anymore or you're going to leave him. I know you love him and he loves you. He always has. That's why you've got to tell him. It's his choice now. He has to take the steps to get his life back together. He caused all this trouble, not you, San."

Sandra was crying on the phone, so distraught about what the future would bring for her and Andy and Lauren. She needed all the emotional support she could get from her family and mine. I was too wrapped up in my own worries to be much comfort to her.

"Where is that boy," Erma said, the anger building in her voice. She wanted to get in her car that minute, drive across five states and kick my butt. "I'm going to tell him how much you and the kids have suffered as a result of his drug use and stupidity with that crook, Bill."

"I've been trying to talk to him, Erma. He's suffering so much right now, I don't want to push him over the edge. Everyone is on his case. He doesn't need me yelling at him, too. I'll never understand why he did all these things. He has always been so blessed. I guess this is the way the Lord has of getting our attention. Everyone falls short of true glory. "

"I think you should get on his case, San. He got himself into this mess. He better figure out how he's going to get out of it."

"I don't want Anderson to rush into any decisions right now. He needs to be patient and figure out what is the right thing to do. One more mistake and it's off to prison for sure. He's always doing things too fast. That's part of his problem. Just like buying those cars and the nightclub.

Before I knew any of it, he'd made the deals."

I returned home just after Sandra and Erma hung up on that Saturday evening. Sandra met me in the garage as I pulled in the gray, 1986 four-door Buick, which I had been thrilled to get from a local dealership. It looked so out of place sitting alone in our three-car garage.

"Anderson, let's talk," she said as soon as I opened the car door. She was dressed in a yellow cotton shorts set. Her face looked so serious and I could tell she had been crying.

I leaned against the car. The steel panel felt warm under my casual black cotton slacks.

"I've been talking with my mother, Erma, and your mother all day," she said. "We all need to be sure of something, Anderson. We want to know if you're going to learn from all these mistakes and become a better person. If you're not, then I don't know if I can stay here with you."

"There's no other place I would rather be than with you," she continued. "Only you know what happened, who did what, and why all those things went on. I'm not a lawyer, but I am a Christian. The Bible says the truth will set you free. Anderson, do you still believe in God and his power?"

I stood mute.

"You, and you alone, have to decide these things, Anderson. We can't do it for you. I pray - we all are praying - that you will do the right thing from this point on, regardless of what happened in the past. We still have a lot to be thankful for. Think of our children."

She looked so beautiful and vulnerable standing before me. More than anything, I always thought of myself as her protector. I would have killed any man who hurt her. And in the end, it was me who hurt her the most.

I hadn't realized until that moment how worried I had been that she would leave, half expecting it, wondering if I would walk in the house someday and find a note saying she and the kids went to Little Rock.

I grabbed her in my arms and kissed her as passionately as when we were teenagers.

"Oh, San, I want to do the right thing. I don't know what that is anymore. Look around, everything I wanted for you and the kids is gone.

I'm just so exhausted. I'm so tired of everything."

"I know this is hard on you, Anderson. It's been hard on all of us. What I'm saying is that if we're going to start over again, it has to be the right way. I don't care if we have a garage full of Mercedes Benzes or not. But it does matter that you and I do right by God."

"Yeah, I know. Tomorrow we'll go to church. That is the one place we can always find relief. Come as you are, huh, Sandy?"

"Yes, Anderson, go as you are. JESUS will fix it for us. He always has. Just be the man I married. Not anyone else."

That was the evening I called Momma for an honest talk about my trouble. And it was the night of my dream of suicide and death.

I had climbed into bed that night and pulled the maroon, goose-down comforter high over my head. I was sweaty hot, but I didn't care. I was hiding from the world, hoping tomorrow wouldn't come.

After Sandra woke me from my nightmare and the medicine soothed my asthma attack, I sat on the side of our wooden king-size bed, which had a small canopy that covered where we rested our heads, and turned the faint light on my side of the headboard. Sandra drifted back to sleep but I sat up for hours.

My mind felt clearer than it had in a long time. And more importantly, I could feel my gut instincts again. All the drug abuse, lying, and scheming had dulled their ability to read people and situations. Now, my instincts were pushing me in a new direction.

I could feel it - knew it for a fact - that Bill Williams was counting on me fighting the criminal charges. If I spent all my time taking down Dr. Bronson and Dr. Holmes, he could piggyback on my efforts and walk away a free man, too.

I had been so busy plotting my legal strategy that I hadn't thought about what tack Bill would take. But that night it came into clear view.

My defense was going to rely on Bill's bounced check for $350,000. Because that showed I tried to repay the bank. I also would attest that I had permission to sign Dr. Bronson's name to legal documents.

Bill was counting on just those two elements himself. He could easily say he thought I did have permission, as college attorney, to sign for the loans and he had no idea that my actions were unauthorized or he would have never entered into the loans in the first place. He discovered too late that I had forged the president's signature. That's why he immediately gave me the $350,000 check to pay them off.

Boy, I could just see Bill up on the stand, playing that part like he was on a Broadway stage. And when I was called to testify, I wouldn't be able to refute his false story. If I rebutted his testimony, by telling the jury how he had schemed and lied and plotted the whole thing, then I'd be slitting my own throat.

If I lied, Bill walked, too. It would be a "win-win" legal scenario for Bill.

And besides helping Bill get off, my legal strategy also wasn't fair to Dr. Bronson.

Even if he had been jealous of my success, that didn't warrant destroying his career. He had been nothing but good to me. To use him as my battering board would be playing right into evil's hands. Dr. Bronson knew nothing of our illegal transactions with NCNB.

It all made sense to me now. That's why Bill hadn't refused to give me the check for $350,000. I thought he gave it to me because I threatened him. He didn't care about that. He was preparing his own escape hatch. Even after the check bounced and the FBI became involved in the case, Bill only asked me once, half-heartedly, for the check back.

That check would ensure his protection.

I made a decision right there at 5:30 a.m. on a Sunday morning, with Sandra sleeping beside me. I knew it would mean I would most likely go to prison and be separated from Sandra, Andy, Greg and Lauren. But once I made up my mind, I never wavered. I used the bible scripture, "What does a man profit to gain the world and then lose his soul?," as my new source of strength.

I CONTACTED the Assistant U.S. Attorney, who was handling the bank fraud case and said I would cooperate with his prosecution of Bill Williams. I had done everything I was accused of and wanted to work out a plea arrangement. I told the prosecutor that Bill Williams had managed to escape criminal charges in the past and I wanted to make sure he was convicted this time.

We worked out a plea bargain regarding my involvement in the North Carolina National Bank forgery. The U.S. Attorney dropped the major count of bank fraud and the seizure of assets charges. I agreed to plead no contest to lesser count of conspiracy to commit bank fraud, a charge that did not carry a mandatory prison term. They also agreed to give me immunity from any other charges that might come from my association with Bill Williams and Bethune-Cookman College.

I met the Assistant U.S. Attorney in Orlando on the day I was supposed to sign the deal. In the room this time was a new face. He introduced himself as Charles Boling, FBI agent from Daytona Beach. He was a middle-aged white guy, with dark hair and wearing a plaid sports coat. He had a folder in front of him. From it, he pulled a piece of paper and handed it to me.

It was the letter which I had written months before to Lou Wenger, the rich developer in New York, who was considering giving Bill Williams a $1 million line of credit. The FBI agent asked me if I wrote the letter. I said I had; the signature on the letter was mine.

He frowned.

"I don't understand. Yes, I had met with Mister Wenger on one occasion in December of '90. He didn't mention to me that he had extended the line of credit to Bill, at that time. But at that time I thought Wenger had backed out of extending the one million dollar line of credit to Bill, which had been one of our schemes to repay the two bank loans. If I recall correctly, he was in Daytona to look around the construction site, and the potential for working on phase II."

"Mister Wenger did not back out of the deal," the agent said. I could tell he was reading my face to see if I was lying to him. "Mister Wenger gave Bill Williams one hundred seventy-five thousand dollars."

"He did it after Bill had told me that the deal had fallen through!" I sounded incredulous. "I'm sorry that I didn't check with Wenger at that time, to alert him that my letter was a hoax, because I thought that had Bill received any money, he would certainly pay the banks. The banks were never paid."

"Yes, Mr. Hill. On or around September twentieth last year, Mr. Wenger sent a wire transfer to Bill Williams for one hundred, seventy-five thousand dollars."

I just shook my head. I thought I had known Bill so well. But his level of scheming continued to amaze even me.

I reiterated that I had received none of the money. Of course, the agent already knew this. He had received a court order to get all of my personal bank records, along with Bill's bank records, and could trace where every cent of the money had been spent.

Bill's bank records showed that he had used the bulk of the money to buy an interest in a large Tampa hotel, which he was now operating. This revelation had served as further proof to me, and now to the prosecutors, that Bill never had any intention of repaying the bank loans. I agreed to repay Wenger as a part of my plea bargain. No criminal charges were ever filed against me in that matter, but Bill was later charged with wire fraud.

The FBI agent also explained another scheme that Bill had initiated. I found it rather ironic and almost chuckled right in front of the investigators and prosecutors.

When Bill had been traveling to the Virgin Islands, looking for work after Hurricane Hugo, he had agreed to rebuild a man's home. Bill received a $50,000 deposit for the work and then disappeared. Turns out the victim in this case was either the U.S. Attorney for that region or one of his assistants. As the FBI agent and Assistant U.S. attorney showed me the documents from this latest fraud case, I could tell they wanted to nail Bill because Bill had victimized one of their own.

I continued to meet regularly with the prosecution team to help prepare for Bill's trial. As we sat in the U.S. Attorney's office during one of these meetings, the young prosecutor explained his theory of the case and his strategy to get a conviction.

"There's an easier way to convict Bill," I said when he finished. "The basis of the indictment is bank fraud. It would be simpler to prove bank fraud when you have a situation that involves Bill receiving double payments for the same work."

The prosecutor, Richard Newsome, and FBI Agent Steve Lanser appeared confused. I could tell Newsome - with his snappy suspenders, and young face, right out of The University of Florida Law School - didn't think I could tell this powerful government machine anything they didn't already know.

They looked at the elaborate charts propped up on easels around the room, detailing where every dollar of the $250,000 NCNB loan had gone. The charts showed Bill had given me $152,000, and that I had turned around and given United American Bank a check for $120,000 from those funds.

The two men looked back at me, waiting.

I put my expanding file on the table and began thumbing through it. As an accountant, and then a lawyer, I had learned to keep detailed and thorough files. I had made personal copies of every document and letter generated from my involvement with Bill. And with my detailed filing system, I could easily retrieve them.

I now pulled out a requisition (pay request) form that was attached to an invoice from Bill Williams. It had been personally signed by Dr. Bronson and myself, authorizing a check for Renselear for $103,500. This was money for site preparation on the Spuds project. Next I pulled out the assignment to NCNB, which Williams had used to secure the $250,000 loan. The two were for the same work criteria, although the prices were inflated for the bank. Bill told NCNB he had not been paid for the Spuds work and would turn the check over to the bank when he got it to repay the loan. At that time, he had already received payment from the college.

The prosecutor turned to Agent Lanser.

"Did you know about this?"

"No, I didn't. I went to the college and requested all their documents regarding Bill Williams. This information was not provided to me," the agent replied.

"I know why you didn't get it. Someone at the college probably did not want to disclose the fact that a large sum of money had been paid to Renselear under my request, when I was administratively no longer involved in the college's construction process. There were several other unethical transactions going on at the time of the disbursement of the college's check to Renselear in March '90 for the Spuds project. One transaction regarded a private shopping center purchase, while the other involved a cash payment of $65,000 to me, by Renselear. The shopping center transaction fell through," I said. "There's no way Bill Williams can wiggle out by playing ignorant because his signature is on both the invoice attached to the college's requisition, and the documents submitted to NCNB. They were requests for double payment of the same services."

I cried when I thought about how my greed had caused me to get caught up in the Spuds construction dilemma. Why didn't I realize that the transaction had gone too smoothly, without any real substantive questions or concerns, when there should have been many? Had I not followed Bill's lead that day, then Tommy would have rightfully kept the contract, and therefore there wouldn't have been a later duplicated contractual invoice to assign to NCNB. I didn't expect the college to have engaged in any type of obstruction of justice, regarding everyone's prior knowledge about the bonding investigation, but had I been given any courtesy of knowing about it, I would have backed off of Bill too, just as quickly as Tommy and Dr. Bronson did. I would not have found myself sitting in the U.S. Attorney's office, as a cooperating witness involved in bank fraud.

AS the trial date arrived, I knew Bill's team of high-price and high-powered lawyers would try to exploit two potential holes in the prosecution's case.

First, Bethune-Cookman College had repeatedly said I had been fired as of June 30, 1990. Although my annual contract had not been renewed on that date, I was still doing work for them until November of that year and continued to receive insurance coverage through the college.

Bill's lawyers would use the college's public statements to try to portray me as a loose cannon, working for my own benefit and, unbeknownst to Bill, therefore I had no authority to be entering into loans on behalf of the college. They would try to convince jurors that I was the bad seed exploiting an innocent and hard-working Bill Williams.

Secondly, Bill's attorneys had a copy of a deposition given by Dr. Bronson in the criminal case involving the fraudulent performance bond used by Bill to get work at the college. Under oath, Dr. Bronson had not been truthful about his business ties to Bill Williams and failed to disclose that he had a signed contract to sell Bill the shopping center. Dr. Bronson had said he had an initial discussion with Bill about the shopping center, but it never went to the negotiation stage. "There were no negotiations," the college president had perjuriously stated.

I had given the U.S. Attorney's Office a copy of the contract signed by Dr. Bronson and his wife dated February 28, 1990, which also spelled out the closing date for the deal on or before March 30, 1990. I assumed Bill had turned over a copy of it to his attorneys, who would use it to impeach the character of Dr. Bronson when he testified against Bill at this trial.

For the first two days of the trial, I waited at home by the phone while the prosecution and defense teams selected a six-person jury. The process had been slow going because some of the potential jurors had read newspaper stories about the case, which disqualified them and Bill's lawyers wanted to make sure and seat educated people who could understand the complex financial arrangements. They had hoped to seat a few blacks, who might be more sympathetic, but in the end agreed to an all-white, twelve-person jury in federal court.

Tuesday mid-afternoon, I received a call that the jury selection had ended. The federal judge would spend a few hours instructing the jury on various matters of law and procedure. The prosecution would begin testimony the next morning at 9 a.m.

I arrived at 8 a.m. at the federal courthouse building, an early 1970s-style drab gray, concrete building that sits in an area dominated by municipal buildings in Orlando. The high-rise county public schools administration center is located on one side. On the other, about a block down, is the city police department and downtown jail annex.

I was sitting in a vinyl and steel chair in the hallway outside the courtroom, reading the morning's *Orlando Sentinel*, when I looked up to see Bill and his lawyers heading my way.

Bill looked immaculate as always, dressed in a dark blue suit, crisp white shirt and a simple matching tie that was more somber than his usual fashion flair. He was between two men I didn't recognize, but assumed were attorneys. Must be hired guns from out of town.

As an attorney, I could easily tell how much other attorneys were billing. Their attire, briefcase and body language gave it away. These weren't $100-an-hour attorneys or even $250-an-hour attorneys like I was. These two were slick, probably from some firm with eight partners listed on the stationary and offices worldwide. Those kinds of attorneys cost $500 an hour, plus expenses.

They strode into the courtroom. The two attorneys - both of them were white - nodded in recognition at me as they walked past. I made eye-contact with Bill, but we did not speak. I could feel Bill reading my demeanor. I had already pleaded no contest to conspiracy to commit bank fraud and was awaiting sentencing. I was looking at possible prison time. Inside, I could feel my spirit had been humbled by my ordeal. And I knew instinctively that Bill could read all that in one quick glance.

I, on the other hand, saw how self-confident he was about the trial. It wasn't smugness that I saw on his face nor anger or resentment at me for agreeing to testify against him. It was more of a self-assured calmness like this trial was a temporary inconvenience for him, which would be over in a few days and allow him to return to more pressing matters.

Looking at the expensive suits around him, I had a sinking feeling in my gut that maybe he was right. The thought pained me intensely. I didn't know if I could handle going to prison if Bill Williams went scot-free. This thought made me want to look at him again, but when I turned that way, the two wooden swinging doors to the courtroom were closing behind them.

As a government witness, I was sequestered, meaning I was not allowed to sit in the courtroom and hear the other witnesses' testimony. I waited in the uncomfortable chair, reading every story in the newspaper.

I was able to follow the progress of the trial. A court bailiff would walk into the hall and call out the name of the next witness. The first witness was the college's accountant, Mr. Patel, who was probably verifying the authenticity of all the checks from the college to Bill Williams. Next was Jo Ann Pyles, who oversaw college development. She outlined Bill's construction ties to the college and how the college had obtained federal grants and loans to pay for the two new buildings.

Tommy Huger was then summoned and I knew I would testify right after him. Now, the jury would begin hearing the crux of the case. Tommy's testimony took more than an hour. He emerged from the courtroom looking strained. I could see the faintest beads of sweat on his face.

"Tommy, how'd it go?" I asked.

"It was hell," Tommy said, and walked off.

The bailiff walked out behind him.

"Anderson Hill," he shouted.

I stood and slowly walked into the courtroom. I was dressed in a black suit, the best one I had, tailor-made, with a heavily starched white shirt and a red, white and black striped tie.

I walked deliberately, but not hastily and glanced at U.S. District Judge G. Kendall Sharp, sitting high up on the wooden bench, as I stepped into the witness box. The judge told me to raise my right hand as a court clerk asked would I tell the whole truth and nothing but the truth, so help me God.

I said I would, turning to look deliberately into the faces of Bill and his two attorneys, each seated on one side of him at the long defense table. I later learned one attorney was Bill's personal attorney; the other represented his Renselear Development Corp.

I also looked over at Richard Newsome, who sat at the prosecutor's table with another assistant U.S. Attorney. FBI Agent Steve Lancer was seated right behind them in the first pew of the audience. Relying on my training from law school, I also made quick and warm eye-contact with each of the white jurors. This helped my credibility.

Richard Newsome finished scribbling some notes on a yellow legal pad, exchanged quick whispers with the prosecutor beside him, and rose. He walked over to the lectern, about three feet from the juror's box and started asking me questions.

I slowly and carefully explained how Bill had paid me more than $800,000 during the course of our 18-month relationship and that $365,000 of that amount, in checks, had not cleared the bank. After I painstakingly outlined the details of the NCNB transaction and how we had been paid for the work by the college months in advance of the false assignment, I decided to go one step further and exploit whatever racist feelings might lie within the jurors.

I diverted from one of Richard Newsome's questions and, looking at the jury, began talking about Bill's two Rolls Royces, his private jet, his sprawling home and extravagant lifestyle.

"It was MR. WILLIAMS," here I pointed at Bill, my voice quivering slightly, "who refused to take his available resources and PAY BACK the bank! MR. WILLIAMS had the resources to EASILY pay the loan back. And he chose not to. I'm not sure why." Here, I paused, looking as disgusted as possible.

My performance was Tony-Award material. I knew the white jurors wouldn't be exactly pleased that a black man owned two Rolls Royces and a private jet. The courtroom got very quiet after I finished my tirade. I could tell by looking at the jurors - a few of whom were sneering in Bill's direction - that my testimony had worked like a charm.

Before the defense attorneys could rise to begin their cross-examination, the judge announced that we would take a 15-minute recess.

"You can step down, Mr. Hill," the judge said to me.

As I walked past the jury box, I hung my head in dramatic fashion. I looked in Bill's direction, shaking my head in disgust. Bill's two lawyers didn't even notice. They were busy whispering into Bill's ears. I knew the lawyers would want to tear into me during cross-examination.

Before I could get out of courtroom, I heard Richard Newsome say that I would be the last prosecution witness. After my cross-examination, the government would rest its case. One of the defense attorneys announced that his first witness would be Dr. Bronson. Dr. Bronson was being summoned for the defense. It had been the government's strategy not to call him because of the conflicts in his testimony.

I waited in the hall, alone, because all the other witnesses had left. Dr. Bronson would arrive from Daytona Beach after lunch. I was curious when the 15 minutes elapsed and I was not called back to the stand. I waited for five, ten, another fifteen minutes, wondering what was happening inside.

Richard Newsome and Agent Lancer emerged with a small crowd behind them and told me Bill's attorneys announced after the break that he would plead guilty to all charges. No plea bargain. No deals. Bill would be held accountable to the max.

The prosecution team offered me their thanks. My testimony had nailed Bill. And I would be spared a blistering cross-examination.

I watched Bill and his attorneys emerge from the courtroom, a few reporters in tow, trying to get Bill to answer their questions. The self-confident expression was gone from his face. He looked rather panicked, like he needed to get outside as soon as possible.

I watched Bill and his attorneys retreat to the elevators. I walked over to a pay phone and called Dr. Bronson's office. He came on the line right away and I could tell he was nervous about giving his testimony.

"You should be getting a call in a minute, Doc. Bill Williams pled guilty. You won't need to come over here."

I explained what happened and recounted my testimony. He was very happy and congratulated me. Anything I did to keep him off the witness stand was most appreciated, he said. He had dreaded being called as a witness. Now, he could concentrate on his college responsibilities. The Bill Williams saga was officially over.

I TOOK great pride in my role in Bill's downfall. But my euphoria was short-lived. I had a bunch of my own problems to deal with. They seemed to come at me in quick succession.

I faced the two pending cases in Daytona Beach for second- and third-degree grand theft for the escrow account check and the credit card advances. After my cooperation in convicting Bill, the U.S. Attorney's Office wrote a letter requesting leniency on my behalf. The State Attorney's Office, which was prosecuting the cases, agreed to recommend that I receive probation to run concurrently with whatever punishment was meted out in the federal bank fraud case.

Again, I pled no contest to the two pending local charges. The judge honored the agreement and sentenced me to probation for four years. The judge also withheld adjudication, a legal term meaning I wasn't technically found guilty of the charges.

Next, I drove to Jacksonville to face disbarment hearings before a local judge there. I went to the hearing on Feb. 20, 1992 and was met outside the courtroom by David McGunegle, who acted as the prosecutor for the Florida Bar.

He told me that he had talked to my attorney, Paul Dubbeld, and knew that I planned to enter a no-contest plea on the charges against me. I nodded in agreement and said I simply wanted to place myself at the mercy of the court.

McGunegle said he would request Circuit Judge Bernard Nachman permanently disbar me. I pleaded for a suspension, instead, which may have allowed me to one day practice law again.

McGunegle said if I tried to fight the matter, the Florida Bar would bring me up on new charges involving the credit card advances. If I agreed to disbarment, the Bar would drop any further proceedings against me.

I knew I had no choice in the matter. I was about to be disbarred.

As we walked into the courtroom, Judge Nachman was seated at the end of a long conference table. The judge read over the charges and asked for my plea. I said I would plead no contest but wanted to offer some mitigating circumstances to help him determine my punishment.

I handed him an affidavit which I had prepared seven months earlier in July 1991, for Dr. Bronson. The eight-page memo outlined, step-by-step, my involvement with Bill Williams, Dr. Holmes, Dr. Bronson, and Robert Billingslea. I had given the synopsis to Dr. Gainous, who told me later that Dr. Bronson disagreed with my account. But, from my point of view, it was the truth and I was sticking by it.

"Frankly, Mr. Hill," the judge started. "I am severely disappointed that a person with your training and professional associations got himself into such a quagmire. I do not believe there are any mitigating circumstances in this case. I have many lawyers in my family, Mr. Hill, and never before have any of us so blatantly violated the rules of ethics. You should be absolutely ashamed of yourself.."

"Of course, I'm ashamed Your Honor. I've made some bad mistakes and fully admit my stupidity in this matter. But I am hoping to salvage my career, Your Honor."

"I do not know if that will be possible, Mr. Hill. I will render an opinion within the prescribed time limit."

His report came not long afterwards and recommended disbarment, which required a formal ruling from the Florida Supreme Court, the ultimate governing body for lawyers within the state. His report did recommend that my disbarment be retroactive to April 1, 1991, the day I was temporarily suspended.

I interpreted this as a glimmer of hope. Under Florida Bar rules, this could decrease the amount of time I would have to wait to reapply for admission. Lawyers who are disbarred must normally wait five years before applying for re-admission. By making the effective date of my disbarment April 1991, instead of February 1992, the judge shaved a year off the time I'd have to wait.

Despite all my mistakes, I knew I would reapply one day to the Bar. I cherished this professional distinction, which had required so much hard work to obtain. I felt that I had wasted so much of my life. I wondered how I could have failed to appreciate all that I had and thrown it away, with or without, the undue influences.

I DREADED my final court hearing to be sentenced on the federal bank fraud charge.

A U.S. probation officer had come to my home months earlier to conduct a pre-sentence investigation, which is a very detailed background report. The officer said, among other things, that he was impressed with my efforts to create a company called the Easy Home Drug Test Corporation. The company was created to advocate the national use of home drug testing, similar to home pregnancy tests, which could be used to deter adolescent drug abuse. I thought, that if a child is aware that a scientific method was available to parents in the home, which could accurately detect the use of marijuana, cocaine, and other illegal drugs in their bodies, it would help them to stop using such drugs. No company or person at that time had marketed such an idea. I even created a catchy slogan for the company which was published that said "Preventing Illegal Drug Use Starts At Home." With this economic drug abuse deterrent methodology for youths, and based on my past cooperation with the U.S. Attorney's Office, I fully expected the probation officer to recommend to the federal district court judge that I receive probation on the federal charge.

I couldn't believe it when I saw a copy of the report and it said I should receive 3 1/2 to 4 years in a federal penitentiary. It was like someone had kicked me in the groin.

I quickly scanned the report. The probation officer had based his recommendation, not only on my conviction on the bank fraud charge, but also on the fact that I had fraudulently obtained money on two occasions from United American Bank. I was stunned! Even though I had told the investigators about those incidents, I didn't think he could use them against me because I had never been charged and convicted of those crimes. It felt like I had been indicted all over again, this time on new charges, even though the U.S. Attorney's Office had promised me immunity.

I felt tricked. I had pled guilty to a class D felony, which came with no mandatory prison time so I could easily have received probation. I wondered if all these white attorneys and prosecutors just wanted to make sure a black man went to prison for trying such scams. I thought my skin tone was influencing my punishments. For example, I knew of a white attorney in Daytona Beach who had bilked customers out of money through some scam. He had received probation on the criminal charges and was merely suspended by the Florida Bar - not disbarred like me.

Still, I had hope. I had received strong letters of support, urging the federal judge to give me probation. The Central Intelligence Agency had written a letter on my behalf, commenting on my involvement with the agency. The one-page letter from the CIA's Office of General Counsel expressed deep appreciation for my services. While an intern, I had been assigned an important project and, based upon my analysis, the agency considered restructuring its procedures for dealing with contracts. I knew there weren't many people, black or white, who could get such a letter from the top secret organization.

I had another letter from Ron Rees, chief executive officer of Halifax Hospital in Daytona Beach, promising to give me strong consideration for a job if I received probation in the case. Letters from Dr. Bronson, Dr. Gainous, my pastor, the YMCA and others also urged the judge to sentence me to probation. And finally, I had our family's asthma and allergy specialist write a letter about my son's severe asthma, which required constant medical attention and costly treatments.

I went to the sentencing hearing alone. Sandra stayed home with the kids. Lots of defendants parade their families before the judge to get sympathy. I had not wanted to use them in such a demeaning way.

My attorney, Paul Dubbeld, had said he'd meet me at the courthouse. When the court clerk called out my case, Paul still had not arrived. In hindsight, I should have asked for a delay. Anxious about a possible prison term, there was no way I could think clearly and argue effectively on my own behalf. That's why attorneys never represent themselves in personal matters.

U.S. District Court Judge Kendall Sharp asked what I wanted to do about my attorney. I guess I felt too confident about my package of letters to him. I figured he'd sentence me to probation and I'd be out of there in 30 minutes.

I said I'd proceed on my own. As a former lawyer, I knew criminal procedure.

Fine, the judge said and pulled out my file from his stack on the bench.

As soon as he started talking, I knew I made a mistake. Despite the letters of support, despite my professional background and my cooperation with the U.S. Attorney's Office, I was just another black man standing before a judge. Consciously or unconsciously, the criminal justice system would use me to send a message to the black community. Blacks who commit crimes - whether they rob a 7-11 at gunpoint or pull off the smartest of white-collar crimes - will be locked up.

"The pre-sentencing investigation recommends three and a half to four years in prison, Mister Hill. What is your position.?"

"Your honor, I would respectfully disagree. The report relies on several incidents for which I was never charged. The U.S. Attorney's Office promised me immunity for my cooperation in the government's case against Bill Williams. I don't believe those incidents can properly be used against me."

"Hmm. Yes, I would have to agree."

I took a deep breath. My emotions were rising and falling like a rollercoaster ride. I was so overwhelmed with fear about going to prison that I couldn't think straight. At that moment, I should have been arguing for probation. But I stood mute while the judge flipped through my file.

"Mr. Hill," the judge said finally. "You are one of the most remorseful persons who has ever come before this court. The court sincerely regrets your involvement in these matters and acknowledges the statements and letters you have offered in support of probation. But the court is obligated ..."

Wait, I wanted to yell. Stop! Please...Stop!

"The court hereby sentences you to ten months in a United States prison. You are hereby remanded to the custody of the United States Marshall. I will allow you a reasonable amount of time to take care of your personal affairs. You shall surrender yourself to a designated prison facility on April fifteenth.

"The court stands in recess. Good luck, Mr. Hill."

BE THERE

Touch me and tell me that you will always be there
Tenderly kiss me and tell me that you forever care.
I mastered this scheme and left you to bare;
all of my troubles that I selfishly forgot to share.
Forgive me my love, but I must pay the price.
It was once for Jesus to die and He did the ultimate
sacrifice.

Sorry that the middle is written this way.
God is writing this book and He alone has the last say.
He has promised that this is the middle and the end is
sure to come.
Like Job He will restore us to what He desires us to be.
Stick with me my love and you will see; that the Lord is
Good and He wants all men to be free.

9 FACING THE TRUTH

"I got what I deserved."

Anderson C. Hill, II, quoted in the *Daytona Beach* News-Journal
after being sentenced to 10 months in federal prison.

THE 16-wheeler rumbled into the driveway at 701 Pelican Bay Drive at 8 a.m. The house was huge and the moving men sighed at the thought of hauling its contents into the Apollo's Moving and Storage tractor-trailer.

A muscular black man, in his early 20s and wearing a red tank top, sat on the passenger side, clipboard on his lap. Another young white guy was squeezed in between him and the driver, a burly white foreman, fifteen years their senior and wearing a Winston Cup auto-racing ballcap.

"I know who this guy is," the young black guy said. "Anderson Hill. I read stories about him in the paper. He worked over at Bethune-Cookman, stole some money, so they say. He ain't telling the whole story, in my opinion. I heard some other folks over at the college took money. They just ain't been caught yet."

"All I know is this is a rush job," the driver replied. "Everything is going back to the storage facility until this guy tells us where he wants us to move this stuff. The paperwork there says most of the rooms are empty, so this shouldn't take us long. Poor guy had to sell off most of his stuff quick."

It was vacate-the-premises-day for the Hill family. Four days, and counting, before I was to surrender myself at Maxwell Air Force Base federal prison in Montgomery, Alabama.

Our street of dreams had come to a dead-end. The Hills, the only black family in the prestigious Pelican Bay gated community, were losing their massive home to foreclosure under a storm cloud of controversy. Pelican Bay Drive would reclaim its lily-white status.

We had tried for months to sell the house and prevent a foreclosure. We circulated fliers, reading "Great Buy." I was willing to sell it below appraised value. But prospective buyers seemed to quickly discern the unsavory details of my demise. They acted like the house had been the scene of a crime; repulsed as if police tape surrounded the property and a chalk outline remained on the floor where a bloody body had laid.

The house reverted to the bank. It would be up to the bank to find a buyer.

I stood at an upstairs window, watching one of the movers lower the dusty steel ramp to wheel furniture into the tandem trailer while the other two men readied the dollies and packing blankets. I glanced across the street and noticed a few neighbors peering out of their windows. They were glad to see us go. None of them came to offer their good-byes.

From our once-opulent furnishings, only a few items remained: A cherry-wood bed, two leather sofas and a big-screen TV. The men had to remove hinges from several inside doors to wheel out the double-sided refrigerator with its darkly tinted glass doors.

The men moved quickly and efficiently and didn't stop once despite their sweat-drenched clothes. In three hours, they were done. I stood in the driveway, watching them go. As they pulled onto the street, the metal undercarriage of the trailer scraped against the rock driveway.

It was like fingernails on a blackboard and sent a shudder through my body. That sound is exactly how I felt. I walked back into the barren house, my footsteps echoing through the drape-less rooms.

Sandra was in the living room, sitting on the last suitcase, which would be crammed into our over-loaded Buick for the 18-hour drive to her mother's house in Little Rock. As I walked in, she turned away from me and looked out the back living-room windows at the golf course. I knew she didn't want me to see she'd been crying.

"I guess that's everything," I said.

"I've checked all the rooms and closets to make sure we didn't leave anything behind," Sandra replied.

"I can't believe we're losing this place. I loved this house more than anything."

"It was our home, Anderson. It will be strange while you're away. The kids and I won't have a home of our own."

Andy and Lauren came bouncing down the stairs. I heard them running from room to room upstairs. As they came into the living room, they must have sensed our somber mood because they grew quiet and still.

"Come here, kids," Sandra said, reaching out her hands so the children would each hold one. "I think we should offer a little prayer before we go."

"I'll say one," said Andy, then 9, and wearing shorts, an Orlando Magic T-shirt and a worn-out pair of sneakers.

We gathered hands and stood in a circle. As our eyes met, my stomach twisted in knots. How could all of this have happened? How could I have caused such pain and upheaval for my family?

"Oh, Lord, please take care of our home," Andy said. "It ain't ours no more. May the next family enjoy this place the way that we did. And please take care of Mommy, Daddy, Lauren and me. Let us find a new place to live. Amen."

Hearing that sweet child's voice humiliated me more than anything else I had suffered, more than the instances when I stood in court as a defendant, sat locked in a jail cell, or read the newspaper headlines about my wrongdoing.

I once earned so much money, I could have paid off the mortgage on the house several times over. Not doing so was another mistake to add to my long list.

Sandra certainly was disappointed in me. She talked about her worries and unhappiness several times. But she only yelled at me once. I can still hear her words:

"How could you place our family in jeopardy, like this? I trusted your judgment, but you let other people lead you astray!"

I also recalled my last words with Dr. Bronson. Sandra and I had gone with the Bronsons to dinner at a local restaurant before leaving town. He sounded like a minister for most of the night, offering us words of encouragement.

"You should not give up hope, Brother Hill. Trust in God. You need to make the best of whatever the future holds for you."

I told him I might get a doctorate in accounting after I was released from prison.

"Young man," he replied, his tone turning sharp and cutting. "You probably need to take some additional courses in ethics."

I knew then that he had not forgiven me, and might not ever, for what I publicly did to him and the college.

I WASN'T looking forward to arriving in Little Rock. Besides the one conversation with my mother, I hadn't fully explained to my family, and Sandra's family the intricate details of my crimes. I prepared for each relative to question me at-length and express their shock and disapproval. I would have to face them for the first time. I didn't have a choice. My family had no place else to go.

I was only there a few days. Luckily, it wasn't as awkward as I feared. My sister, Erma, as it turned out, had been receiving newspaper clippings about me for more than a year from a guy she knew in Daytona Beach. All that time I was trying to keep Erma and Momma in the dark about what was happening to me, they knew everything.

Sandra also kept her mother informed and talked to her by phone regularly for moral support. I was spared from having to recount the whole ordeal. I was greeted with warm and optimistic demeanors, although I sensed the pain right under the surface.

They uttered only words of encouragement to me. It was far too late to offer much else. "Keep your family together, whatever you do. Everybody makes mistakes and time heals all wounds, because soon they are forgotten."

We got the kids enrolled in school and I left two days later on a morning flight to Montgomery, Alabama. It was April 15, 1992, the due date for millions of Americans to pay their taxes. The U.S. District Court judge had ordered me to surrender myself at the base prison that day. It was also the same day that hotelier Leona Helmsley and boxer Mike Tyson reported to prison for their various criminal offenses.

Before I boarded the plane, I kissed Sandra and hugged Andy and Lauren. We hadn't told the kids I was going to prison. We had said I was going to work in another state. But you know kids, I'm sure they heard someone talking about me going to prison.

Lauren squirmed out of her mother's arms and wrapped her little arms tightly around my leg.

"Daddy don't go! Please don't go! Please stay with us! Don't leave us daddy!"

I hugged them all.

"Daddy will be back," I said. "Daddy has to go. I can't stay, Lauren. But Mommy, Mamama, Granny, Aunt Genie', and Branndii will take care of you until I come back. I'll be back as soon as I can."

I was one of the last people to walk aboard the small DC-9 jet. I was assigned a window seat, which happened to face the terminal, and I could see Sandra and the kids waving at me from behind the large plate glass windows. A steady stream of tears filled my eyes and I steeled myself to stop from sobbing right there in front of the other passengers.

I didn't know if I'd ever see them again. We had never been separated for more than a weekend. Now I faced ten long months. Boy, I felt bad. My heart longed to stay and I was so fearful of what lay ahead. I recalled my father's stories about prison and all the violent prison scenes I had watched in movies and read about in books. I felt queasy for the entire two-hour flight.

The plane landed in Montgomery about 11 a.m. I had no luggage or possessions. A letter from the U.S. Bureau of Prisons said not to bring anything. The prison would provide me with the basics.

I procrastinated for an hour before heading out to the prison. I sat in an airport restaurant and ordered a full breakfast, thinking it may be my last decent meal for a long time. I wandered through the few gift shops in the terminal and finally went outside to hail a cab.

The driver was a friendly black man with a deep Southern accent. I told him I needed to go to Maxwell Air Force Base. "Are you in the military?", he asked.

"No, I'm a United States prisoner."

I expected a cool response, but he began talking about the prison facility. It's not that bad, he said. They even give furloughs to prisoners out there from time to time. I said I hoped to get one myself to visit my wife and kids.

He drove all the way across the base to an isolated area with ten red brick buildings, ranging from one to three-stories high. There was no razor-wire fencing or guard towers. It could have been another military dorm compound.

The driver knew just where to take me. He stopped at the main office. I handed him a $20 bill and walked inside. The lobby area was institutional gray with plastic chairs pushed against the wall. Three pay phones were lined against a far wall near the restrooms and water fountain.

I walked up to the reception desk, enclosed in thick glass with a small round speaker in the middle to talk through. I expected a white red-neck guard and was surprised when a short young, good-looking black woman walked up and smiled. Her hair weave was freshly done and looked great.

I told her my name and said I was supposed to report today to start serving my term.

"Come on in. Welcome to Maxwell Federal Prison."

She pushed a button and I heard a steel door to my right buzz open.

This won't be bad, I thought. I hope there are lots of good-looking girls guarding us. I almost chuckled out loud, suddenly cheerful after several days of anguish.

My mood didn't last long. The pleasantries stopped at my arrival.

I was led into a room where a guard standing and watching me, I was told to get undressed. As I stood there naked, the guard went through all my clothes to make sure I hadn't tried to sneak anything in. Another attendant told me to spread eagle and began probing every orifice in my body, including using a rectal probe.

I was handcuffed and led into a small steel, cage-like cell. I was still naked and was left to sit there for several hours. I felt like an animal, which was precisely the intended effect. Sure, they needed to search me for security reasons. But more importantly, they wanted to make a lasting psychological impression. I was no longer the man I had been an hour earlier, when I enjoyed the liberty of personal choices, civil rights and freedom to come and go whenever I wanted.

Prison requires a change in mindset. I no longer had any control over my life. In such a confined existence, time slows to a fraction of what it is on the outside. A second becomes a minute, a minute an hour, an hour a day, a day a week and a week is a month.

After sitting there for four hours, a guard opened the door and handed me a dark-green, two-piece uniform to wear. I then followed him to pick up my bedroll. He left me at the back door of the building, telling me to report to Mobile Unit C and pointing towards another building.

From my limited knowledge of prisons, I knew it was time to "Walk Down the Lane."

Sure enough, I noticed men stopping their work along the compound and looking out the windows of the dormitory. A new prisoner had arrived. Time for everyone to check me out.

I could feel their eyes crawling over my body like ants. My face contorted into its meanest scowl. I puffed out my chest, although I was already a big guy. The months of inactivity had added even more pounds to my overweight frame. I had become very fat and out of shape.

I relied on what I learned as a teenager about the need to carry myself in such a way that if someone messed with me, I'd retaliate swiftly and viciously. As a man, you have to stand down other guys if you're ever to live a peaceful existence. That was the approach I adopted now. I walked through the compound, alert like a cheetah, ready to spring on the first person who messed with me.

A guard gave me a tour of my dorm and told me to settle in. The dorm consisted of one huge room, divided into small cubicles, maybe 10 feet by 12 feet, with two bunk beds per cubicle. Every four cubicles, or 16 men, shared one bath.

Crammed into such a setting, privacy was non-existent. I barely talked to anyone the rest of the day and sat alone at dinner in the large prison cafeteria. Every seat was full in the dining hall, meaning the prison was at its capacity of 800 men.

Lights went out at 10 p.m. It took me awhile to finally fall asleep. It seemed like I had just nodded off when I was startled awake by a big black guy standing beside the bunk. I slept on the top bed.

"Hey, mother fucker," he yelled at me. "You keeping everyone awake with that snoring, goddammit. Now shut up."

I was lying on my stomach. I quickly rolled over and, with my elbow, slammed him in the jaw. He fell backward, slamming into our short brown lockers. I jumped off the bed. I swung at him and missed. Before he could come at me, I shoved him down on the floor and pounced on him, fists flying.

The commotion woke up the other prisoners. Two guys grabbed my shoulders and pulled me off.

I towered over the guy and said in a loud voice, the craziest look possible on my face: "Nigger, I'm here because I already killed me one nigger! Don't fuck with me because I'll kill your goddamn ass too! Don't nobody in here *fuck* with me. I'm not putting up with no shit! Whichever one of you mother fuckers, wants to bother me, Bring It On. I am NOT to be fucked with! I'm nobody's joy-boy and I don't care who you are, what you're about, if I find anybody fucking with me while I'm asleep, I'm going to kill your mother fucking ass!"

I was scared to death.

My biggest fear was gang rape. I had heard the prisoners saying, "What is the greatest joy? A tooty-fruity, big fat, booty boy!"

My response to Big Foot Joe had the desired effect. No one else ever complained about my snoring nor did they hassle me. Plus, within a few days, it spread through the dorm that I was a former attorney. In prison, if you have a legal background, inmates flock to you and want to be friends. My reputation in prison was sealed.

My next dilemma was work detail. The military decided to open these kinds of minimum-security prisons on its bases to get a free labor pool. The military relied on prisoners to maintain the base grounds.

I hoped my education, coupled with my allergies and asthma, would land me a clean job in an office or the prison library. But I noticed right away that the white inmates got the clean jobs. The black men cut grass and picked up litter.

On my second day, the alarms rang at 5:30 a.m. The prisoners quickly got dressed, used the bathroom and headed for the dining hall. At 6:15 a.m., they loaded onto old school-style buses, painted drab military green, and went to work around the base.

I was supposed to report to the main office, where I would be assigned a job for my 10-month sentence. An elderly white man, who wore half-rimmed glasses and looked at me over the top of his spectacles, wasn't sympathetic to my request for clean work.

"I could care less about your training," he said. "I'm going to assign you where ever I choose."

My intake report listed my severe allergies. So, instead of working on the grass-cutting crew, the old guy assigned me to garbage detail. I worked in the recycling section, going from office to office on the base, picking up garbage and recyclables for eight hours a day. After a few weeks, I decided the assignment was risky to my health because I was breathing so much dust.

I went back to the elderly guy and requested a job in the prison library. He sneered at me. I could read his thoughts: How dare some nigger come to him with an attitude? He said he'd think about my request. Until then, I was to stay on the garbage truck.

If he denied my request, I knew I'd be powerless to appeal it.

Prisoners learn quickly to fear, not only prison guards, but also all prison employees from secretaries to maintenance men to the warden. Every employee has the power to write up a prisoner and send him into solitary confinement.

Prisoners who got written-up sometimes were sent to what they called, Diesel Therapy. The prisoner would be loaded on a bus and transferred from prison to prison until he ended up at a medium-security facility, which offered far fewer privileges than our minimum-security one.

I resented the old white guy for treating me disrespectfully. But as I left his office, I acted humble and told him whatever he decided would be acceptable to me. Two days later, I got word that I would be transferred to the kitchen. Dishwasher detail.

At first, I was mad as hell and wished I'd kept my mouth shut and stayed on the garbage detail. The first day on my new job, though, I realized it was one of the best jobs in the compound.

Cafeteria workers could eat as much as they wanted. And even better, the job required prisoners to work different hours from the rest of the population. When the other prisoners were off, we worked to prepare the meals, feed them and clean up. Conversely, while they worked, we enjoyed our free time.

When the alarms sounded at 5:30 a.m., I could stay in bed. Once everyone left, I'd get up and take a shower in solitude. I'd watch a little TV and then head to the dining hall to start washing dishes. This bit of privacy was comforting in such an environment.

For those reasons, the cafeteria attracted some impressive workers. The former governor of West Virginia, for example, was assigned to wipe down the tables after meals.

It may sound funny for a former lawyer to say, but I took great respect and dignity in my kitchen detail. Some of the inmates would laugh at me because I was so joyful and happy in my work. I'd rush back and forth from the serving line to the kitchen, keeping the racks full of glasses. Once the racks were loaded, I'd stand there and hand each inmate a glass for his tray. In this way, I got to know most of the inmates in the facility.

I wanted them to know that if I could behave congenially during my prison time, so could they.

My days blurred into a predictable routine. When I wasn't working in the kitchen, I was lifting weights and playing racquetball, and
became the camp's racquetball champion in both singles and doubles. In
the evenings, I'd find a seat in the crowded TV room. Television is a
mainstay for prisoners. We'd watch different programs and for a few
hours escape into the television set and become a part of the program.

I'd also help a few inmates with their legal cases. I limited my
assistance because I grew tired of hearing so many people protesting
their innocence. I wasn't going to waste my time doing legal research for
con artists. I also volunteered my time to help inmates learn to read and
understand educational materials for such things as getting their general
equivalency diploma, or GED. I regularly attended Sunday church
services and was even allowed to lead the prayer one Sunday.

It's hard to describe the isolation felt in prison. Prisoners get so
lonely for their families and can become despondent over their inability
to get home during personal tragedies. For instance, the telephone room
was always crowded during calling hours. It was a huge room with 50
pay phones that only allowed collect calls. You could see the happiness
and the pain on the faces of prisoners as they talked to their loved ones
back home.

One time, an inmate started beating on the phone and ripping it
out of the wall. He had called his home. A man answered, said his wife
was unavailable and hung up on him. He grew frantic when the man
wouldn't accept his collect calls. All prisoner phone calls are monitored
by the guards, so it didn't take long for the guards to haul him out. I
never saw him again.

During one of my first telephone calls to Little Rock, I learned
that Sandra had fractured her ankle in a bad fall and had to undergo
emergency surgery. A small metal plate was implanted to hold her foot
bones together.

Her fall happened the day before she was scheduled to start work
at Philander Smith College, a small, private college supported by the
United Negro College Fund. She was offered a good position and salary
as a development associate, a position that she had once held at Bethune-
Cookman College.

She was walking down the steep incline of the driveway at her
mother's house, which her parents purchased shortly before her father

died in 1986. Located in an upscale section of town, the five-bedroom, two-story home had a stone facade and natural rock driveway, which was slippery when wet. Sandra was carrying a small child. When she began to lose her balance, she was so focused on protecting the baby, she fell awkwardly and broke her ankle. Thank heavens the baby wasn't hurt.

The fall ended her job opportunities. She was confined to bed for a month and then started rehabilitative therapy. Unable to work, Sandra went on welfare to support herself and the kids, and to qualify for Medicaid coverage.

I tried to get an emergency furlough to go home and see her, but it was denied.

The warden denied another request for a furlough when Andy was hospitalized for severe asthma. I called the hospital to talk to Sandra, who was on crutches. I could hear my son in the background, yelling and screaming out of control. The doctors eventually realized he was allergic to the asthma medication that he had been given. It caused Andy to go into delirium.

The helplessness I felt was overwhelming. As I listened to my son hollering and talking out of his head, the doctors and nurses in the background trying to figure out what was wrong with him, I just wanted to run out of the compound and head home. I stayed because I didn't want to be sent for Diesel Therapy.

That was the closest I came to contemplating an escape. I stayed in turmoil for weeks, thinking about how my once happy and carefree family was now on welfare and food stamps. I could do absolutely nothing to help them in their time of greatest need.

I tried to find comfort in God. I remembered how I had ended up in trouble because I rushed into so many destructive decisions. This philosophy strengthened my faith and helped me believe that something good might come out of all of this.

It wasn't too long afterwards when I received a letter from U.S. District Court Judge Kendall Sharp. I had written to him shortly after my arrival when I learned that I would have to serve at least eight months of my 10-month prison term. I had thought I could serve five months in prison and five months in a halfway house. When the prison refused my request, I wrote to the judge and asked him for a split sentence.

When I read his letter granting the split sentence, I jumped and hollered and screamed for joy. I knew I would remain at Maxwell only a short while longer. The judge's order also said my time at a halfway house would be on a least-restrictive status, meaning I could travel to and from a job, and possibly receive a furlough to see my family.

Exactly five months to the day of my arrival at prison, I was handed a one-way bus ticket to Orlando and set free. Five months may not sound like a long time. But it took its toll. I'll never forget that experience - the feelings of being trapped, of having no personal control and of constantly being treated by the prison staff like I wasn't even human.

Upon my release, I felt absolutely glorious. Almost like being a child when the whole world is fresh and new. My system was clean of cocaine or alcohol. There were times when I had access to alcohol and cocaine at Maxwell prison. But I vehemently refused to participate and quickly distanced myself from anyone who did. I was determined to make a positive change in my life and swore off drugs and alcohol for the rest of my life. I lost my cravings for beer, tequila and cocaine, and I didn't want them back. I could see the tremendous number of mistakes that were caused by my constant abuse of liquor and drugs.

In many ways, the prison sentence was a blessing for me. If I had been placed on probation and allowed to remain free, I most likely would have returned to using drugs and alcohol. I was in better shape than I'd been in almost a decade. I walked into prison weighing a hefty 275 pounds and left weighing a firm 220 pounds.

I had plenty of time to think in prison. I read many different books, including the New Testament of the Bible from cover to cover, and tried to glean from them a beneficial message. I read Washington, D.C., Mayor Marion Barry's book. Drugs tricked him into an unfortu-nate set of circumstances, too. Drugs always seem to lead to a bad outcome, no matter what people tell themselves while they are using them. Just being around illegal drugs is enough to land people in serious trouble.

I wasn't serving time for illegal drugs, but I might as well have been. Had I not been using drugs, I would have not become involved with Bill Williams and would not have made so many bad decisions.

I also read *The Jordan Rules* by Michael Jordan. I had taken graduate level courses in economics, but I learned things from Michael Jordan that I never learned in college. His point was that whenever he did something, he clearly thought out what effect it would have on other things. For example, if he wore a particular outfit or brand name shoe, how would it affect his marketability of other products? I decided from this point forward, I would approach my decisions much more methodically.

UNDER the U.S. Bureau of Prison rules, I could have gone to any halfway house with an opening in the country. I chose to return to Central Florida. Many people like to start fresh after their release from prison. They choose to go to a new town where the residents don't know their sordid history.

I needed to return to my community. I wanted my old friends and acquaintances to see me make good. I planned to reapply to the Florida Bar and practice again as an attorney. And I hoped to help my son, Gregory, then a freshman at Bethune-Cookman College.

I was assigned to a federal halfway house in the city of Maitland, just north of Orlando. I was told to immediately find a job if I wanted to remain there. I wasn't sure what to do. I recalled my unsuccessful job searches after my disbarment. As a convicted felon just released from prison, I'd face an even harder time.

I figured my only hope would be to ask an old acquaintance for a job, someone who knew me before I got in trouble. I called Harry Morall and Jane Carey, two attorneys who had worked part-time in my law firm years before and now shared a law practice in Orlando. Harry said he may be able to take me on as a paralegal, doing legal research and handling simple legal work, but he'd first have to talk to Jane, his wife.

He came by the halfway house a few days later. He kidded me about being a convicted felon. We recalled the days when we both attended law school at the University of Florida and played grueling games of one-on-one basketball. I assumed by his jovial manner that he had come to tell me I had a job with his office. I had no idea what a big job it would be.

His office had taken on a case that was gaining tremendous

publicity nationwide and would set an important precedent. At first, I thought Harry was telling fishermen's tales. But it turned out he wasn't exaggerating a bit.

The case involved a boy, named Gregory Kingsley, who lived for years with foster parents in a nearby community. The boy decided he wanted to be adopted by this family and the family wanted to adopt him, too. To do so, Gregory needed to sever legal ties with his parents. His father agreed, but his mother, Rachel Kingsley, refused. An attorney for Gregory filed suit - Kingsley versus Kingsley - and, in effect, asked a judge to allow the boy to "divorce" his mother. The case was a novel one and would set an interesting precedent, namely, whether kids have the right to choose different parents.

I saw Rachel a few days later, when I started working for Morall and Carey in downtown Orlando. Rachel was a white lady in her early 30s and appeared very distressed over the prospect of losing her son forever.

Based upon what I knew of the complaint, I was not sure whether the young child had adequate grounds to have his mother's parental rights terminated. The case involved a two-step process in which the court would first have to decide whether Rachel's abandonment of the boy warranted termination of her parental rights. The second part of the litigation involved the adoption of Gregory by his foster parents.

During the Kingsley trial, the outside of the Orlando courthouse looked like the area around the Super Bowl on Super Bowl Sunday. The parking lot and adjacent streets were filled with big TV trucks with satellite dishes on top, and crowds of reporters milling around. When we arrived in the morning, hundreds of them would surround our car and shout questions at Rachel from the time she stepped from the car until she could retreat inside the courthouse.

The case had been featured prominently on a variety of national news shows. Harry, Jane and Rachel were guests on every major talk show, explaining again and again why she should have the opportunity to keep her son. The trial was also televised on Court TV.

Just a week after my release from federal prison, I was regularly seen on national television, seated at the defense table in the courtroom and walking behind Rachel into the courthouse. I received many phone calls at the halfway house from Sandra, my mother and other relatives back in Little Rock. I even got a few messages from my friends back at Maxwell prison. They couldn't believe I was involved in this landmark case. And neither could I. It made me want to be a lawyer all over again.

I took it as a good omen.

People never know where they will end up. I had told myself in prison that *quitting is just one step away from success.* The very next step you take may bring about success. I still faced an uphill climb to rebuild my life. But I took great pride in being able to do legal research and analysis for the Kingsley versus Kingsley case, which, by the way, Rachel eventually lost, both at trial, and on appeal.

MY life had come apart piece by piece. It would be rebuilt the same way.

The first priority was my family. I started seeing Gregory right away. He was then attending Bethune-Cookman College and was facing a difficult time in the shadow of his father's tarnished reputation. He would come by the halfway house and I would offer whatever support and advice I could.

I soon was granted a furlough to travel to Little Rock to be reunited with Sandra, Andy and Lauren. When my flight arrived and I walked out of the gate, I was so overjoyed to see them.

Andy and Lauren ran up and hugged me. Both of them had grown several inches since I'd last seen them.

"Daddy, we're ready to go home," Lauren said.

"When are you going to take us home, daddy?" Andy asked.

I had to tell them I was only visiting for a few days and would have to leave them again. But I promised to be back very soon to get them for good.

There were many details to resolve before they could join me. I was still being held at the halfway house and needed to find a good-paying job. Morall and Carey were paying me minimum wage. They didn't need another employee and only hired me as a favor.

I liked the job but it would not support my family. With my criminal history, I was turned down for many jobs. Eventually, I realized my only option was to open my own business. Luckily, the director of the halfway house, Mr. Procknow, was supportive of my decision. He could have denied my request because, as a condition of the halfway house, I had to contribute 25 percent of my gross pay to the facility. Allowing me to start my own business meant the halfway house would receive less income from me.

I called my business Prime Time Paralegal. Even though I had been disbarred, I could do legal research for attorneys and handle simple legal procedures, as approved by the Florida Supreme Court. That way, I could capitalize on my law experience, by working directly for other attorneys and hopefully continue my march toward re-admission into the Florida Bar. I mainly found myself doing business consulting, by work-ing with my brother-in-law Lloyd, at his architectural firm called Lam Design, Inc., in Atlanta, Georgia. Lloyd gave me a chance to fly to Atlanta often, while his firm worked on planning for various construc-tion projects, related to the '96 Summer Olympic Games. That was a delightful experience for me, which Lloyd had no obligation to do.

I found a three-bedroom home to rent in a nice Orlando suburb. I stretched my budget as far as I could to afford the house, not wanting my family to suffer too much shock after being accustomed to Pelican Bay. Our new home was much smaller, but it was attractive, and in a nice neighborhood, where the homes started at $100,000.

The day after my release from the halfway house, I flew to Little Rock and drove my family back home. I was so happy to be with them again, although my joy was tempered by Gregory's recent decision to leave Bethune-Cookman and return to Oklahoma.

I'll never forget my mother's words just before we left Little Rock with a U-Haul trailer in tow behind our old blue Buick.

"Brother, whatever you do, keep your family together. This separation was very hard on Andy. He came over to see me all the time and cried about missing his daddy. I was so worried about him. I was worried about all of you.

"I can't live through this type of situation again. You had better not get in any more trouble. If you do, you are going to end up killing your mother."

"Momma," I told her. "You don't have to worry. I'm going to keep my nose clean and take care of my family. I don't ever want to leave them again. Believe me."

We set off down the highway, singing songs and elated to be a family once more. I felt like I was getting to know them all over again, and I'm sure they felt that way about me.

WE were broke. No doubt about it. I made just enough to cover our living expenses and nothing more. Andy became very ill again with his asthma and had to be hospitalized in Orlando for a week. The bills were tremendous and I certainly didn't have the money to pay them.

Because my family had been on welfare in Arkansas, the hospital encouraged me to apply again for Medicaid and food stamps. The Medicaid coverage allowed Andy to receive all the necessary medical treatment while the food stamps helped us make ends meet.

I certainly wasn't proud to be receiving state assistance. I didn't like it at all, to be quite honest. But I refused to let my pride stand in my way as I had done in the past when I refused to give up the Mirage and all my expensive possessions even though I couldn't afford them. I was now prepared to do whatever necessary for my family, as long as it was legal. I knew we'd eventually get off welfare, which we did, but we needed it at that point.

We joined a church with a long and rich black heritage in Orlando. It was called the Mount Pleasant Missionary Baptist Church and was much like our Greater Friendship Baptist Church in Daytona Beach. I told our new pastor all about my past. I was honored when he invited me to join the church's board of deacons.

The pastor, Walter Prince, even urged the congregation to vote for me.

That was a great day for me when the church voted me in. In many ways, I felt like the vote was a sign that I had been forgiven. This gave me deep strength and encouragement to continue along the narrow path of my rehabilitation.

I began to speak at various functions around town. I was even asked to give a speech at the 30th anniversary of Pastor Bentley at the Greater Friendship Baptist Church in Daytona Beach. It was a chance for me to speak directly to so many people who had personally witnessed my fall from grace. Even Dr. Bronson attended the service that morning.

I was very nervous before the speaking engagement but knew what I wanted to say.

The Bible says it is good to be a witness for the Lord. I truly believe that people need to tell others about the mistakes they've made and the difficulties they've suffered. Things surely did not go as I had planned in my life, but God stayed beside me and helped me through. God granted me peace in a time of storm. He will certainly do that for anyone else who asks.

GETTING BACK

Can I go back to what I was in past tense?
I fight hard everyday to gain my former stature.

You left me here to disdain in my tears.
You were a vital element in the downfall.
You refuse to claim your part.
You are not telling the truth from your blinded heart.

I want my former self again.
Not the liar, cheater, beast of a man.
You still have your life, why can't I have mine?

Law is an integral part of me.

I want to lavish my wife with laughter.
Cherish my children with sunshines.
Give relief to the poor.
I have learned my lesson oh so well.

Get me back to the place where I first began.
I can make all things new.
The light that guides me does not dim at every whim
of pleasure.

Sought after the truth and the truth sought me.
Discovered fountains of wisdom, knowledge, and the
courage to do the correct thing.

10 TO SERVE AGAIN

"Between truth and the search for the truth, I opt for the second."
Bernard Berenson, American art critic (1865-1959)

THE Governor and Cabinet of Florida convene in a long rectangular auditorium in the Capitol, a high-rise 1970s-looking building that towers up from behind the beautiful, historic old Capitol.

The group sits at a rounded conference table, with the governor in the middle. The room is paneled in wood and has high ceilings, which gives it the feeling of the tremendous power of the state of Florida.

I stood at a lectern before the state's most powerful elected officials. Gov. Lawton Chiles was in charge, and seated on both sides of him were the Attorney General, the Secretary of State, the Commissioner of Education, the Commissioner of Agriculture, the Comptroller and the Treasurer.

Their seven white faces turned my way, appearing slightly bored yet antsy to conclude the lengthy meeting. I was here to ask them to restore my civil rights. As a convicted felon, I was prohibited from voting, holding office or being admitted to the Florida Bar. Only a vote from this body could restore my rights. If they turned me down, my dreams of being readmitted to the Florida Bar would be dashed forever.

Convincing them to vote for me would be difficult, but then, it was quite a task just to get here.

Once my family and I settled into our new life in Orlando, I applied to the state and federal courts for early termination of my probation, which was supposed to last for four years. The courts granted my request, which cleared the way for me to apply to the Florida Parole Commission's Office of Executive Clemency to have my civil rights restored.

I did not meet the criteria for this rather stingily-granted special exception. Under the rules, applicants must have served their complete sentence and have made full restitution. I still owed $425,000 in my federal case and $75,000 in my state cases. I proceeded with my application under a financial hardship clause. With my current income, it could take me decades, maybe my whole life, to pay off those debts. Plus, I faced a growing $324,000 tax lien from the Internal Revenue Service, which had audited me after my release from prison and slapped me with the big tax bill for unreported income during my involvement with Bill Williams.

At first, the Parole Commission denied my application. The only way I could keep my application alive was to receive a waiver of the rules, which required the approval of the Governor and three of the six Cabinet members.

They turned me down, too.

I applied for another waiver hearing. After several months of correspondence between myself and the staff in Tallahassee, the state capital, a second hearing was granted. Finally, I got the waiver. Now, I'd ask them to restore my civil rights.

I received letters of support from Dr. Bronson and the FBI, which initially had responded coolly to my attempt to have my civil rights restored. The FBI asked if I would be willing to talk about my complex crimes to a gathering of FBI agents. I said sure and flew out to San Francisco for one seminar and later spoke at another one in Miami. Afterward, the FBI wrote a nice factual letter, outlining my helpful assistance to the bureau's investigations of my crimes.

The only other possible obstacle could come from Walt Disney World. About six months before my second Cabinet hearing, I sent a notice to Disney, alerting the conglomerate that I intended to file suit, because its representative, Bob Billingslea, had used his position as trustee for Bethune-Cookman College to misrepresent Bill Williams. And, according to Bill and O.J. Tate, Bob had received payments for his false statements. It made me mad that Bob never was held accountable for his role in the mess. I accepted and admitted my culpability in the whole affair. I wanted Bob to do the same.

Of course, I was treading on dangerous ground. In Orange County, Florida, not many people go to battle with Disney. The sprawling vacation land is king of the county, well-endowed with money and resources to squash any potential troublemakers. I saw myself as the biblical "David," and of course, Disney, was "Goliath!" My slingshot had to be the "Truth," in order for me to have any reasonable chance of success.

The day after I sent the notice, a female attorney from Disney's legal department called. Carol Pacula, who I discovered was in my '82 law class at The University of Florida, said she wanted me to explain my legal basis for the proposed litigation. Basically, I intended to rely on Billingslea's malicious interference with my business opportunities, as an agent of Disney.

We talked several more times during the next month. She requested a variety of documents from me and I promptly sent them along. I figured Disney wanted to settle this matter out of court to avoid any negative publicity.

She finally called me three months later. Her voice did not have the jovial and friendly tone that it had in the past. She said she had forwarded all of my documents to Disney's corporate counsel in California and had just received his response.

If I filed suit, Disney would make sure I never practiced law again in the state of Florida, she said. Disney would not tolerate me trying to "blackmail" the company.

I told her immediately that I had no intentions of blackmailing anyone. I was willing to submit to a polygraph test to attest to the veracity of my statements.

"I can't believe Disney would make such a volatile statement about using its powerful influences to stop me from practicing law. It's definitely not Disney's decision whether I am ever re-admitted to the Florida Bar. This isn't right," I protested.

But she had nothing else to say and hung up. Disney had indeed flexed its corporate muscles. The company hadn't conducted a legal evaluation of my claim, it conducted a psychological evaluation. I'm sure company officials had read the stories in the local media about my desires to get back into the Bar. One phone call from Disney could submarine those plans. It wouldn't take much to keep a convicted black felon from re-entering the Bar.

Disney's strategy worked. I didn't file the suit nor did I tell anyone about what had happened with Disney. My energy was focused on battles on other fronts - namely convincing the Governor and Cabinet to restore my civil rights.

This would be my last shot with them. As I stood at the lectern looking at their white faces, I knew my chances were slim.

I needed a dramatic performance, something to shake them out of their apathy and at least listen to me. I'd have maybe 60 seconds before their eyes glazed over and one of them hastily cut me off.

I started speaking.

"Your honorable Governor and Cabinet members, I am here for restoration of my civil rights. Without this, I will never be able to pay the amount of restitution that I owe nor will I be able to fulfill my dream of practicing law again in this state.

"I acknowledge that I do not deserve restoration. I have made many mistakes and fully admit my guilt. I have served my time in prison and am desperately trying to rebuild my life for my benefit and that of my wife and three children."

At this point, I stepped away from the podium. I slowly bent down, getting on my knees on the carpeted floor.

"You are like Caesar and I am like the fallen warrior. I beg of Caesar to spare my life. You, Caesar, can simply give me a thumbs down for death or a thumbs up to spare my life. I am here to beg of you, Oh Caesar, please give me a thumbs up and allow me to hopefully someday have a chance on re-entering the Florida Bar."

I stood up and quickly collected my papers off the podium. I bowed to them and turned and walked out of the room.

This appeal seemed like my only hope. It made an impact; that I'm sure of. It was quite something to see this big black man begging the white man to help him. My actions were sincere and not just a ploy. I hoped they could feel the pain I felt for all of my mistakes. And not too long afterwards, I received a letter in the mail that they had granted my request.

THE U.S. Attorney's Office called me one day and said more criminal charges were being filed against Bill Williams in Cleveland, Ohio. Bill had served 18 months in federal prison at a minimum-security military base in the Florida Panhandle, similar to the prison where I was.

He had since been released and was preaching the gospel as a newly ordained minister. I guess he found something within himself. Whether it was JESUS, I don't know.

The new charges stemmed from Bill's involvement with Airship

Enterprises, the blimp company that sold advertising. Evidently, Bill had used the same kind of loan scams on them as he had with me. I was totally unaware that Bill used his brother-in-law, without the man's knowledge, in running this scheme in Cleveland, at the same time Bill and I, were defrauding the banks in Orlando.

I was asked to travel to Ohio and testify against Bill. I agreed. I didn't need to be convinced that Bill was a crook and would do anything to get money, even if it meant destroying everyone around him.

Bill claimed he was innocent in the Cleveland case. I heard through mutual acquaintances that Bill blamed me for all the crimes in Orlando. Bill's jail-yard story was that I masterminded the schemes. He even claimed at one sentencing hearing that I had forced him into at least one of our fraudulent bank loans, which was just not true.

I traveled to Cleveland in the fall of 1995 to recount my ordeal to the jury.

After I finished my testimony, I sat in the hallway waiting to be called back in for cross-examination by Bill's lawyers.

I heard the courtroom door open and expected to hear the bailiff call my name to return to the witness stand. Instead it was Bill. The hallway was vacant except for the two of us.

We made eye contact. I was sitting 10 feet away from him. He looked exactly the same. I felt like prison had aged me a bit.

"You are a no good mother fucker," Bill said, a meanness in his eyes. "I am going to get you someday."

I simply smiled at him and didn't say a word. Bill walked back into the courtroom. I've never seen him since that day. When I got back to Orlando, I learned that he'd been convicted of eight counts of wire fraud, bank fraud and money laundering. He received a lengthy sentence at a federal prison in Georgia.

Bill has five children. His family looked up to him as a role model. His wife and children were surely devastated to see him going back to prison so soon after his release.

I can only say I have forgiven Bill for what he did to me and my family. I am not blaming him totally for the problems I brought upon myself. I just hope that Bill someday will realize the mistakes he has made and will begin using his talents in a good way, rather than in a destructive way.

I cannot live my life with hatred or absolve myself by shifting blame to someone else. I could have prevented everything, if I had been in the right frame of mind and had not allowed greed to lure me away from my values and my true goals.

I AM trying hard to pass these lessons and values on to my children, who I came to treasure even more than ever, along with my wife, during our ordeal. It is truly a miracle, for which I thank God, that we managed to survive these experiences with our family intact. I can take no credit for that. It is a testament to Sandra's strength.

It is easy for me to say I love her because she has done so much for me and the children. She was the one who suffered the most for my ignorance and greed. She has never rubbed salt in my wounds, even though she warned me many times to stop snorting cocaine, stop trying to hang onto the Mirage, and stop associating with Bill Williams. She has never used my mistakes against me in an argument. I think that says a lot about her as a person.

She is a very strong woman who took her marriage vows very seriously. So many marriages have failed over far less. The irony is that she's a beautiful woman who could easily have found another man.

When I think of all the years she sat at home crying and wondering where I was and when I'd be home, I feel so remorseful. How could I have done those things to her and my family? I wish there was a way to change the past, but I can't. That's why everyday is special to me. I lost valuable time worrying about material possessions and unfortunately allowed valuable moments with my family to fall by the wayside. These days getting home from work and having dinner with my family makes me feel the best.

"Anderson, all of those things we used to have did not mean a lot to me," Sandra has told me. "You and the kids are what's important. Sure, I'd be lying if I said I didn't enjoy the house, the jewelry, the money and all the other stuff we had. But the way we were trying to keep those things, it wasn't worth the pain. It's better to have a little and be happy, than to own a lot and be miserable. I was miserable with our life back then. You just would not listen and I didn't push you because I love you.

"When you were younger and we were dating, you would tell me that one day something was going to happen in our lives that would be mind-blowing. At first, I thought you were going to become president of Bethune-Cookman, have a big law practice or do well with the Mirage. I came to realize that it wasn't any of those things. The Lord has something great in store for you and I want us to find it together."

Sandra is the type of person who doesn't like to take credit for the things she does. But I must say, if not for her, everything would be lost.

I know our marriage would not have survived if I had gone back to drinking and doing drugs. In 1996, I started to attend the Florida Lawyers Assistance (FLA) program to help keep me sober. It is good to have a safety net outside of my home. Sandra, my mother and my sister are proud that, regardless of what I did in the past, they can rest assured that I kicked some awful habits.

Economics is the biggest problem facing my family. As a convicted felon, it is hard to find employment. No one wants to give me the benefit of the doubt. But I count my blessings, because by not being employable at the level I wish to be employed, I seek new ground. There are opportunities which exist for me, but my challenge is to find them and support my family.

I will probably struggle financially for the rest of my life. It goes along with having a criminal record, a personal blemish that I think about daily.

Because every day there are telltale signs to remind me. I see and hear from old acquaintances and they ask how we're doing. I cannot answer without remembering where we've been. My criminal record will follow me no matter where I go. It is a fact that I will always have to disclose. If I don't tell, then I'm trying to be someone I'm not.

Of course, I miss the lifestyle we once had. But all those possessions weren't mine to keep. If I knew then what I know now, I would have made sure we kept our home. Losing our home was the worst blow. A home is an anchor for a family.

Rather than securing our home, I reached out for other investments. That shows how messed up my thinking was. Home comes first, then branch out to other ventures. That's my philosophy today. If I ever

do enjoy financial success again, I won't waste my money on possessions that really have no value. A car is a car. The make and model
doesn't mean much to me anymore. I used to love automobiles. Now, I
see them for what they really are - transportation.

I bought all those Mercedes Benzes to show off. I was trying to
show the world I had made it. But I hadn't made it. Success isn't a
Mercedes Benz. It's keeping a marriage together and raising your children to be productive citizens.

We spend a lot more time together as a family now. We occasionally go out to eat and to the movies. Andy and I work out at the basketball club together on a regular basis. Lauren and I are involved in many
discussions about her being a young lady and watching out for the boys.
I'm enjoying them while I can.

They'll be busy with their own lives before too long. Andy is in
the tenth grade while Lauren is in the eighth. Both are musically in-
clined. Andy plays the trombone; Lauren the flute.

Just recently, Sandra and I sat them down and talked about what
happened to me in Daytona Beach five years ago. We had to. A story
about me was about to appear in an Orlando newspaper. I was scared to
death to tell them. But Andy, then 13, and Lauren, 12, said they already
knew. They'd heard it from their cousins and friends.

"Your Daddy's in prison," Lauren said one of her cousins said.

It frightens me to think what they'll face in their lives, especially
Andy. So many young black men end up in trouble with the law. Sometimes I use the phrase "Bait for the system" like my mother used to say.

I tell Andy to run at the first sign of trouble. That's the only way
to stay clean. I don't want him to face what my father, Gregory, and I
have faced. We must break this cycle. But there is no clear-cut solution.
All I can do is be a good father, teach him to obey the law, and trust in
God. Gregory told me that he is writing a book. I cannot wait to see it.
I pray Lauren will avoid trouble in her life.

I HAVE applied to be re-admitted to the Florida Bar. I took the
Bar exam for a second time, after many years of waiting, and passed all
the sections of it, on the first try. My admission remains a long shot,

though, especially because I have not made restitution in my criminal cases, or paid my creditors, as required by the Board of Bar Examiners procedures. The Board also has stringent character investigations for all applicants. I have tried to show the community, that I am of good character and not financially irresponsible, since my rehabilitative efforts commenced.

Still, I pray the Florida Supreme Court will give me the benefit of the doubt and allow me a second chance. Practicing law was second nature to me. I lost a part of myself when I was disbarred. A long time dream of being a lawyer vanished. Years of hard work were wasted. My heart aches at the thought that I may die without ever walking into a courtroom again as an attorney.

Even if I'm readmitted, my path will be difficult because my life will always be under a microscope. I'll never be "clean-cut Anderson Hill" again.

Whatever the outcome, I have come to terms with what I did and believe I am a better person for it. It has been painful. I had to dig deep within my soul to go on. I struggled from time to time to remain truthful and optimistic. I would have rather kept much of this a secret, such as my drug use.

In life, you have to take risks. By taking a risk and being honest in this book, I hope people can learn about the pitfalls that can occur in life. I know my honesty could jeopardize my chances of re-entering the Florida Bar because I don't know how the Board will view some of the statements I've made. I was very careful not to make any confidential disclosures, unless they are in dispute between me and the person(s) under discussion. It is my hope that my words shall be acceptable, in God's sight, the sight of others, as well as in the sight of others who can learn from them.

I will never be satisfied with my position in life until I reach my grave. I still want to make something of my life, a big part of which will be helping others. We cannot find success solely within ourselves because success is allowing others to see us as we really are. For them to see us as successful, it is required that we reveal our true and complete selves. That's what I'm attempting to do. I may fall short of my goal, but I am honestly reaching for it.

APPENDIX

IN SEARCH OF THE TRUTH

A Real Life Story About What an Attorney Should "NOT" Do!

PRIME TIME PUBLISHERS, Inc.

TAC's MISSION

THE AMERICAN CONSCIOUS, INC.
Do you have a Conscious? If not, get one soon...
Remember to put a "TAC" in it!

750 S. Orange Blossom Trail, Suite 120
Orlando, FL 32805, USA
web pages @ http://www.iag.net/~tac

Telephone (407) 426-8597
Fax same as above, e-mail: tac@iag.net

MISSION STATEMENT

The Mission of The American Conscious (TAC), Inc. is to align itself with well established community based organizations as a joint effort in providing alternative choices for at-risk individuals through informative seminars and motivational lecture series. TAC considers all persons to be at-risk based upon the experiences of its founder, Anderson C. Hill, II, J.D., M.B.A. TAC seeks to combat the criminal mind-set by advocating higher education and promoting strong family support structures. It is our belief that through the timely disclosure of personal truthful affirmative statements shall lead to increased prevention of irreparable bad acts. When TAC is too late to prevent non-conforming social behavior, the company believes in being the catalyst for developing an organizational system of personal recovery, for the vast amount of human resources, which may have already fallen by the wayside. TAC teaches methods of conscious social recovery as a part of its congruent philosophies.

WILLIE LYNCH SPEECH

I greet you here on the banks of the James River in the year of our Lord, 1712.   I shall thank you the gentlemen of the colony of Virginia for bringing me here.   I'm here to help you solve some of the problems with the slaves.   Your invitation reached me on my modest plantation in the West Indies where I have experimented with some of the newest and still oldest methods of controls of slaves.

Ancient Rome would envy us if my program is implemented.   As our boat sails South on the James River, named for our illustrious king, whose version of the Bible we cherish, I saw enough to know that your problem is not unique.   while Rome used cords of wood as crosses for standing human bodies along it's old highways in great numbers; you were here using the tree and the rope on occasion.   I caught a whiff of a dead slave hanging from a tree a couple of miles back.   You're not only losing valuable stock by hanging, you are having uprisings, slaves are running away, your crops are sometimes left in the fields too long for maximum profit, you suffer occasional fires, your animals are killed.   Gentlemen, you know what your problems are; I don't need to elaborate.   I am not here to enumerate your problems, I am here to introduce you to a method of solving them.

In my bag here I have a fool proof method for controlling your black slaves.   I guarantee everyone of you that if installed correctly, it will control the slaves for at least 300 years.   My method is simple.   Any member of your family, and any overseer can use it.   I have outlined a number of differences among the slaves and I take these differences and make them bigger.   I use fear and distrust and envy for control purposes.   These methods have worked on my modest plantation in the West Indies, and they will work throughout the South.

Take this little list of differences, think about them.   On the top of my list is age, but it is there only because it starts with an "A".   The second is color, or shade, there is intelligence, size, sex, size of plantation, status on plantation, attitude of owner, whether the slave live in the` valley or on the hill, East, West, North, South.   Whether they have fine hair or coarse hair, whether they are tall or short.   Now that you have a list of differences, I shall give you an outline

WILLIE LYNCH SPEECH

of action. But before that, I shall assure you that distrust is stronger than trust, and envy stronger than adulation, respect or admiration. The black slave, after receiving this indoctrination, shall carry on and will become self-refueling, and self-regeneration for hundreds of years, and maybe thousands. Don't forget, you must pitch the old black male verses the young black male, and the young black male verse the old black male. You must use the dark skin slave verses the light skin slave, and the light skin slave verses the dark skin slave. You must also have your white servants and overseers distrust blacks; but it is necessary that they trust and depend on us. They must love, respect, and trust only us. Gentlemen, these kits are your controls; use them, have your wives, and your children use them; never miss an opportunity. My plan is guaranteed, and the good thing about this plan is that if it is used intentionally for one year, the slave themselves will remain perpetually distrustful.

Willie Lynch 1712
From the Smithsonian Institute

HILL'S AWARD LETTER

GRADUATE SCHOOL OF BUSINESS ADMINISTRATION

UNIVERSITY OF FLORIDA · GAINESVILLE 32611
Robert F. Lanzillotti, Dean · 904-392-2397

April 9, 1982

Mr. Anderson Hill
286-10 Corry Village
Gainesville, Florida   32603

Dear Mr. Hill:

   Congratulations on your successful completion of the Juris
Doctorate/Master of Business Administration degree. It is with
honor that the Graduate School of Business acknowledges you as
the premier black graduate of this program. You are a commendable
role model for students to follow.

   It is therefore my pleasure to inform you that your
accomplishment will be recognized formally at the Ninth Annual
Minority Students Recognition Program on Sunday, April 18, 1982
at 2:30 p.m. in the Reitz Union.

   We look forward to seeing you at the ceremony. Good luck and
much success in your future endeavors.

                                        Sincerely yours,

RFL:ji

cc: Kraft, J.
     Armstead, G.

Equal Employment Opportunity / Affirmative Action Employer

HUGER'S RESIGNATION

Bethune-Cookman College

DAYTONA BEACH, FLORIDA 32015

OSWALD P. BRONSON, PRESIDENT

MEMORANDUM

TO: DR. OSWALD P. BRONSON, SR., PRESIDENT

FROM: THOMAS A. HUGER, DIRECTOR
      CONSTRUCTION/RENOVATIONS

RE: RESIGNATION

The foremost quality of professionalism and leadership is LOYALTY. If this trait is not forever present trust/faith, and productivity will never be at a high level.

Am I to understand that my work environment/supervisor must be changed in order to produce the utmost efficiency? It is not very practical to change horses in the middle of the stream, and by making this change, it is logical to perceive disruption in the normal process of the ongoing projects.

The Living/Learning Complex (LLC) was a very expensive educational experience. Without the direct guidance and leadership of Anderson Hill, the College could have easily had a project in the $4,600,000 range (according to R. S. Means Building Cost Data Reference Manual 1988 edition, the median unit cost was $61.45 per square foot. This building was actually 69,582 Sq Ft. Please include site work, extra roads, fencing, furniture, fixtures and equipment).
Dr. Bronson, Anderson Hill is the most loyal (to you) Cabinet Member, Administrator, Faculty or Staff person that I have met or have known to this day. Realizing that I have been around and associated with B-CC since 1957. THE LEGACY LIVES ON. By instituting a change of this severe magnitude you will definitely be doing the College a great injustice.

If it is your decision to proceed with this change, I request to stay in place for the remainder of my employment which will terminate June 30, 1990. Upon my departure you may announce that the LLC project overrun was my direct responsibility.

HOLMES' PUBLIC OUTCRY

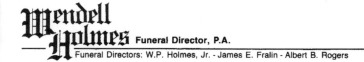

Wendell Holmes Funeral Director, P.A.

Funeral Directors: W.P. Holmes, Jr. - James E. Fralin - Albert B. Rogers

July 14, 1989

I NEED YOUR HELP!!!

First, though, at the risk of being considered presumptuous, I'd like to take the liberty of giving you some limited indication of the kind of things that I have been doing, as well as the kind of person that I am.

For example:

> First Black to be elected as a member of a School Board in the State of Florida - Duval County, 1969 to present

> Served as Chairman of the Duval County School Board for four years

> Presently serving as Chairman of the Bethune-Cookman College Board of Trustees with 12 years of service as a member of the Board

> Presently serving as 2nd Vice Chairman of the Hampton University Board of Trustees with 14 years of service as a member of the Board

> Prime mover and Founding Chairman of the Board of Directors of Century National Bank, 1976-1984, Florida's first Nationally Chartered Black-owned bank

> Past Chairman, Board of Directors, Jacksonville Opportunities Indsutrialization Center, Inc. (OIC), Charter member of the Board

"Where Service And Satisfaction Excel"
2719 W. EDGEWOOD AVENUE • P.O. BOX 2704 • JACKSONVILLE, FLORIDA 32209 • PH. 765-1641

HOLMES' PUBLIC OUTCRY

Page -2-

> Charter member, Jacksonville Community
  Relations Commission

> Immediate past Chairman, Administrative
  Board, Ebenezer United Methodist Church

> President, WENDELL P. HOLMES FUNERAL
  DIRECTOR, P. A., 33 years

> Former member, Community Economic Develop-
  ment Council

Additionally, I feel that I should also tell you that I am 67
years of age, a victim of cancer, and have a wife who is permanently disabled due to multiple sclerosis.

You will see from this profile, that a considerable portion
of my life has been devoted to public and civic service, and
helping people, particularly those who are less advantaged
and in need of a boost to make them more productive, self-
sufficient, motivated members of the Community in which they live.

Now, I am in a situation which requires assistance--hopefully
assistance which your office can give.

Briefly, with a view and focus toward entrepreneurial and economic development within the black community of Jacksonville,
and in conjunction with five other investors, we were able to
get approval of a loan through the SMALL BUSINESS ADMINISTRATION
to open a "CHICKEN GEORGE CHICKEN" franchised restaurant.
Subsequently, the parent company, JOLOG INDUSTRIES, D/B/A
CHICKEN GEORGE CHICKEN, headquartered in Baltimore, Maryland,
filed for bankruptcy.

Due to that and other reasons, our proposed restaurant did not
materialize, and the building which we had purchased, remodeled
and expanded was subjected to foreclosure proceedings by FLORIDA
NATIONAL BANK, then purchased and re-sold by the SMALL BUSINESS
ADMINISTRATION.

The three investors who negotiated the loan through the SBA
have been sued by the SBA for a recovery of monies due the
agency in the amount of $111,689.

Robert Perkins and Jack Walsh, the other two guarantors on
the loan, have settled with the SBA for $12,000 and $15,000
respectively, with re-payment scheduled over a period of
approximately 10 years.

HOLMES' PUBLIC OUTCRY

Of the total of **$171,437,** which the several investors contributed toward the project, **I personally invested $132,817,** in a vain attempt to keep the project from failing. Much of that was borrowed money, which I am presently re-paying at a considerable sacrifice.

To date, the **SBA has refused to consider a settlement of any kind with me,** in spite of the settlements which have been made with **Perkins and Walsh,** and in spite of the terrible disparity between my contributions and that of the other two guarantors in this unsuccessful venture, although we were all supposed to have invested <u>equally</u>. The fact is, **Perkins invested $4,050 and Walsh invested $11,675.**

This loss, coupled with the heavy financial loss which I suffered as the result of the closing of Century National Bank, has been devastating to my personal resources.

When one considers the complete set of circumstances which surround this case, it seems to be patently unfair for the SBA to maintain the hard-line attitude which they have in refusing a reasonable settlement with me.

Additionally, the SBA has been awarded a Summary Judgment against me by the Federal District Court for the full amount of the indebtedness, which is now under appeal.

It also is very clear that the efforts which I have put forth in the two business endeavors mentioned above were designed to create jobs and provide economic benefits for the black community of Jacksonville, and for that my own exonomic future and security are in deep jeopardy. **IT JUST ISN'T FAIR!!**

AGAIN, I NEED YOUR HELP!!! If there is anything at all that you can do to help right what seems to be a terible wrong, I shall be eternally grateful. **TIME IS OF THE ESSENCE.**

I have attached a detailed resume' in the event that additional information regarding me as an individual may be needed.

Thank you for your consideration.

With best wishes,

Respectfully,

WENDELL P. HOLMES, JR.

ATTACHMENT

REPLY FOR HOLMES

Heron, Burchette, Ruckert & Rothwell

Austin, Texas
Sacramento, California
Phoenix, Arizona
Mesa, Arizona
Omaha, Nebraska

Suite 700
1025 Thomas Jefferson Street, N.W.
P.O. Box 96670
Washington, D.C. 20090

Lincoln, Nebraska
Rapid City, South Dakota
Denver, Colorado
Colorado Springs, Colorado
Moscow, U.S.S.R.

(202) 337-7700
TWX 710-822-9270
FAX (202) 898-7723

October 15, 1989

Mr. Eric Benderson
Associate General Counsel
Office of Litigation
Small Business Administration
1441 L Street, N.W.
Room 716
Washington, D.C. 20416

Dear Mr. Benderson:

Per our conversation of October 11, 1989, I am forward to you casework regarding an SBA case for recovery of funds involving Mr. Wendell Holmes of Jacksonville, Florida.

As noted from our discussion, Mr. Holmes has attempted on several occasions to negotiate a settlement of his case. To date, there have been no formal responses to Mr. Holmes settlement offers and your assistance in achieving a resolution to this ongoing matter.

Should you have any questions regarding the enclosed materials, please feel free to contact me.

Sincerely,

Steven L. Pruitt

cc: Wendell Holmes, Jr.
    Bill Williams
    Anderson Hill

-253-

IN THE CIRCUIT COURT, SEVENTH
JUDICIAL CIRCUIT, IN AND FOR
VOLUSIA COUNTY, FLORIDA

CASE NO.: 91-1499-CI-CI
DIVISION: F

BETHUNE-COOKMAN COLLEGE, INC.,
a Florida not for profit
corporation,

       Plaintiff,

v.

ANDERSON C. HILL, II, and CAMP,
a Florida general partnership,
and ANDREW METROPOLE, CARL R.
ROBBIE, PETER ECONOMAKIS,
CONSTANTINOS TRAKAKIS, GEORGE
ROUFOS, PANAGIOTIS GEORGOPOULOS,
and DINO TRAKAKIS, as general
partners of CAMP,

       Defendants.

STIPULATION FOR SETTLEMENT AND ENTRY OF JUDGMENT
BETWEEN PLAINTIFF AND DEFENDANT, ANDERSON C. HILL, II

The undersigned parties, plaintiff, BETHUNE-COOKMAN COLLEGE, INC., and defendant, ANDERSON C. HILL, II ("HILL"), join in this stipulated judgment to be entered into the record in the above referenced matter and agree that the terms shall be binding upon them and upon the issues as set forth herein with respect to such lawsuit. The parties contacted counsel to negotiate and advise them of this stipulation, read and understand the terms of the stipulation, and freely and willingly execute the same. The undersigned parties hereby agree to settle the pending dispute

RLL\SMN\STIP\45240.1   1

between them and the entry of a judgment against defendant, HILL, and stipulate to the facts as follows:

1.   On or about June 9, 1989, defendant, CAMP, entered into a Contract for Sale and Purchase whereby defendant, CAMP, was to sell to plaintiff certain real property commonly known as 609-611 Volusia Avenue, Daytona Beach, Volusia County, Florida. A copy of the Contract for Sale and Purchase with Addendum to Contract is attached hereto as <u>Exhibit A</u>.

2.   Pursuant to the Contract for Sale and Purchase, plaintiff and defendant, HILL, entered into a written agreement whereby defendant, HILL, as escrow agent and attorney for plaintiff, agreed to hold $35,000.00 belonging to plaintiff until certain conditions set forth in the Contract for Sale and Purchase were performed or the time for performance had expired.

3.   According to the terms of the Contract for Sale and Purchase, plaintiff made a Deposit of Earnest Money in the amount of $35,000.00 to be held in escrow by defendant, HILL, in an interest bearing account in a bank or savings and loan association in Volusia County, Florida.

4.   The Addendum to the Contract for Sale and Purchase states that the contract is wholly contingent upon final approval by the federal government but, if not so approved, then the contract shall be considered void with the deposit being returned to plaintiff.

5.   Prior to the date for closing, plaintiff was unable, despite a good faith effort, to obtain final federal approval as required by the Contract for Sale and Purchase. Plaintiff notified

defendant, CAMP, and defendant, HILL, that the federal government failed to issue final approval of the Contract for Sale and Purchase under public law and requested that defendant, HILL, return to plaintiff the deposit being held by defendant, HILL, as escrow agent.

6.   Plaintiff and defendant, CAMP, entered into a Stipulation for Settlement and Entry of Judgment whereby defendant, CAMP, stipulated and agreed that plaintiff is entitled to the $35,000.00 Earnest Money Deposit and one-half of the interest on the deposit being held by defendant, HILL,

7.   Defendant, HILL, has failed and refused to return the Earnest Money Deposit of $35,000.00 held in escrow to plaintiff as per the terms of the Contract for Sale and Purchase and the Addendum to Contract despite repeated demands therefor. Defendant, HILL, has also failed and refused to remit plaintiff's one-half of the interest and defendant, CAMP's, one-half of the interest on the Earnest Money Deposit as per the terms of the Contract for Sale and Purchase.

8.   As a result of defendant, HILL's, failure to return the Earnest Money Deposit according to the terms of the escrow agreement, plaintiff has suffered damages of $35,000.00 with accrued interest.

9.   Plaintiff retained the services of the undersigned attorneys to pursue this action and defendant, HILL, is liable for the reasonable amount of fees incurred by plaintiff in this action.

10.   The parties hereto stipulate and agree to the terms set

B-CC SETTLEMENT w/HILL

forth in the Stipulation for Settlement and Entry of Judgment Between Plaintiff and Defendants, CAMP, ANDREW METROPOLE, CARL R. ROBBIE, PETER ECONOMAKIS, CONSTANTINOS TRAKAKIS, GEORGE ROUFOS, PANAGIOTIS GEORGOPOULOS and DINO TRAKAKIS.

11. The parties hereto stipulate and agree to the entry of a judgment in favor of plaintiff, BETHUNE-COOKMAN COLLEGE, INC., and against defendant, HILL, for $35,000.00 in principal, one-half (1/2) of the total interest, from June 9, 1989 to March __5__, 1992 at the rate of % __6__, in the amount of $ __5,755.25__ and plaintiff's attorneys' fees in the amount of $ __7,000.00__ for a total of $ __47,755.25__, for which execution shall issue forthwith.

By: _____
ANDERSON C. HILL, II

STATE OF FLORIDA
COUNTY OF VOLUSIA

The foregoing instrument was acknowledged before me this 5th day of March., 1992, by __Anderson C. Hill__, who is personally known to me or who has produced __license__ as identification and who did take an oath.

NOTARY PUBLIC:

Sign: _____
Print: _____
State of Florida At Large
(Seal)
My Commission Expires:
Title/Rank: __Notary Public__
Serial Number: __CC024499__

B-CC SETTLEMENT w/HILL

BETHUNE-COOKMAN COLLEGE, INC.　　　COBB COLE & BELL

By: _Oswald P. Bronson Sr_　　By: _Robert W. Lloyd_
　　DR. OSWALD P. BRONSON, SR.　　　ROBERT W. LLOYD
　　President　　　　　　　　　　FLA. BAR. NO. 881708
DATED: _3/16/92_　　　　　　　150 Magnolia Avenue
　　　　　　　　　　　　　　　　Post Office Box 2491
　　　　　　　　　　　　　　　　Daytona Beach, FL 32115-2491
　　　　　　　　　　　　　　　　(904) 255-8171
　　　　　　　　　　　　　　　ATTORNEYS FOR PLAINTIFF

BRONSONS' CONTRACT FOR WILLIAMS

BETTER BUSINESS FORMS
Orlando FL - (407) 281-9044

CONTRACT FOR SALE AND PURCHASE

PARTIES: OSWALD P. & HELEN W. BRONSON, HUSBAND AND WIFE ('Seller')
of 107 PINE CONE COURT, DAYTONA BEACH, FL (Phone) (904)756-255
and BILL WILLIAMS, JR. ('Buyer')
of 7380 SANDLAKE ROAD, SUITE 350, ORLANDO, FL (Phone) 407)363-1110

hereby agree that the Seller shall sell and Buyer shall buy the following real property ('Real Property') and personal property ('Personalty') (collectively 'Property') upon the following terms and conditions which INCLUDE the Standards for Real Estate Transactions printed on the reverse or attached ('Standard(s)') and any addendum to this instrument.

I. DESCRIPTION: (a) Legal description of Real Property located in Volusia County, Florida:
E 90 ft of Lots 1 and 2 of Blk 2 BOSTROMS SUB
HAND TRACT FITCH GRANT MB 2 PG 153 PER OR
2233 PG 199

(b) Street address, city, zip, of the Property is: 323 to 329 Yonge Street, Ormond Beach, FL

(c) Personalty ALL PERSONAL PROPERTY ON PREMISES AT TIME OF
CLOSING BUT NOT THAT OF TENANTS PERSONALTY

II. PURCHASE PRICE $135,000.00

PAYMENT:

(a) Deposit(s) to be held in escrow by ANDERSON C. HILL, II, if any required by seller in the amount of $

(b) Subject to AND assumption of mortgage in favor of FL NATIONAL BANK
in names of sellers having an approximate present principal balance of $79,583.66

(c) Purchase money and mortgage and mortgage note bearing annual interest at ___% on terms set forth herein, in amount of $

(d) Other 2nd mtg. held by seller with 6 month balloon at 12% $45,416.34
interest on principal balance

(e) Balance to close (U.S. cash, LOCALLY DRAWN certified or cashier's check), subject to adjustments and prorations $10,000.00

III. TIME FOR ACCEPTANCE; EFFECTIVE DATE: If this offer is not executed by and delivered to all parties OR FACT OF EXECUTION communicated in writing between the parties on or before March 2, 1990 , the deposit(s) will, at Buyer's option, be returned to Buyer and the offer withdrawn. The date of this Contract ('Effective Date') will be the date when the last one of the Buyer and the Seller has signed this offer.

IV. FINANCING: (a) If the purchase price or any part of it is to be financed by a third party loan, this Contract for Sale and Purchase ('Contract') is conditioned on the Buyer obtaining a written commitment for the loan within n/a days from Effective Date, at an initial interest rate not to exceed n/a % term of n/a years, and in the principal amount of $ n/a Buyer will make application within _____ days from Effective Date, and use reasonable diligence to obtain the loan commitment and, thereafter, to meet the terms and conditions of the commitment and to close the loan. Buyer shall pay all loan expenses. If Buyer fails to obtain the loan commitment and, promptly notifies Seller in writing, or after diligent effort fails to meet the terms and conditions of the commitment or to waive Buyer's rights under this subparagraph within the time stated for obtaining the commitment, then either party may cancel the Contract and Buyer shall be refunded the deposit(s).

(b) The existing mortgage described in Paragraph II(b) above has (CHECK (1) OR (2)): (1) ☐ a variable interest rate OR (2) ☒ a fixed interest rate of _____ % per annum. At time of title transfer some fixed interest rates are subject to increase. If increased, the rate shall not exceed n/a % per annum. Seller shall, within _____5 days from Effective Date, furnish a statement from all mortgagees stating principal balances, method of payment, interest rate and status of mortgages. If Buyer has agreed to assume a mortgage which requires approval of Buyer by the mortgagee for assumption, then Buyer shall promptly obtain all required approvals and diligently complete and return them to the mortgagee. Any mortgage charge(s) not to exceed $ n/a shall be paid by buyer (if not filled in, equally divided). If the Buyer is not accepted by mortgagee or the requirements for assumption are not in accordance with the terms of the Contract or mortgagee makes a charge in excess of the stated amount, Seller or Buyer may rescind this Contract by prompt written notice to the other party unless either elects to pay the increase in interest rate or excess mortgage charges.

V. TITLE EVIDENCE: At least ___15 days before closing date, Seller shall, at Seller's expense, deliver to Buyer or Buyer's attorney, in accordance with Standard A, (Check (1) or (2)): (1) ☐ abstract of title OR (2) ☒ title insurance commitment.

VI. CLOSING DATE: This transaction shall be closed and the deed and other closing papers delivered on 3/30/90 , unless extended by other provisions of Contract.

VII. RESTRICTIONS; EASEMENTS; LIMITATIONS: Buyer shall take title subject to: zoning, restrictions, prohibitions and other requirements imposed by governmental authority; restrictions and matters appearing on the plat or otherwise common to the subdivision; public utility easements of record (easements are to be located contiguous to Real Property lines and not more than 10 feet in width as to the rear or front lines and 7½ feet in width as to the side lines, unless otherwise specified herein); taxes for year of closing and subsequent years; assumed mortgages and purchase money mortgages, if any; other n/a

provided, that there exists at closing no violation of the foregoing and none of them prevents use of Real Property for leasehold/commercial purpose(s).

VIII. OCCUPANCY: Seller warrants that there are no parties in occupancy other than Seller, but if Property is intended to be rented or occupied beyond closing, the fact and terms thereof shall be stated herein, and the tenant(s) or occupants disclosed pursuant to Standard F. Seller agrees to deliver occupancy of Property at time of closing unless otherwise stated herein. If occupancy is to be delivered before closing, Buyer assumes all risk of loss to Property from date of occupancy, shall be responsible and liable for maintenance from that date, and shall be deemed to have accepted Property in their existing condition as of time of taking occupancy unless otherwise stated herein or in a separate writing.

IX. TYPEWRITTEN OR HANDWRITTEN PROVISIONS: Typewritten or handwritten provisions shall control all printed provisions of Contract in conflict with them.

X. INSULATION RIDER: If Contract is utilized for the sale of a new residence, the Insulation Rider or equivalent may be attached.

XI. COASTAL CONSTRUCTION CONTROL LINE ("CCCL") RIDER: If Contract is utilized for the sale of Property affected by the CCCL, Chapter 161, F.S. (1987), as amended, shall apply and the CCCL Rider or equivalent may be attached to this Contract.

XII. FOREIGN INVESTMENT IN REAL PROPERTY TAX ACT ("FIRPTA") RIDER: The parties shall comply with the provisions of FIRPTA and applicable regulations which could require Seller to provide additional cash at closing to meet withholding requirements, and the FIRPTA Rider or equivalent may be attached to this Contract.

XIII. ASSIGNABILITY: (CHECK (1) or (2)): Buyer (1) ☐ may assign OR (2) ☒ may not assign Contract. 1)This contract is wholly contin-
XIV. SPECIAL CLAUSES: (CHECK (1) or (2)): Addendum (1) ☒ is attached OR (2) ☐ is not applicable. gent upon buyer being able to assu
THIS IS INTENDED TO BE A LEGALLY BINDING CONTRACT. by Fla bank. Initials
IF NOT FULLY UNDERSTOOD, SEEK THE ADVICE OF AN ATTORNEY PRIOR TO SIGNING.
THIS FORM HAS BEEN APPROVED BY THE FLORIDA ASSOCIATION OF REALTORS AND THE FLORIDA BAR.

Approval does not constitute an opinion that any of the terms and conditions in this Contract should be accepted by the parties in a particular transaction. Terms and conditions should be negotiated based upon the respective interests, objectives and bargaining positions of all interested persons.

COPYRIGHT 1986 BY THE FLORIDA BAR AND THE FLORIDA ASSOCIATION OF REALTORS, INC.

X Oswald P. Bronson Sr. X 2-28-90 Date
OSWALD P. BRONSON, SR.
Social Security or Tax I.D. # X

X Helen W. Bronson X 2-28-90 Date
HELEN W. BRONSON
Social Security or Tax I.D. # X

X Bill Williams Jr. CEO X 3-2-90 Date
BILL WILLIAMS, JR.
Social Security or Tax I.D. # X 59-2873388
Renculean Dev Corp
(Seller) Date
Social Security or Tax I.D. #

Deposit(s) under Paragraph II received, IF OTHER THAN CASH, THEN SUBJECT TO CLEARANCE ANDERSON C. HILL, II (Escrow Agent)
By: A.C. Hill, II

BROKER'S FEE: (CHECK & COMPLETE THE ONE APPLICABLE)
☐ **IF A LISTING AGREEMENT IS CURRENTLY IN EFFECT:**
Seller agrees to pay the Broker named below, including cooperating sub-agents named, according to the terms of an existing, separate listing agreement;
OR
☐ **IF NO LISTING AGREEMENT IS CURRENTLY IN EFFECT:**
Seller shall pay the Broker named below, at time of closing, from the disbursements of the proceeds of the sale, compensation in the amount of (COMPLETE ONLY ONE)
_____ % of gross purchase price OR $ _____ for Broker's services in effecting the sale by finding the Buyer ready, willing and able to purchase pursuant to the foregoing Contract. If Buyer fails to perform and deposit(s) is retained, 50% thereof, but not exceeding the Broker's fee above provided, shall be paid Broker, as full consideration for Broker's services including costs expended by Broker, and the balance shall be paid to Seller. If the transaction shall not close because of refusal or failure of Seller to perform, Seller shall pay the full fee to Broker on demand. In any litigation arising out of the Contract concerning the Broker's fee, the prevailing party shall recover reasonable attorney fees and cost.

n/a n/a n/a
(firm name of Broker)

-259-

B-CC CONTRACT FOR RENSELEAR

THE AMERICAN INSTITUTE OF ARCHITECTS

AIA Document B801

Standard Form of Agreement Between
Owner and Construction Manager

1980 EDITION

THIS DOCUMENT HAS IMPORTANT LEGAL CONSEQUENCES; CONSULTATION WITH AN ATTORNEY IS ENCOURAGED.

This document is intended to be used in conjunction with
AIA Documents A101/CM, 1980; B141/CM, 1980; and A201/CM, 1980.

AGREEMENT

made as of the 1st day of March in the year of Nineteen
Hundred and Ninety

BETWEEN the Owner: BETHUNE-COOKMAN COLLEGE, 640 SECOND AVENUE
DAYTONA BEACH, FL 32115

and the Construction Manager: RENSELEAR DEVELOPMENT CORPORATION
7380 SANDLAKE ROAD, SUITE 350
ORLANDO, FL 32819

For the following Project:
(Include detailed description of Project location and scope.) Spuds Educational Center approximately 6,000
square feet with 5 classrooms, 2 science laboratories, storage areas,
media center sith production/workroom, career counseling area, administration and faculty office with toilet facilities.

the Architect: CRAIG T. WATSON, AIA
748 RENEGADE
PORT ORANGE, FL 32127

The Owner and the Construction Manager agree as set forth below.

AIA DOCUMENT B801 • OWNER-CONSTRUCTION MANAGER AGREEMENT • JUNE 1980 EDITION • AIA⊕
©1980 • THE AMERICAN INSTITUTE OF ARCHITECTS, 1735 NEW YORK AVE., N.W., WASHINGTON, D.C. 20006   **B801 — 1980 1**

B-CC CONTRACT FOR RENSELEAR

ARTICLE 16
OTHER CONDITIONS OR SERVICES

(List Reimbursable Costs and costs not to be reimbursed.)

Article 9 is hereby wholly deleted and if any disputes
hereby arie herefrom the subject matter of this agreement
then it shall be resolved by legal litigation with the
non-prevailing party responsible for all attorney fees and
costs thereby incurred by the prevailing party.

This Agreement entered into as of the day and year first written above.

OWNER	CONSTRUCTION MANAGER
BY _(signature)_	BY: _(signature)_
OSWALD P. BRONSON, SR., PRESIDENT	BILL WILLIAMS, PRESIDENT
BETHUNE-COOKMAN COLLEGE, INC.	RENSELEAR DEVELOPMENT CORPORATION

AIA DOCUMENT B801 • OWNER-CONSTRUCTION MANAGER AGREEMENT • JUNE 1980 EDITION • AIA®
©1980 • THE AMERICAN INSTITUTE OF ARCHITECTS, 1735 NEW YORK AVE., N.W., WASHINGTON, D.C. 20006

B801 — 1980   9

B-CC PAYMENT FOR RENSELEAR

PURCHASE REQUISITION

BETHUNE-COOKMAN
COLLEGE
DAYTONA BEACH, FLORIDA

HOME OF THE

FIGHTING WILDCATS

27332

BUDGET ACCOUNT NO: _____

DEPARTMENT: SPUDS CONTINUING CENTER ADVISE A. C. HILL, II   ON DELIVERY

DATE ISSUED 3/13/90   DATE REQUIRED 3/13/90

QUANTITY	DESCRIPTION	QTY. X UNIT PRICE	TOTAL
	PLEASE EXECUTE CHECK PAYABLE TO RENSELEAR,		
	DEVELOPMENT CORPORATION IN ACCORDANCE WITH		
	THE ATTACHED PAYMENT REQUEST FOR $ 103,500.00		

APPROVED: SIGNED: A. C. Hill II

_____ DEPARTMENT CHAIRMAN

WHATEVER IS DESIRED
MUST BE FULLY EX-   _____ VP FOR ACADEMIC AFFAIRS/DEAN OF FACULTY
PLAINED BY THE PER-
SON INITIATING THE   _____ VP FOR FISCAL AFFAIRS
REQUISITION.

_____ PRESIDENT

REQUISITIONER'S COPY

Independent Printing Co

COPY

IN THE CIRCUIT COURT, SEVENTH JUDICIAL CIRCUIT
OF FLORIDA, IN AND FOR VOLUSIA COUNTY, FLORIDA
CASE NO. CRC91-1080CFAES

STATE OF FLORIDA,   )
)
            Plaintiff,   )
)
vs.   )
)
BILL WILLIAMS,   )
)
            Defendant.   )
_____)

251 North Ridgewood Avenue
Daytona Beach, Florida   32114
July 31, 1991
2:10 p.m.

DEPOSITION OF OSWALD P. BRONSON, SR.

The above-styled cause came on for hearing before me,
Tammy Fiacco, Deputy Official Court Reporter of the Seventh
Judicial Circuit of Florida, and Notary Public, State of
Florida at Large, at the time and place above indicated for
the purpose of taking testimony.

1   needs to be done, must be done and that the college will

2   cooperate and we would open all our files and make certain

3   that whatever data is needed to satisfy their investigation

4   that we would provide it.

5   Q   Who first made you aware that there might be some

6   kind of a problem with the bond?

7   A   Jake Ross.

8   Q   Was that in a meeting or telephone call or what?

9   A   I think he was in my office. He came by to alert

10   me that he had received some information that we may have a

11   problem there.

12   Q   Do you remember about when that was?

13   A   Oh, some time -- March 1990, maybe.

14   Q   What was the status of construction when you --

15   A   I cannot say at that point. I'm not in a position

16   to say. Because I was gone much of the time.

17   Q   Jake Ross was the first person to --

18   A   To alert me, yes.

19   Q   -- alert you to any problem.

20   You never heard about a problem from Anderson Hill

21   before that?

22   A   You mean about this particular construction?

23   Q   About the bond problem.

24   A   I cannot say at the moment. I know Jake Ross was

25   the first person that brought it to my attention.

BRONSON DEPO. EXCERPTS

1   Q How about Thomas Huger? Did you hear anything

2 from him or from Dr. Cook?

3   A I think along the way Thomas Huger also mentioned

4 it. He, perhaps, had heard from Cathy Smith, who was with

5 the government, that they had received some information or

6 calls that the insurance company did not exist.

7   Q Did that come directly to you? Or did you hear

8 that from one of the other --

9   A Jake Ross was the first person that brought it to

10 my attention.

11   Q Okay. And you had never even seen the papers

12 before that?

13   A No.

14   Q That would be handled by the construction

15 department?

16   A That's true.

17   Q After this came to your attention, what did you

18 do? Did you ever meet with Mr. Williams?

19   A No. I simply told Jake Ross that whatever the

20 State Attorney's Office needs in order to get this

21 information out before the State Attorney's Office as

22 needed, that we would cooperate. We assured him that we

23 would cooperate.

24   Q Did you ever --

25   A Fully.

```
 1          Q    Have you, yourself, ever been in any other kind of

 2    business ventures with Bill Williams, other than this

 3    fine-arts center?

 4          A    No.

 5          Q    Have y'all ever discussed doing any business

 6    together?

 7          A    Well, I discussed -- get these ideas on some real

 8    estate that I had at one time.  But, I backed away from

 9    that.

10          Q    What real estate are you talking about?

11          A    No.  I had a shopping strip in Ormond that we, at

12    one -- that I discussed with him, if he had interest in

13    buying it.

14               But, after going home and thinking about it, I

15    said, No, I better back away, because he's doing work for

16    the college.  I'm the president.  So, I didn't go through

17    with that at all.  And then he indicated he did not have

18    interest in that.

19          Q    What was the deal?  You were going to sell it to

20    him?

21          A    Or get him to help me find somebody to buy it.

22          Q    How far did those negotiations go?

23          A    It never -- it didn't get to the negotiation

24    stage.  It was just an initial conversation.  There were no

25    negotiations.
```

BRONSON DEPO. EXCERPTS

1   Q   Who else was present during those negotiations.

2   A   They were not negotiations.

3   Q   Conversations?

4   A   Conversations is a better word, or a conversation.

5   Q   Who else besides you and Mr. Williams were present

6 during those?

7   A   Anderson Hill may have been present. He may have

8 been present.

9   Q   How far did the conversation go?

10   A   The conversation did not go any further than

11 getting his ideas on it and seeing whether he may have

12 interest or know someone who wanted to buy it.

13   Q   When did these take place?

14   A   In the -- maybe late '89, early '90.

15   Q   Did you ever get to a point of exchanging any

16 papers or anything?

17   A   No. There was no negotiations. There was no

18 discussions of how much you pay me for this or that. I just

19 wanted to know if he had interest or had somebody who may

20 have interest in buying it. That was it.

21   Q   Okay. The situation where the bond developed, did

22 you ever review any papers at all about this bond?

23   A   You mean prior to -- prior to it being brought to

24 my attention by Jake Ross?

25   Q   After it was brought to your attention, did you

NEWSPAPER ACCOUNT

NOVEMBER 28-DECEMBER 4, 1991   •   PRICE 50 CENTS

Did Bronson Lie Under Oath In Deposition?

BY TONEY ATKINS
of the Daytona-Times Staff

Did Bethune-Cookman College President Oswald P. Bronson Sr. lie under oath in a deposition related to a lawsuit filed against the college over delinquent loans made to the construction manager of the college's new fine arts center?

In an interview Tuesday, Bronson said an emphatic "no," especially regarding a personal business relationship with Bill Williams Jr., president of Renselear Development Corp.

NCNB National Bank of Florida and United American Bank of Central Florida are asking for a total of $600,000 from B-CC, Renselear Development Corp. and Williams.

Despite a contract showing the signatures of Bronson and Williams in the sale of Bronson's shopping strip in Ormond Beach to Williams for $135,000 dated Feb. 28, 1990, and March 2, 1990, Bronson said in a deposition on July 31, 1991 that he had never been involved in any other kind of business ventures with Williams, other than the fine-arts center.

"Have y'all ever discussed doing any business together?" Bronson was asked during the deposition.

"Well, I discussed — got these ideas on some real estate that I had at one time. But I backed away from that."

"What real estate are you talking about?" the B-CC president was asked.

"No. I had a shopping strip in Ormond that we, at one — that I discussed with him, if he had an interest in buying it," Bronson responded. "But after going back home and thinking about it, I said, 'No, I better back away, because he's doing work with the college. I'm the president. So I didn't go through with that at all. And then he indicated he did not have interest in that."

"What was the deal? You were

See BRONSON ON Page 3A

Bronson —————— Cont. From Page 1A —————

going to sell it to him?" Bronson was asked.

"Or get him to help me find somebody to buy it," Bronson said in the deposition.

Asked how far the negotiations went, Bronson said, "It never — it didn't get to the negotiation stage. It was just an initial conversation. There were no negotiations."

He said Attorney Anderson Hill II "may have been present" during the conversations, and he told interrogators, "The conversation did not go any further than getting his ideas on it and seeing whether he may have interest or know someone who wanted to buy it."

He said the conversations took place "in the — maybe late '89, early "90."

Asked during the deposition if he got to the point of exchanging any papers or anything, Bronson replied, "No. There were no negotiations. There were no discussions of how much you pay me for this or that. I just wanted to know if he had interest or had somebody who may have interest in buying it. That was all."

Questioned by the Daytona Times about his deposition and the contract for sale and purchase of the shopping strip, Bronson said, "That was canceled. We did not go through with that. We did not consummate the deal."

Bronson added, "We backed away from that because we saw it could be a conflict of interest, and I was looking out for the integrity of the college. I can't recall the exact date of our conversations, but we backed away in view that we were talking about doing a job on campus."

He said, "Anything I would say now would be through the maze of time that has rusted my memory."

He acknowledged that he had been warned against doing business with Williams.

Williams' company was hired by the college to do both the Dr. Mary McLeod-Bethune Fine Arts Center and the Wildcat Student Center, and the contracts were signed Sept. 14, 1989, months before the contract between Bronson and Williams on Bronson's property was signed.

Bronson declined further comment Tuesday.

On June 13, 1990, Bronson said the college had originally talked about having Renselear do the entire $15 million project. "We're reevaluating our approach," he said then.

But it wasn't until two days later that Bronson sent Williams a letter regarding the construction manager's agreement on the Wildcat Student Center in which he wrote, "The college hereby elects to terminate this agreement in all parts and all respects, and this letter shall constitute notice of that termination."

It also was revealed on June 13, 1990, that Williams' Orlando-based company got the job without having to go through any bidding process and has a history of problems with the Internal Revenue Service, despite the fact that millions of dollars in federal money were being spent on the fine arts complex.

In addition, B-CC's former internal attorney, Hill, and the college's full-time director of construction and renovation, Thomas Huger, admitted to having personal business relationships with Renselear Development Corp. However, they contend they had nothing to do with the company's being hired and, until just before the matter became public, were unaware of the legal and IRS problems faced by Renselear and its president.

College officials say the delinquent loans made to the construction manager were obtained partly by forging Bronson's signature and that the college had no knowledge of the loans until it was served with the lawsuits last December.

Hill could not be reached for comment as the *Times* went to press Tuesday.

B-CC'S LETTER TO HILL

Bethune-Cookman College

DAYTONA BEACH, FLORIDA 32015

MARY McLEOD BETHUNE, FOUNDER
OSWALD P. BRONSON, SR., PRESIDENT

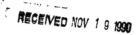

RECEIVED NOV 1 9 1990

WENDELL P. HOLMES, JR.
CHAIRMAN, BOARD OF TRUSTEES

November 15, 1990

ANDERSON C. HILL, II, ESQUIRE
429 NORTH RIDGEWOOD AVENUE
DAYTONA BEACH
FLORIDA   32014

Dear Mr. Hill:

It has been called to our attention at BETHUNE-COOKMAN COLLEGE, that there may be a need to clarify your professional relationship with the institution.

The Administrative action taken with respect to your status at the college and confirmed by the Board of Trustees was a change from that of a regular employee as Internal Attorney to a status of your being called upon for legal service on an at-need basis.

I am certain that you can readily understand and appreciate the necessity to make this distinction as to your relationship with the college.

We continue to be grateful for your loyalty and diligent efforts on behalf of BETHUNE-COOKMAN COLLEGE, and look forward to maintaining a mutually beneficial association in the years ahead.

With best wishes,

Sincerely,

WENDELL P. HOLMES, JR.

WPH,JR/mt
cc: Dr. Oswald P. Bronson, Sr.

PLEASE REPLY TO: POST OFFICE BOX 2704, JACKSONVILLE, FLORIDA 32203-2704

-270-

PRESIDENT'S LETTER TO HILL

Bethune-Cookman College

DAYTONA BEACH, FLORIDA 32015

MARY McLEOD BETHUNE, FOUNDER
OSWALD P. BRONSON, SR., PRESIDENT

OFFICE OF THE PRESIDENT

December 26, 1990

263-923

HAND DELIVERY
Anderson C. Hill,III, Esquire
429 N. Ridgewood Ave.
Daytona Beach, Fla. 32114

Re: United American Bank of Central Florida v. Renselear
Development Corporation, Case No.: 90-1684

Dear Mr. Hill:

We have recently learned that without authorization from or knowledge of the college, you accepted service of the complaint in the referenced lawsuit on behalf of Bethune-Cookman College, Inc. and have been representing it in the lawsuit. We hereby demand that you immediately withdraw your unauthorized representation of Bethune-Cookman College, Inc. in this lawsuit. We are concerned that you have been representing the college without our knowledge or authorization, that you stipulated to and then permitted a judgment to be entered against the college, and that my signature has been forged on the Stipulated Judgment and other pleadings and exhibits.

We have retained Cobb Cole and Bell to represent Bethune-Cookman College, Inc. in this lawsuit. Accordingly, we request that you immediately make your files on this lawsuit available to them. We also request that you cooperate with Cobb Cole and Bell in having them appear as counsel for Bethune-Cookman College, Inc.

Sincerely,

Oswald P. Bronson, Sr.

cc:
Scott W. Cichon, Esquire

S2\scich\26300C

-271-

AFFIDAVIT OF PROCESS SERVER

A F F I D A V I T

STATE OF FLORIDA   )
)   ss.
COUNTY OF ORANGE   )

BEFORE ME, the undersigned attesting officer duly authorized to administer oaths, personally appeared J. SCOTT McKNIGHT, and stated as follows:

1.   That this Affidavit is based upon my personal knowledge.

2.   That on or about March 16, 1990, I was employed as a process server for Southland Process Service whose mailing address is Post Office Box 560514, Orlando, FL 32856.

3.   That in the case of United American Bank of Central Florida vs. Renselear Development Corporation, et al, CI-90-1684, I received a subpoena to be served on the President of Bethune-Cookman College in Daytona Beach, Florida for a March 26, 1990 appearance.

4.   That on or about March 16, 1990 I served on Senorita W. Locklear, Administrative Secretary to the President of Bethune-Cookman College the subpoena for deposition. A copy of the Affidavit of Service is attached hereto as Exhibit "A". A copy of the subpoena for deposition is attached hereto as Exhibit "B".

5.   That I served this subpoena in the course and scope of my employment with Southland Process Service.

6.   That I was of legal age and not a party to the above referenced action at the time of service.

AFFIANT FURTHER SAYETH NAUGHT

_____
J. SCOTT McKNIGHT / AFFIANT

The foregoing instrument was acknowledged before me this 16th day of July, 1993, by J. SCOTT McKNIGHT, who is personally known to me or who has produced _____ as identification and who did (did not) take an oath.

_____
Notary Public
Commission No. _____ NOTARY PUBLIC, STATE OF FLORIDA.
MY COMMISSION EXPIRES July 22, 1995.
BONDED THRU NOTARY PUBLIC UNDERWRITERS.

TERRI L. Howard
(Name of Notary typed, printed or stamped)

(SEAL)

-272-

BOUNCED CHECK TO HILL

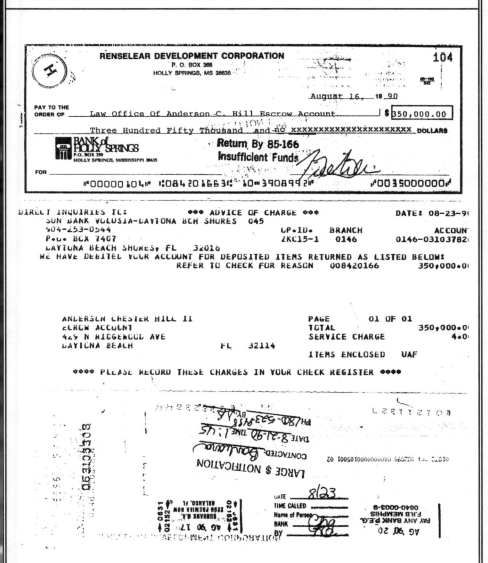

RENSELEAR DEVELOPMENT CORPORATION
P. O. BOX 368
HOLLY SPRINGS, MS 38635

104

August 16, 19 90

PAY TO THE
ORDER OF _Law Office Of Anderson C. Hill Escrow Account_ $ 350,000.00

Three Hundred Fifty Thousand and no xxxxxxxxxxxxxxxxxxxxxx DOLLARS

BANK of
HOLLY SPRINGS
P.O. BOX 250
HOLLY SPRINGS, MISSISSIPPI 38635

Return By 85-166
Insufficient Funds

FOR _____

⑈000000104⑈ ⑆084201663⑈ 10⑈390899 2⑈ ⑈0035000000⑈

DIRECT INQUIRIES TO: *** ADVICE OF CHARGE ***   DATE: 08-23-9(
   SUN BANK VOLUSIA-DAYTONA BCH SHORES   045
   904-253-0544   OP.ID.   BRANCH   ACCOUNT
   P.O. BOX 7407   2KC15-1   0146   0146-031037820
   DAYTONA BEACH SHORES, FL   32016
WE HAVE DEBITED YOUR ACCOUNT FOR DEPOSITED ITEMS RETURNED AS LISTED BELOW:
                    REFER TO CHECK FOR REASON   008420166   350,000.00

   ANDERSON CHESTER HILL II   PAGE   01 OF 01
   ECROW ACCOUNT   TOTAL   350,000.00
   429 N RIDGEWOOD AVE   SERVICE CHARGE   4.00
   DAYTONA BEACH   FL   32114
                                          ITEMS ENCLOSED   UAF

   **** PLEASE RECORD THESE CHARGES IN YOUR CHECK REGISTER ****

WILLIAMS' DENIAL

BILL WILLIAMS
P.O. Box 691191
ORLANDO, FLORIDA   32819

June 7, 1994

CERTIFIED MAIL # P 297 500 722
RETURN RECEIPT REQUESTED

Anderson Hill II
750 South Orange Blossom Trail
Suite 259
Orlando, Florida   32805

Re: Fraudulent Check

Dear Mr. Hill:

This letter is with reference to your certified letter P 942 068 977 regarding a check drawn upon the Bank of Holly Springs.

This is the first time I received notice to this check.

This check is fraudulent and was never authorized for payment to you or to the Law Office of Anderson C. Hill Escrow Account. No check request was ever made to issue a check to the Law Office of Anderson C. Hill Escrow Account, therefore no payment was made or due.

Whoever affixed your name and Law Office of Anderson C. Hill Escrow Account to this check, did so fraudulently. This is a severe and gross mistake for anyone to have done such a serious transaction. This check #104 from Renselear Development Corporation, P.O. Box 366, Holly Springs, MS was never issued by me or anyone authorized from Renselear Development Corporation to give a check to the Law Office of Anderson C. Hill Escrow Account.

No money is owed to you or due you from Renselear Development Corporation or Bill Williams. If you know who and why someone presented this check to you, please write me so that I can turn it over to the Authorities.

Sincerely,

Bill Williams

BW/rp

HILLS' RECOVERY FOR CHECK

IN THE CIRCUIT COURT FOR
ORANGE COUNTY, FLORIDA

NATIONSBANK OF FLORIDA, N.A.,
as successor in interest to NCNB
NATIONAL BANK OF FLORIDA,

                    Case No.: CI95-7378

        Plaintiff,   Division: 33

vs.

RENSELEAR DEVELOPMENT CORP., an
administratively dissolved Florida
Corporation, **BILL WILLIAMS, Jr.,**
and **ANDERSON C. HILL, II,**

        Defendants.

_____/

FINAL JUDGMENT AGAINST RENSELEAR DEVELOPMENT CORPORATION

    This action was heard after entry of default on Defendant/Cross Plaintiff **ANDERSON C. HILL, II's**, motion for entry of a default by the Court and

    IT IS ADJUDGED that Defendant/Cross Plaintiff **ANDERSON C. HILL, II**, recover from Defendant/Cross Defendant **RENSELEAR DEVELOPMENT CORPORATION**, an administratively dissolved Florida Corporation, the sum of **$1,067,500.00** with costs of **$20.00**, making a total amount of **$1,067,520.00**, that shall bear interest at the rate of _10_ % a year, for which let execution issue.

    DONE and **ORDERED** in chambers, Orlando, Orange County, Florida this _8_ day of ____Jan.____ 1997.

                           Circuit Judge

Copies to: Ronald B. Cohn, Esquire
            Anderson C. Hill, II
            Renselear Development Corporation c/o Bill Williams
            Bill Williams

STATE OF FLORIDA, COUNTY OF ORANGE I HEREBY CERTIFY
That the above and foregoing is a true copy of the original
Dated 1/8/97 By _____ Circuit Court

U.S. Department of Justice

United States Attorney
Middle District of Florida

Orlando Division
201 Federal Building
80 North Hughey Avenue
Orlando, Florida 32801-2280

407/648-6700

June 10, 1993

Don Alan Hyman, Esquire
Assistant Director for Lawyer Regulation
    Florida Bar
650 Appalache Parkway
Tallahassee, Florida 32399-2300

    Re: Anderson C. Hill, II
           Case No. 91-173-Cr-Orl-18

Dear Mr. Hyman:

    This letter regards Anderson C. Hill, II.

    Please be advised Anderson C. Hill, II, has been and is currently a cooperating witness with our office. Mr. Hill's cooperation arose from an investigation of Bill Williams, Jr. and several construction projects Mr. Williams' performed for Bethune-Cookman College. During the time period in which Mr. Williams was performing these construction projects Anderson C. Hill, II was the general counsel for Bethune-Cookman College.

    Our investigation resulted in the indictment of Bill Williams, Jr., Renselear Development Corporation, and Anderson C. Hill. As Mr. Hill has informed you, he pleaded guilty to the indictment and agreed to provide the government with restitution of several hundred thousand dollars. Mr. Hill was also sentenced to a period of incarceration.

    Mr. Hill's cooperation was complete and truthful; he went above and beyond his obligation under the plea agreement in terms of providing the government assistance with the prosecution of Mr. Williams. In fact, in my four years as a federal prosecutor, Mr. Hill has proven to be one of the most cooperative and helpful of any of the witness

LETTER CONCERNING HILL

who has assisted me in a case. Mr. Hill continues to provide cooperation, and periodically calls my office to ascertain whether he may be of assistance.

Thank you for your attention to this matter, and please do not hesitate to contact me if you have any questions regarding Mr. Hill or his cooperation with this office.

Very truly yours,

ROBERT W. GENZMAN
United States Attorney

By

C. Richard Newsome
Assistant United States Attorney

CRN:aiw

cc: Anderson C. Hill, II
        35 West Pine Street
        Suite 213
        Orlando, Florida 32801

NOTICE OF LAWSUIT BY HILL

PRIME TIME

PARALEGAL CORPORATION

35 WEST PINE STREET
SUITE 213
ORLANDO, FLORIDA 32801

ANDERSON C. HILL, II, J.D., M.B.A. / PRESIDENT   (407) 423-1758   Fax 423-1863

REPLY: 750 S. ORANGE BLOSSOM TRAIL, SUITE 259, ORLANDO, FLORIDA 32805 TELEPHONE: (407) 426-8597

August 24, 1993

Mr. Richard Nunis
Chairman of the Board
Walt Disney World Co.
c/o Legal Department
P.O. Box 10,000
Lake Buena Vista, Florida 32830-1000
Certified Mail No. P 128 688 712

and

Dr. Oswald P. Bronson, Sr.
President
Bethune-Cookman College, Inc.
640 Dr. Mary Mcleod Bethune Blvd.
Daytona Beach, Florida 32015
Certified Mail No. P 128 688 713

RE: NOTICE OF PENDING LITIGATION HILL v. WALT DISNEY WORLD CO. and ROBERT BILLINGSLEA

Dear Mr. Nunis and Dr. Bronson:

I very much regret that I must take the enclosed legal action against Walt Disney World Co. and Mr. Billingslea. The sworn complaint, with its attachments, are self explanatory. Notice is required under the contract, that is being sued upon, per Plaintiff's exhibit "A", between Disney and the College at paragraph 12.

Pursuant to paragraph (9)(A) of the complaint, I have made an offer to take three professional "lie detector" examinations, to prove the truthfulness of my allegations, if Mr. Billingslea, will also submit to the same. Disney can select an examiner, I can, and then the Court shall designate the third. The results of the evaluations can be used at trial.

Hopefully, the relationship between Bethune-Cookman and Disney will not suffer because of Mr. Billingslea's actions. The public records show that I have admitted to my mistakes, but none of which would have ever occurred, if Mr. Billingslea had been truthful, with his introductions and recommendations.

NOTICE OF LAWSUIT BY HILL

AUGUST 24, 1993
Page 2
Disney & Bethune—Cookman

Thank you for your time and consideration in this matter. I am
willing to discuss the matter, if a timely response can be made
after the receipt of these documents, within twenty four (24) hours
at the reply telephone number above.   The proposed time limit is
not to push any response, but out of concern for other legally
related matters.

Cordially,

Anderson C. Hill, II

cc: Scott Cichon, Esquire, Certified Mail No. P 128 688 714

DEMANDS FOR RESIGNATIONS

August 30, 1993

Mr. Scott W. Cichon, Esquire
Cobb Cole & Bell
150 Magnolia Avenue
Daytona Beach, FL 32114
visa vis facsimile (904) 258-5068 at 11:45 a.m., two pages...

RE: HILL v. WALT DISNEY WORLD &
     ROBERT BILLINGSLEA, B-CC
     REQUESTED CONSIDERATIONS

Dear Mr. Cichon:

This letter comes pursuant to our conversation on August 28, 1993.
I wanted to put the same in writing, so that my legal positions
will not be misinterpreted by anyone, in regards to the above
referenced litigation sent to you by certified mail number P 128
688 714. My purpose in all this is to culminate the activities of
Bill Williams, Jr., as related to myself, my family and Bethune-
Cookman College, Inc.

The college has been given notification of the litigation in
accordance with the terms of the contract. Bethune-Cookman will be
a very important factor in the litigation. The college's opinions
on the various issues will be critical to my successful outcome.
It is my firm legal opinion that the college needs to make
decisions on the related issues. For purposes of the litigation
the college is requested to consider and issue legal opinions on
the following:

(1) In accordance with Walt Disney employment policies for
previous Disney related employment accusations, I stated that I
will take a polygraph examination, to statistically determine the
truthfulness of the allegations in the compliant. Robert
Billingslea is requested to simultaneously submit to the same. It
is well known that B-CC cannot influence Disney as to whether it
can require employee Billingslea to submit to polygraph, but B-CC
can make a determination as to whether Billingslea remains as a
trustee member. I think that Mr. Billingslea should irrevocably
resign/terminate his B-CC Trustee membership.

(2) B-CC has issued or caused to be issued, in the Daytona Beach
News Journal, on 7/24/91, 10/17/91, 10/19/91, 3/3/92, 1/3/92, and
1/10/92, along with related articles in the Daytona Times and other
newspaper publications, that I was fired from my position at B-CC
**"when college officials became concerned about the extent of my
relationship with Williams/Contractor"**. This statement amounts to
the truth for the college's reason for terminating my employment
contract, without any written notice, in accordance with well

DEMANDS FOR RESIGNATIONS

established college policy. I think that the college should affirm this matter and inform Disney Officials of the same. My employment was terminated as a result of my association with Bill Williams, before any recorded or known information was published about our illegal activities. The economic report was not the true basis for termination.

(3) I would like to be temporarily reinstated as a probationary member of the faculty, as an assistant professor of business, with the terms of reinstatement to be resolved at a later time, if B-CC decides to make such offer of employment.

(4) Dr. Wendell P. Holmes, Jr., should tender his irrevocable resignation/termination as chairman and trustee member to the college. My reasons for this request is based upon Dr. Holmes fostering the relationship between Bill Williams and myself, for the personal benefit and gains of Holmes, which commenced on or around August 29, 1989. Williams used this relationship between Williams and Holmes, to gain my participation in the UAB matter. Your civil discovery, in the past UAB v. B-CC litigation, should have disclosed disbursements from the loan on 9/21/89 going to, among others, myself, Billingslea, and Williams' law firms known as Heron, Burchette, Ruckert & Rothwell and/or Laxalt, Washington, Perito & Dubac, in care of Steve Pruitt, Esquire. Holmes can disclose to you the nature of his involvement thereof.

The above four numbered requests will conclude any and all allegations that I have, concerning any persons now connected with B-CC, as a part of to the wrongful misconduct of Bill Williams, Jr., and Renselear Development Corporation. This letter comes as full disclosure to your office of my concerns as related to the institution.

Time is of the essence in these matters. I plan to be in Daytona Beach on August 31, 1993, to file the lawsuit, unless other developments occur. Thank you for your time and consideration in this urgent legal dilemma.

Cordially,

Anderson C. Hill, II

CORROBORATING AFFIDAVIT BY TATE

AFFIDAVIT
of
OLIVER J. TATE

STATE OF FLORIDA
COUNTY OF ORANGE

Before me, the undersigned authority, personally appeared OLIVER J. TATE, who was sworn and made the following statements for use by Anderson C. Hill, II, in his investigations of Robert L. Billingslea and Walt Disney World, Inc., of Orlando, Florida and says:

(1)   That Tate was an employee of Renselear Development Corporation, with Bill Williams, Jr., President, through approximately November 1989.

(2)   Tate is aware, by virtue of his said former employment position, that Bill Williams, Jr., had a relationship with Robert L. Billingslea, who at all times held and publicized that he was the Director of Equal Employment Opportunities Programs/Corporate for Walt Disney World Company in Lake Buena Vista, Florida and a trustee for Bethune-Cookman College, Inc., Daytona Beach, Florida.

(3)   Tate is aware that Billingslea and Williams did travel to Daytona Beach, Florida for the purpose of meeting with College officials.

(4)   Tate is aware that Billingslea had full knowledge of Williams bad reputation and dealings with third parties, before the initial introduction to Hill.   Billingslea was aware that Williams had several severely questionable acts once Williams arrived to reside in Orlando, which include the Timberleaf Project and Williams residential arrangements.

(5)   Tate heard Williams specifically state on several occasions, in a derogatory manner, and it was known throughout the community, that Williams had paid Billingslea for his introduction to Hill along with other recommendations by Billingslea, in the amount of $5,000.00.

(6)   Tate specifically asked Billingslea, if had received money from Williams, based upon Williams statements in paragraph (5), and Billingslea advised Tate that at first Billingslea had not, but immediately subsequent, Billingslea admitted to receiving money from Williams, but only referred to the money as pocket change.

(7)   Tate advised Billingslea to inform College Officials of Williams bad reputation and acts in accordance with a set of newspaper publications shown to Billingslea by Tate, concerning Williams from Ohio.

CORROBORATING AFFIDAVIT BY TATE

(8) Tate had not spoken with or seen Hill since a visit by Hill to Tate's office in approximately December 1989, until a telephone conversation with Hill on August 5, 1993. During the office visit Tate advised Hill to be careful with Williams but did not discuss the matters disclosed herein with reference to Billingslea.

further affiant sayeth not.

_____
OLIVER U. TATE
(407) 352-6612

Sworn to and subscribed before me this 6th day of August, 1993, A.D.

_____
NOTARY   PUBLIC

CINA A. PODLASECK.
PRINTED NAME OF NOTARY PUBLIC

The affiant produced the following identification: Personally known to me.

My Commission Expires: 1/24/97

My Commission Number is: CC249260

CINA A. PODLASECK
MY COMMISSION # CC 249260
EXPIRES: January 24, 1997
Bonded Thru Notary Public Underwriters

THANK YOU FROM BCC

THOMAS T. COBB
W. WARREN COLE, JR.
SAMUEL P. BELL III
JAY D. BOND, JR.
JONATHAN D. KANEY JR.
J. LESTER KANEY
JOHN J. UPCHURCH
JAMES M. BARCLAY
C. ALLEN WATTS
LARRY D. MARSH
KEVIN X. CROWLEY
THOMAS S. HART
TERRENCE M. WHITE
THEODORE E. MACK
JANET E. MARTINEZ
KENNETH R. ARTIN
GREGORY D. SNELL
SCOTT W. CICHON
JAY A. DECATOR III
JUDSON D. KING
ROBERT A. MERRELL III
J. JOAQUIN FRAXEDAS
CAROL A. FORTHMAN
NORMA STANLEY
RENEE K. FEHR
BRUCE A. HANNA
JAMES A. PETERS
ANN-MARGRET R. EMERY
ROBERT W. LLOYD
DENNIS K. BAYER
GARY L. BUTLER

LAW OFFICES

COBB COLE & BELL

150 MAGNOLIA AVENUE

POST OFFICE BOX 2491

DAYTONA BEACH, FLORIDA 32115-2491

TELEPHONE (904) 255-8171
DELAND (904) 736-7700
TELECOPIER (904) 258-5068

September 14, 1993

TALLAHASSEE OFFICE

131 N. GADSDEN STREET
TALLAHASSEE, FLORIDA 32301
(904) 681-3233
TELECOPIER (904) 681-3241

ORLANDO OFFICE

SUITE 122
900 WINDERLEY PLACE
POST OFFICE BOX 940639
MAITLAND, FLORIDA 32794-0639
(407) 661-1123
TELECOPIER (407) 661-5743

OF COUNSEL
PHILIP H. ELLIOTT, JR.
CASEY J. GLUCKMAN
PAUL N. UPCHURCH

MEDIATION COUNSEL
C. WELBORN DANIEL
ROBERT P. MILLER
MICHELLE JERNIGAN GROCOCK

000263-923

Mr. Anderson C. Hill
750 Orange Blossom Trail
Suite 259
Orlando, Fl

Re: United American Bank v. Bethune-Cookman College
     Case No.: CI90-1684

Dear Mr. Hill:

As you know, we have successfully settled the above matter. We would like to take this time to thank you for all your assistance in this lawsuit. We appreciate all the valuable time you contributed to helping us resolve this matter. Good luck in your future endeavors.

Sincerely,

Scott W. Cichon

SWC:smn

cc: Dr. Oswald P. Bronson

SCI\SMN\LETR\104340.1

-284-

PIPS II

```
10/08/97                CORPORATE DETAIL RECORD SCREEN              4:15 PM
NUM: L29290        ST:FL INACTIVE/FL PROFIT      FLD: 11/09/1989
LAST: ADMIN DISSOLUTION FOR ANNUAL REPORT        FLD: 10/11/1991
FEI#: 59-2979035
NAME      : PIPS II, INC.
PRINCIPAL: % JOAN LOWE
ADDRESS    429 N. RIDGEWOOD AVE
           DAYTONA BEACH, FL
RA NAME   : LOWE, JOAN
RA ADDR   : 429 N. RIDGEWOOD AVE
           DAYTONA BEACH, FL
ANN REP   :                                   (1990) I  10/24/90
```

```
10/08/97                OFFICER/DIRECTOR DETAIL SCREEN             4:15 PM
CORP NUMBER: L29290          CORP NAME: PIPS II, INC.
TITLE: D        NAME: HILL, ANDERSON C., II
                      429 N. RIDGEWOOD AVE
                      DAYTONA BEACH, FL
TITLE: D        NAME: PATTEN, EDWARD
                      10824 HEATHER RIDGE CIR
                      ORLANDO, FL
TITLE: D        NAME: GUEST, WILLIAM
                      10824 HEATHER RIDGE CIR
                      ORLANDO, FL
TITLE: D        NAME: MITCHELL, CHARLES H.
                      902-F LAKE DESTINY DR
                      ALTAMONTE SPRING, FL
```

MONEYS RECEIVED FROM WILLIAMS

IN THE CIRCUIT COURT
SEVENTH JUDICIAL CIRCUIT
IN AND FOR VOLUSIA COUNTY, FLORIDA

Case No.   92-30337-CICI
Division   F (J. Johnson)

ALLEN GREEN CONSTRUCTION
COMPANY, INC., a Florida corporation

      Plaintiff,

vs.

BETHUNE-COOKMAN COLLEGE, INC.,
a Florida corporation,

      Defendant.

_____/

SUPPLEMENT TO
MEMORANDUM AND PROFER OF EVIDENCE
REGARDING PUNITIVE DAMAGES
ALLEGED IN THE THIRD AMENDED COMPLAINT

      Plaintiff, Allen Green Construction Company, Inc. ("AGC"), respectfully submits this Supplement to Memorandum and Profer of Evidence Regarding Punitive Damages Alleged in the Third Amended Complaint.

INTRODUCTION

      At the hearing on Defendants motions to the Third Amended Complaint this court instructed counsel for the plaintiff, AGC, to file with the court any addition documentation or information related to punitive damages as they were discovered.

      All capitalized terms used herein, unless the context indicates otherwise, shall have the meanings ascribed in the Memorandum And Profer Of Evidence Regarding Punitive Damages Alleged In The Third Amended Complaint ("Profer").

1

green\grprof2.doc

MONEYS RECEIVED FROM WILLIAMS

AGC has uncovered substantial additional monies being paid to Hill and Huger by Renselear. Even though there are accounts and times for which bank records have not yet been obtained, the documented monies discovered to date which were paid by Renselear to Hill are **$807,437** and to Huger **$12,500** (which does not include the $60,000 annual salary paid by Renselear to Huger.

AGC has set forth below in chronological order the monies paid to Hill and Huger. The paragraphs below correlate numerically to the tabs attached hereto unless the context indicates otherwise.[1]

These monies substantiate AGC's allegations that Hill and Huger were receiving monies from Rensclear, both before AGC was terminated and thereafter, contrary to their deposition testimony in this case however in conformance with their testimony in Federal court. AGC has not yet, however, obtained copies of the checks evidencing the $60,000 annual salary Huger testified he was receiving from Rensclear in 1990.

MONIES RECEIVED BY HUGER AND HILL FROM RENSELEAR

1.   On May 1, 1989, Renselear issued a **$10,000** check to Hill, of which $3,500 was deposited into his law firm account and $6,500 into his personal account. (This was 4 days before Bethune entered into the Renselear Part A Contract [relative to the Fine Arts Project].)

2.   On May 11, 1989, (one day after Renselear received $40,000 from Bethune on the Renselear Part A Contract) Hill negotiated a cashier's check from Renselear, as remitter, for **$40,000**--of which **$7,500** went in the form of a cashier's check from Hill, as remitter, to Huger; $11,500 into Hill's personal account; and $21,000 to Hill's law firm account.

---

[1]   The copies attached hereto as exhibits 1-4 and 6-15 arc copies received from Sun Bank in response to a subpeona regarding Hill's accounts.

MONEYS RECEIVED FROM WILLIAMS

3.   On June 6, 1989, a Renselear check made payable to Sun Bank of Volusia County in the amount of **$15,000** was negotiated by Hill--of which $6,315.47 went to Dordevic to pay Hill's mortgage and $8,684.53 went into his firm account.

4.   On June 12, 1989, Hill negotiated a cashier's check from Renselear, as remitter, for **$15,000**, which was deposited into his firm account.

5.   On July 10, 1989, Huger negotiated a **$5,000** check from Renselear.

6.   On July 21, 1989, Hill deposited a **$25,000** cashier's check from Huger, as remitter, which was drawn from a Renselear account-- of which $6,500 was deposited to Hill's personal account and $18,500 to his firm account.

7.   On August 11, 1989, (the same day Renselear received an improper payment from Bethune of $86,447--See paragraph 36 of Profer) Hill negotiated a **$41,000** cashier's check from Equal Dux, as remitter, which was deposited $10,500 to his personal account, $22,000 to his firm account, $2,000 for cash, and $6,500 unaccounted for. (Paragraph 8 of the Profer establishes this check $41,000 came from Renselear.)

8.   On August 18, 1989, (the same day Renselear received a payment from Bethune of $200,000 purportedly to complete the Project after AGC was terminated--See paragraph 39 of Profer) Hill negotiated a **$80,000** cashier's check from Equal Dux, as remitter, which was deposited $1,000 to his personal account, $5,000 to his firm account, $757.30 to cash, and $73,242.70 to pay down Hill's credit line (Paragraph 8 of the Profer establishes this $80,000 check came from Renselear.)

9.   On September 1, 1989, (one day after Renselear received a payment from Bethune of $47,000 purportedly to complete the Project after AGC was terminated--See paragraph 39 of Profer) Hill negotiated a **$4,500** cashier's check from Renselear, as remitter, which was deposited to his personal account.

10.   On October 19, 1989, Hill received a wire transfer of $5,000 from Renselear as the originator.

3

r.reen\grprof2.doc

MONEYS RECEIVED FROM WILLIAMS

11.   On December 1, 1989, Hill negotiated a cashier's check from Renselear, as remitter, in the amount of $47,000, which was deposited into his personal account.

12.   On December 6, 1989, Hill negotiated a cashier's check from Renselear, as remitter, in the amount of $30,000, of which was $6,000, which was deposited into his personal account, $22,000 was paid to Grezik, and $2,000 was converted to cash.

13.   On January 26, 1990, Hill negotiated a cashier's check from Renselear, as remitter, in the amount of $15,000, which was deposited into his personal account.

14.   On March 19, 1990, Hill negotiated a cashier's check from Renselear, as remitter, in the amount of $65,000, which was deposited into his personal account.

15.   On July 3, 1990, Hill deposited into his escrow account a $152,000 cashier's check from Renselear, as remitter, of which Hill took a $31,990 as a closing fee on a $250,000 loan.

16.   On August 16, 1990, Hill deposited into his law firm escrow account a Renselear check in the amunt of $350,000.   AGC has not yet documented to where these funds were then dispersed.

4

green\grprof2.doc

MONEYS RECEIVED FROM WILLIAMS

CERTIFICATE OF SERVICE

I hereby certify that a copy of the foregoing was served by U.S. Mail to the following:

Michael S. Orfinger Esquire
MONACO, SMITH, HOOD, PERKINS,
  LOUCKS & STOUT
444 Seabreeze Boulevard, Suite 900
P.O. Box 15200
Daytona Beach, FL 32115

Attorney for Defendant

this _1st_ day of December, 1993.

Daniel J. Webster, P.A.
COBLE, WOODS, SEPS, WEBSTER,
  CLAYTON & TEAL, P.A.
P.O. Drawer 9670
Daytona Beach, FL 32120
Fla. Bar No. 0382132
(904) 253-0661
Attorney for Plaintiff

green\grprof2.doc

5

-290-

STATEMENT OF HILL'S CHARACTER

CENTRAL INTELLIGENCE AGENCY

WASHINGTON, D.C. 20505

Office of General Counsel

24 May 1991

Anderson C. Hill, Esquire
429 North Ridgewood Avenue
Daytona Beach, Florida 32114

Dear Mr. Hill:

In response to your request of 26 March 1991, we are providing you with the following statement of your performance and character while an Urban Fellow at the Central Intelligence Agency during the period 4 June 1984 through 1 August 1984. This statement is limited to your performance during the two months you worked at the Agency and should not be interpreted as a commentary on any later activities. Please feel free to forward this letter to any Florida Bar officials you deem appropriate.

There are two memoranda commenting on your performance from which I have excerpted. In the first memorandum, the Agency's Chief of Procurement stated that you completed a special study for the Agency entitled "Analysis of Deliveries for Production Contracts." He stated your work was completed in an excellent fashion. Although you had no background in Federal Government contracting, you quickly completed the necessary legal research to understand the complexities of enforcing the terms and conditions of Federal contracts. He went on to state that your enthusiasm for the task was apparent from the beginning, that you gathered the necessary data to do this analysis with skill and diplomacy and with little or no guidance. The Chief of Procurement stated that your report would be of great value in helping to focus management attention on contract deliveries and that your efforts were much appreciated.

The second memorandum evaluating your performance states that you completed two reports -- the delivery analysis mentioned above and an examination of potential problems regarding spare parts acquisition by the Agency. The reviewer stated you prepared both reports in a timely and complete fashion and demonstrated a clear understanding of the issue which needed to be resolved. The memorandum states that both reports evidenced a conscientious and detailed examination of the problem in which you identified and examined issues and also supplied management with recommendations to solve the problems which had been identified.

Should you wish to discuss this excerpting, please do not hesitate to contact me on ███████████.

Sincerely,

Diane E. Florkowski
Office of General Counsel

THANK YOU FROM FBI

U.S. Department of Justice

Federal Bureau of Investigation

In Reply, Please Refer to
File No.

FBI Academy
Quantico, Virginia 22135

August 31, 1995

Mr. Anderson Hill
7345 Woodworth Way
Orlando, Florida   32818

Dear Mr. Hill:

  This letter is to express the appreciation of the FBI
Academy for your assistance in the recently conducted training
seminar to address fraud in financial institution. The group of
approximately sixty Criminal Investigators from the FBI, United
States Secret Service and numerous state and local Criminal
Investigators along with bank examiners from all the
investigative agencies were very appreciative of the information
you provided. Several expressed special appreciation for your
candid and forthright assessment of how individuals are drawn
into criminal actively and some of the signs that should have
warned others that criminal acts were in progress.

  Thank you for the sacrifice in time required for you to
prepare and deliver in excellent presentation to those attending
this seminar.

     Sincerely yours,

     Gary J. Kruchten
     Supervisory Special Agent

ACKNOWLEDGEMENT OF EFFORT

U.S. Department of Justice

United States Attorney
Northern District of Ohio

1800 Bank One Center
600 Superior Avenue, East
Cleveland, Ohio 44114-2600
September 29, 1995

Mr. Don Alan Hyman, Esq.
Assistant Director for Lawyer Regulation
Florida Bar
650 Appalache Parkway
Tallahassee, Florida 32399-2300

      Re: Anderson C. Hill, II
           (former Bar #372110)

Dear Mr. Hyman:

Please be advised that Anderson C. Hill, II, testified on behalf of the United States in a recent federal fraud prosecution trial in the Northern District of Ohio, United States v. Bill Williams, Jr., case no. 1:94CR377.

Mr. Hill appeared voluntarily, not as part of any plea agreement or non-prosecutive agreement in this district. While the scope of his testimony was limited, nonetheless, his contribution to the trial, which resulted in the jury finding the defendant, Williams, guilty on all eight counts of the Indictment, was extremely valuable.

Mr. Hill's testimony was forthright and sincere. Furthermore, Mr. Hill was exceptionally cooperative, and made himself available to assist the government in reviewing documents and briefing me on the defendant's background.

At the conclusion of the trial, Mr. Hill asked me if I would consider writing this letter to advise you of his assistance, and I was very happy to do so.

If you have any questions, please feel free to contact me.

Very truly yours,

Thomas E. Getz
Assistant U.S. Attorney
216/622-3840

TEG:tlk
cc: Anderson C. Hill, II
       750 Orange Blossom Trail, Suite 259
       Orlando, Florida 32805

ETHICS PRESENTATION

UNIVERSITY OF FLORIDA

College of Law
Offices of the Faculty

March 20, 1997

PO Box 117625
Gainesville, FL 32611-7625
(352) 392-2211
Fax (352) 392-3005

Mr. Anderson Hill
750 S. Orange Blossom Trail
Suite 120
Orlando, FL 32805

Dear Mr. Hill:

Thank you for presenting your story "A Fall From Grace" for the students enrolled in our ethics course this spring. We were, indeed, pleased with the turnout of over 200 students and the feedback has been quite positive.

You are to be commended for your courage and dedication to the cause of improved professional responsibility. Your story provided some context for issues which appear abstract and removed from the average student's sense of reality. It is beneficial for the students to put a personal face on ethical dilemmas and what better way to accomplish this goal than to have a person formerly involved in ethical violations present their story. Most of the students see these issues in a different light now. They are struggling to get beyond the surface issues and to identify the many intricate details which contribute to overstepping ethical boundaries.

I thought you might like to have a copy of the video tape that was made of the presentation. Accordingly, I have requested that our Media Center forward one to you. We keep a copy on file in our audio-visual library, so that students and other library users may view it.

Again, it was a pleasure meeting you. Please accept our sincere appreciation for presenting this excellent talk to our students. Good luck on all of your future endeavors.

> "In every adversity, look for the benefit that can come out of it. Even bad experiences offer benefits; but you have to find and cease them."

Sincerely,

Phyliss Craig-Taylor
Professor of Law

LETTER OF SUPPORT

BLACK LAW STUDENT ASSOCIATION

UNIVERSITY OF
FLORIDA
College of Law

141 E. Bruton-Geer Hall
Gainesville, FL 32611
Phone: (904) 392-7114

March 29, 1997

Anderson C. Hill, II, J.D., M.B.A.
750 S. Orange Blossom Tr.
Suite 120
Orlando, Florida 32805

Dear Mr. Hill:

I am writing on behalf of the W. George Allan chapter of the Black Law Students Association at the University of Florida, in order to convey our deepest and most sincere appreciation for your participation in our 1996-97 Alumni Reunion Weekend. Alumni Reunion Weekend is one of the most important series of events and productions of the year. Your presence and participation helped make this years weekend the best ever.

You have gained a great deal of respect from the UF Law community for your unselfish sharing of the story of your rise and unfortunately fall as an attorney. The impact of your presentation is still being felt here in Gainesville as on any given day, students are still engaged in dialogue with regards to your story and the application of the model rules of professional conduct. In other words, your story was an outstanding supplement to the legal education we are receiving here at UF Law.

The greatest contribution you made to the students, faculty, staff, administrators and the community at large, is your recognition of your mistakes, taking the punishment and now turning what could have been a totally negative experience into a teaching tool for all those who come into contact with you or hear of your story. Mr. Hill your perseverance alone has inspired the students of UF Law to visualize and reach even higher levels of achievement.

The members of BLSA encourage you to share your message with as many students entering the legal profession as will listen. We further realize as a result of your presentation, as has been stated many times, "To whom much is given, much is required." We are encouraging our professional responsibility instructors to continue using your materials and telling your story due to the realism it brings to legal courses offered here at UF Law.

Once again, we thank-you for your enriching contributions to our Alumni Reunion Weekend. We hope to see you next year! From BLSA, we wish you Peace, Love and Blessings.

Sincerely,

LeVoyd L. Carter, II
BLSA President 1996-97

LETTER OF ACKNOWLEDGEMENT

UNITED STATES DEPARTMENT OF EDUCATION

WASHINGTON, D.C. 20202-_____

APR - 3 1997

Mr. Anderson C. Hill, II
750 S. Orange Blossom Trail
Suite 120
Orlando, Florida 32805

Re: Florida Magazine Article

Dear Mr. Hill:

Thank you for providing me with a copy of the September 1, 1996, 'Florida Magazine' section of The Orlando Sentinel. I found the article to be a very captivating story of your life's triumphs and troubles. Clearly your story is a reminder to all professionals who hold positions of trust, that severe consequences will await those who violate that trust. It is indeed encouraging to read of your stated repentance and of your enterprise to warn others of the slippery slope that can easily lead to harm and ruin.

You are to be commended for your recent efforts to offer your life experiences as an educational benefit to others. Although I have no first hand knowledge of your presentations, based upon the information you shared with me, your program has the potential of being successful in making lasting impressions of ethics and of the need for sound judgement in the minds of those professionals who are everyday operating in positions of trust. God Bless you in your endeavors.

Sincerely,

Raymond C. Pierce
Deputy Assistant Secretary
Office for Civil Rights

LETTER OF RECOMMENDATION

Louis A. Wenger
770 Railroad Avenue
W. Babylon, NY 11704(
516) 661-0100

April 12, 1997

Ms. Kathryn E. Ressel
Executive Director
Florida Board of Bar Examiners
1891 Eider Court
Tallahassee, FL 32399-1750

RE: ANDERSON C. HILL, II - FILE NO. 72911

Dear Ms. Ressel:

This letter comes in support of Mr. Hill's re-admission to The Florida Bar. As you are
aware, Mr. Hill was engaged with gentleman known as Bill Williams, Jr. and Renselear
Development Corporation. Williams introduced me to Hill, and based upon the
representations of both gentlemen on behalf of Bethune-Cookman College, my company
extended to Mr. Williams a line of credit for $1,000,000.00.

Williams did receive $175,000.00 as an initial draw on the line of credit. To say the
least, Williams never repaid the advance and I subsequently requested that the Federal
Bureau off Investigation's review of the matter. Williams was prosecuted for the offense
and plead guilty in Federal Court. Hill was never prosecuted, but agreed to provide
restitution back to me based upon another Federal Charge involving Williams.

Hill has remained in close contact with me throughout the years and has pursued
Williams through other matters involving the Courts.

I definitely feel that Hill did not possess any bad intent in the transaction with Williams.
It appears that Williams had pulled Hill into the scheme, similar to the way I was duped.
As a result of Hill's contact with me and ; his apparent remorse for this involvement, I
assigned Hill the rights to the contract I had with Williams for collection purposes.

It is my opinion that Hill should be re-admitted to the Bar Association in Florida.
Everyone makes mistakes. At times there must be forgiveness, if the person repents, and
does his best to rectify the wrongful nature of their involvement. Anderson Hill has done
the best that he could with limited resources and obvious constraints on his professional
abilities. I do not know any further circumstances of your investigations, but from my
knowledge of Hill, he deserves another chance to practice law.

Thank you for allowing my comments. If you need anything further, please contact me.

Sincerely,

Louis A. Wenger

-297-

CLARIFICATION REQUEST OF DISNEY

ANDERSON C. HILL, II
REPLY: 750 S. ORANGE BLOSSOM TRAIL,
SUITE 259, ORLANDO, FLORIDA 32805
TELEPHONE: (407) 426-8597

December 22, 1994

WALT DISNEY WORLD CO. and **WALT DISNEY ATTRACTIONS, INCORPORATED**
c/o Mr. Frank S. Ioppolo
Registered Agent for both Companies
1375 Buena Vista Drive
4th Floor North
Lake Buena Vista, FL 32830

HAND DELIVERED TO ABOVE ADDRESS ON DECEMBER 27, 1994 AT 12:07
P.M. TO ~~Mrs Roebuck - Receptionist~~ by MICHAEL LIEB of
INFINITY INVESTIGATIONS, INC., 1025 S. SEMORAN BLVD., SUITE 1093,
WINTER PARK, FL 32792, (407) 677-4992
_____   12/27/94
Michael Lieb   Date

**RE: LEGAL NOTIFICATION BASED UPON
LACK OF FORMAL RESPONSES TO
ATTACHED COPIES OF CERTIFIED MAIL
NO.S Z 716 410 825 and Z 710 410 828**

Dear Mr. Ioppolo:

Please find attached hereto true and correct copies of the
documents that were forwarded to and received by Mr. Richard "Dick"
Nunis, Chairman of Walt Disney Attractions, Inc. and Ms. Carol
Pacula, Esquire, Director of your Legal Department. Said documents
were mailed by certified U.S. mail on December 7, 1994 and received
by said parties on December 8, 1994. Verifications of the mailings
and receipts are attached hereto.

A written response to the same was requested within 48 hours of
delivery and to date no such response has been received by me. I
am very concerned about the matters I disclosed therein and will
not legally allow the same and/or lack of professional/unethical
treatment to continue. The threats made by Disney are very serious
and given the size of your conglomerates, I must act with extreme
caution in making known the emotional distress over the unlawful
acts known to the appropriate authorities.

I demand a written reply to the attached correspondence no later
than December 30, 1994, before 5:00 p.m. Please govern yourself
accordingly.

Cordially,

Anderson C. Hill, II
Attachments-letter dated December 7, 1994

DISNEY'S POSITION TO HILL

 Walt Disney World Co.

January 4, 1995

Mr. Anderson C. Hill, III
750 S. Orange Blossom Trail
Suite 259
Orlando, Florida 32805

Dear Mr. Hill:

In your December 7, 1994, letter to Mr. Nunis and me, you ask for Disney's position regarding certain disclosure. Our position is as follows:

1. The greater part of your letter is simply untrue. In fact, other than the dates of correspondence and the fact that we have had communication, it is difficult to find anything in it which we could agree is not a false assertion or characterization.

2. You came to us. You asserted a claim. After a lot of investigation and conversation, I informed you, albeit less bluntly than I put it here, that there was absolutely no basis for your claim and therefore no reason to discuss settling it.

3. I made no threats to you. I have not been in touch with any bar association about you.

4. I do not understand why you draw some connection between Disney and the Sentinel article.

5. Other than your letters to us, I have no idea what documents you are referring to about disclosure.

6. I would remind you that any statements that you may choose to make about Disney should be known to you to be truthful and accurate.

P.O. Box 10,000 / Lake Buena Vista, Florida 32830-1000

Part of the Magic of The Walt Disney Company

DISNEY'S POSITION TO HILL

Mr. Anderson C. Hill, III
January 4, 1995
Page 2

    7.   Disney does not authorize you to make public anything Disney was given to understand was intended to be confidential.. Equally important is that Disney has no fear of the truth.

Personally, I am very disappointed with the content and purport of your letter and only regret that you seem to have chosen a dishonorable course of conduct.

Very truly yours,

Carol S. Pacula

Carol S. Pacula
Director - Legal

CSP:CV

APPENDIX DOCUMENTS

To Succeed in Life Journey, is Required to Find the Truth...

Looming in my future at arms length;
A force beckons my wispy tongue to partake
of the nectar that appears sweet to the lips
of desperate dreamers.
The approach is subtle, cunning and wry.
I didn't get the opportunity to ask the question of just why?
I became the prostitute of an evil that exists among mortals.
Evil's persuasion to exchange my birthright for fool's gold
was a complete attempt to steal my confused soul.

Didn't expect the pain to come so very soon!

The passion was insatiable, desiring and sweet.
The asps venom was bequeathed from generation to generation,
I tried desperately to destroy the tradition.
The son of perdition's contact was exact
and transparent as the wind.
Caught in the rights of passage that were not mine to claim.
Sheaths of scales covered my eyes.
Globs of gloom clogged my ears.
My lifespan has been cut short by the space of ten thousand years.
In search of the beginning I could not find an ending in the
evergreen forest of lies.
The truth seemed many miles away.
Humbly I glance back at my yesterdays
and cautiously step into the mysteries of tomorrow.

No fear overtakes my soul!

I have my dear wife and children who have always been
beside me to help me focus;
and face the truth as it touches the ventricles
of my inner being.
The great and almighty GOD shadows over me and provides
rational wisdom to my marrow.
I now discern the truth from lies.

EPILOGUE

"If a man does not keep pace with his companions, perhaps it is because he hears a different drummer. Let him step to the music which he hears, however measured or far away."
Henry David Thoreau, American writer (1817-1862)

WRITING a book is a most difficult task. I commend all of the authors that have engaged and somehow completed the task, whether large or small. It normally takes great inspiration to begin the book, and blessed fortitude to end.

One of my biggest motivations came when Walt Disney World's legal counsel advised me of their position regarding my claim against them. When they said a resounding "no", among other statements previously mentioned, my mind raced to answering the question, "how can I deal with what has happened?" Disney's reply helped me put my situation into a different perspective. I should not have stated in the opening jurisdictional statement of the courtesy compliant sent to them, that the action exceeded $30,000,000.00. That was not a procedurally acceptable phrase to get into Florida Circuit Court at that time, but the standard language is simply that the action exceeds $15,000.00. After making the procedurally acceptable phrase a person would then move forward to prove the amount of damages, whether actual or punitive, later in the litigation. I never got that chance. My feelings were that I had been greatly damaged by the intentional misrepresentations of their agent, Robert Billingslea, with some of his statements and employment demands for Bill Williams. The college stated in various newspapers that my termination was based upon my association with Williams. Few, if any, of the articles mentioned the recommendation of the trustee committee on employment downsizing. I never received any formal notice from the college regarding my employment position in accordance with personnel policies. At the time of the non-renewal of my contract, the only people who knew about the illegal acts which had taken place with the bank were Bill and me. Had a civil court permitted a jury to consider punitive damages based upon the alleged malicious interference with my business opportunities, then who knows what the final award could have been. In paranoid anticipation, it was important for me to get their attention. This way the case would have had close evaluation at the highest possible level. So I tried to strike a nerve at the top. Touché', the mouse struck mine, instead.

Concluding the Disney controversy made me begin to analyze other factors which caused my fall from grace. It certainly was more than Billingslea and Williams. In fact, God made me clearly see that it was MY fault. No one else can be blamed for MY personal mistakes. I pray that those persons who have been effected by my stupidity and greed can truly forgive me. This book is not intended to shift the blame to anyone or cause punishment or anguish. The other persons who are also responsible will have to live with, and be accountable to, themselves, for they know these are accurate accounts of what happened. In my certified cover letter to Disney, I offered to take three polygraph examinations. I wanted them to know my claim was reliable. A third party affidavit was also submitted in corroboration of the claim. Conscience is always present, albeit since I have accepted God's forgiveness regarding certain events, it may become suppressed, however it is forever there. I am now humbly able to live with myself.

BETHUNE-COOKMAN COLLEGE is still very important to me. It is a great school, with a magnificent heritage. That is why I wanted my son, Gregory, to attend. I encourage others to obtain their higher education there. No one person is bigger than the institution. However, I felt it was important for me to give my side of the story. One day I shall repay the monies which I have duly acknowledged in court that I owe. I have not been privy to the internal explanations regarding my conduct. I feel the record deserves a public explanation from all sides, in order to protect the reputation of this worldly institution. My tenure at the college ranged fourteen plus years and I am proud of my affiliation during the majority of those years.

The dream job, law license, home and material possessions were lost because of the evil which existed in me and others. The grace of God saved my precious marriage and family relationships. My wife's and my relationship suffered greatly, but love acted as a sturdy safety net. I believe the way to combat depravity is to bring it into the light.

My book helped me to accomplish my battle, even though the war of good versus evil rages on. My lead in this novel comes from the book of Ephesians, fifth chapter. My brother-in-law, John Myers, a fellow Mason, explained the Holy verses to me through a writing he faxed me. His review of text from Ephesians pointed out that one should have nothing to do with darkness, but rather expose it. For it is shameful even to mention what the disobedient do in secret. But everything exposed by the light becomes visible. Evil cannot survive in the light. Another way to think of it, is that evil is not strong enough to successfully stand in opposition with the truth. Truth causes evil to crumble. I definitely do not want evil to exist in me, and therefore with my limited talents and resources I then took off *in search of the truth*. This book serves as an example of darkness, enlightened by the Light, and the examples can be molded to fit anyone's circumstances. Because we are human, we are all subject to err. I felt that if a person has the opportunity to see the mistakes that I have made, then hopefully they will not make the same or similar ones. If someone has already made errors or committed sinful acts, then I trust that this book will assist with their recovery.

With the rough draft for the text completed, my next problem was actually finishing and publishing this literature. I became frustrated in my dissertation. It began to appear that the book would never be completed. There were dead ends after dead ends. Potential investors for publishing the book were sought, but all doors seemed to close. But I kept remembering saying in prison that *quitting is just one step away from success, because the very next step you take might end in success.* Art Finley was the next step I took that lead to success with this project.

One day while dining at my favorite restaurant, next door to my office building, the strangest set of events started to occur. I had recently started my new life in Orlando, Florida, and at the McDonald's drive-through window, I noticed the person in the car was Art. He did not see me. I was not sure whether to say anything to him or not. Art was Bill's closest friend from childhood and Bill had persuaded Art to move to Orlando. I thought that Art may be hostile towards me because of what happened with Bill. But I got his attention anyway. From that day forward he and I have become very close friends. On many occasions, Art has told me his opinion of what happened between Bill and me. He certainly knows both sides of the story. Art told me that Bill had vehemently cried over the telephone, like a baby, when Art had once mentioned my name. I had asked Art to ask Bill if he would give me a copy of the canceled check, if any, that Bill had paid Robert Billingslea, for his introduction to me. But Art said, Bill, after several moments of prolonged whimpering, said that I was the reason for his problems and that he would never do anything to assist me.

YEARS later, Art called me and said that he had had a meeting with a white Christian businessman named Ken Guthery. They had met by chance at a car wash. Art said that Mr. Guthery had deeply impressed him with his obvious excitement over being an Alpine Industries dealer. He had told Ken about me and wanted all three of us to get together and talk about being dealers. At first I was unsure about meeting Mr. Guthery, but I could tell from Art's tone of voice, that this man had something important to say.

They came to my office and I noticed that Mr. Guthery was very sharply dressed, in an expensive gray suit, with a full glowing white beard and he was old enough to be my father. After a couple of hours Ken, convinced me to become an Alpine dealer. He surprisingly said that he would financially back me so I could get started, since I didn't even have a checking account. Earlier Ken had demonstrated the air purifier unit. I am an asthmatic. It amazed me how the unit cleaned the air and allowed me to breathe better. I have not turned the units off since he installed them in my home and office.

During our meeting Art left the office for several minutes. As Ken and I sat there, the Spirit moved me to be totally up front and open with him. I told Ken about my recent past and the troubles which sent me to prison. A part of my explanation consisted of showing him the magazine article which had been written about me in the *Orlando Sentinel*. I explained to him that I had almost finished writing an autobiography, but finances were stopping me from its completion. He looked at me and said, "How much would it cost?" I gave him a projection of time and costs and without hesitation he said, "I will finance it for you."

It is impossible for me to express the feelings of joy and happiness that overcame me. Ken could see the tears in my eyes. I was so choked up and excited, because I knew that he was serious. After having gone through so much emotional trauma for so many years, and then just like that, here was an immediate unforeseeable break! God truly works in mysterious ways! All we have to do is to believe in Him and His power. Ken looked at me and said, "Did you see the movie Jerry Maguire?" I said yes. He then responded, "I am Jerry Maguire and you are Cuba Gooding!" As our level of emotions increased, we both began acting out the parts. Our voices intensified, we started jumping up and down and laughing, like little kids. His message to me was loud and clear. We found ourselves on the same spiritual wave length. The joy of finally publishing this book, in the right tone and objective, was divinely designated. We both knew it and simultaneously felt the presence of God. What a glorious feeling! It was like being in church and hearing that song or message from the preacher, which touches your heart. Towering over Ken, I gave him a big bear hug and said "You are an Angel!" That moment I knew that God had sent an Angel to at last open doors which had been closed to me and my family for so long. Ironically, it has come from a white man, who was not really exposed to black people until he was about twenty years old. I could tell that he did not see any racial barriers and was willing to give me another chance.

I have learned so many lessons from my life experiences. Love and respect for people must be color blind. We are all frail human beings. You never know where your help might come from. God works through many different people and He does not choose His messengers by the color of their skin. God chooses messengers to carry out His decisions based upon the contents of their hearts. Many people, both black and white have supported me, and all are <u>deeply</u> appreciated. I extend to them my love and prayers. People who have supported me, are my source of strength to prevent me from ever traveling down the road of crime again. I will not keep secrets from them as I did in the past. That was wrong, especially not having open discussions with my wife, because this created confusion and unnecessary anxiety. Whenever I feel that something is amiss, I will find the courage through my relationship with God to promptly discuss, the warning signals, with people that I know truly care. Even if those people can't advise me on problem resolutions, at least the problems will be out in the light. Writing this book has allowed me to explore and get to know my inner being and for that I am eternally grateful, and trust that others will benefit from my exploration. My oath is to God, family and community. My oath is to do what is right and not let the dollar warp my conscience, which is the message I give when I speak to groups. We <u>must</u> listen to our inner selves, which are God-guided and will always keep us on our Spiritual Paths!

"I thank you the reader for your time and I thank God for His continued support and most of all, His Love. I am Blessed!"

BIBLIOGRAPHICAL REFERENCES

Anderson C. Hill, II, author, is currently engaged in seeking additional authors for publication. He is a dealer for Alpine Industries, which sells air purification systems. This gentleman is a life member of Kappa Alpha Psi Fraternity. Hill hopes to one day be re-admitted to The Florida Bar Association. Business development and public speaking are his favorite pastimes, when he is not with his family or in church. He can be reached at Prime Time Publishers, Inc., in Orlando, Florida.

The American Conscious (TAC), Inc., editor, was founded in 1996 by the author. It consists of many different persons, with many different talents, that came together to edit this book. The primary objective of the company is found in the appendix. Its mottoes are: "Do you have a conscious? ...if not, get one soon!"; and "Remember to put a TAC in it!" The company is one of the author's mechanisms to urge prevention of bad acts or rehabilitation through conducting public speaking engagements and seminars. The corporate logo, at the beginning of the appendix, shows the company's creativity. Call for more information.

Gina's Inkwell, poet, is located in St. Petersburg, Florida. The poet specializes in a concept called "Personalized Poetry". The poetry is designed specifically for individuals, as seen throughout this book. According to Gina, "The Holy Spirit knows everybody. I strictly rely on the prompting of the Spirit. He instructs me on what to write."
Gina is the mother of one son, Aubrey, and two daughters, Ashley and Airess.

Michael G. Cothran, illustrator, is an extremely talented individual, as is Gina (above). He presently serves as a freelance illustrator and designer in the city of Pittsburgh, Pennsylvania.

"IN SEARCH OF THE TRUTH: A Real Life Story About What an Attorney Should 'NOT' Do!" details a life from rags to riches to reality. It is a colorful depiction of what it is like to live as an African-American male who attempts, unsuccessfully, to avoid following in the footsteps of his father who went to prison. This realistic self-analytical autobiography lacks the rage or darkside which so commonly colors the writings of authors who have experienced what Anderson Hill experienced and should, therefore, become required reading for educators, aspiring lawyers, and all professionals, regardless of race or status, who are concerned about ethics and values. During seminars for the F.B.I. Academy at San Francisco, California and Miami, Florida in 1995, Hill described his real life experiences which included serving as Urban Fellow with the United States Central Intelligence Agency, Assistant to the President and Attorney on Staff for Bethune-Cookman College where, for 14 years, he was groomed for the college's presidency. Although he has an insider's view of complex legal issues, this former attorney demonstrates in a very simple way problems which must be dealt with and decisions which must be made while coping with the imbalance between greed and ethics. You'll be glad you read this life story and recommend it to anyone who is concerned about values and morality. Order today!

**PRIME TIME
PUBLISHERS, Inc.**

ORDER FORM

Quantity	Description	Cost Each	Total
	Standard Edition	14.95	
	Autographed Edition	19.95	
	Deluxe Edition (Personalized and Autographed)*	24.95	
	Shipping & Handling per Copy	3.95	
	(Florida Residents Only) 7% Sales Tax		
	TOTAL		

* Deluxe Edition may be addressed to recipient. Please indicate recipient's name here:

PAYMENT METHOD

❑   Check or Money Order (make payable to PRIME TIME PUBLISHERS, Inc.)

Charge to my: ❑ Visa   ❑ Mastercard   ❑ American Express   ❑ Discover   ❑ Optima

Print Name (as it appears on card):

Card Number:	Exp. Date:
Authorized Signature:	Today's Date:

SHIPPING INFORMATION

Name:

Address:

City:	State:	Zip:

Daytime Telephone Number: (   )

FAX Order Form to (813) 988-8422 • Phone: (813) 988-8148 or (800) 635-2639
MAIL Order Form to: **PRIME TIME PUBLISHERS, Inc.**
Attn: Clearing House • 4205 E. Busch Boulevard • Tampa, Florida 33617-5937